Mary Ann Glendon

THE INTELLECTUALS
AND THE MASSES

THE INTELLECTUALS AND THE MASSES

Pride and Prejudice among the Literary Intelligentsia, 1880–1939

JOHN CAREY

ST. MARTIN'S PRESS
NEW YORK

THE INTELLECTUALS AND THE MASSES. Copyright © 1992 by John Carey.
All rights reserved. Printed in the United States of
America. No part of this book may be used or reproduced
in any manner whatsoever without written permission
except in the case of brief quotations embodied in critical
articles or reviews. For information, address St. Martin's
Press, 175 Fifth Avenue, New York, N.Y. 10010.

Library of Congress Cataloging-in-Publication Data

Carey, John.
The intellectuals and the masses : pride and prejudice among the
literary intelligentsia, 1880–1939 / John Carey.
            p.   cm.
"A Thomas Dunne book."
ISBN 0-312-09833-2
1. English literature—20th century—History and criticism—
Theory, etc.   2. English literature—19th century—History and
criticism—Theory, etc.   3. Criticism—Great Britain—History—20th
century.   4. Criticism—Great Britain—History—19th century.
5. Great Britain—Intellectual life—20th century.   6. Great
Britain—Intellectual life—19th century.   7. Canon (Literature)
I. Title.
PR471.C37   1993
820.9′00912—dc20   93-29090   CIP

First published in Great Britain by Faber and Faber Limited.

First U.S. Edition: December 1993

10   9   8   7   6   5   4   3   2   1

Contents

Preface

This book is about the response of the English literary intelligentsia to the new phenomenon of mass culture. It argues that modernist literature and art can be seen as a hostile reaction to the unprecedentedly large reading public created by late nineteenth-century educational reforms. The purpose of modernist writing, it suggests, was to exclude these newly educated (or 'semi-educated') readers, and so to preserve the intellectual's seclusion from the 'mass'.

The 'mass' is, of course, a fiction. Its function, as a linguistic device, is to eliminate the human status of the majority of people – or, at any rate, to deprive them of those distinctive features that make users of the term, in their own esteem, superior. Its usage seems to have been originally neither cultural nor political but religious. St Augustine writes of a *massa damnata* or *massa perditionis* (condemned mass; mass of perdition), by which he means the whole human race, with the exception of those elect individuals whom God has inexplicably decided to save.[1] Even in modern times, the belief that God is implicated in the condemnation of the mass lingers on among intellectuals, as I show in Chapter 4. Those not saved will, Augustine trusts, burn in Hell. This well-established Christian precedent for disposing of the surplus 'mass' by combustion was, as my final chapter notes, given practical expression in our century in Hitler's death camps.

My first four chapters are based on the T. S. Eliot Memorial

Lectures that I gave at the University of Kent in November 1989. I added the remaining 'case studies' because I wanted to see how the ideas in the lectures would apply to a number of individual writers, each of whom was conscious (though in contrasting ways) of the 'mass' as a new and challenging presence, and none of whom I had had a chance to write on before.

I should like to thank Mrs Valerie Eliot, Matthew Evans, Robert McCrum and the other directors of Faber and Faber for inviting me to give the Eliot Lectures. For my generous welcome at Canterbury, and for enthusiastic feedback and criticism, I am indebted to Shirley Barlow, Master of Eliot College, Bill Bell, Keith Carabine, David Ellis, Krishnan Kumar and Michael Irwin. I greatly enjoyed and benefited from my stay among them.

The first of my two chapters on Wells was given, in shorter form, as the 1990 Henry James Lecture at the Rye Festival. I am grateful to Dr Ione Martin and to Anthony Neville, that prince of booksellers, for endowing the lecture and asking me to give it. Dr Martin and her husband kindly entertained me at Lamb House, where I had the unexpected (and, given this book's general tenor, rather inappropriate) honour of sleeping in Henry James's bedroom.

To record all the friends and colleagues I have pestered and gained stimulus from would make an embarrassingly long list, but six I cannot omit – David Bodanis, David Bradshaw, Martin Green, David Grylls, Peter Kemp and Craig Raine, for whose wisdom and encouragement, much thanks.

John Carey,
Merton College, Oxford,
March 1992

PART I
Themes

The Revolt of the Masses

The classic intellectual account of the advent of mass culture in the early twentieth century was by the Spanish philosopher José Ortega y Gasset. His book was called, in its English translation, *The Revolt of the Masses*, and it was published in 1930. The root of its worries is population explosion. From the time European history began, in the sixth century, up to 1800, Europe's population did not, Ortega points out, exceed 180 million. But from 1800 to 1914 it rose from 180 to 460 million. In no more than three generations Europe had produced 'a gigantic mass of humanity which, launched like a torrent over the historic area, has inundated it'.[1] Other writers, of quite different casts of mind from Ortega y Gasset, viewed this phenomenon with similar dismay. H. G. Wells, for example, refers to 'the extravagant swarm of new births' as 'the essential disaster of the nineteenth century'.[2]

In Ortega's analysis, population increase has had various consequences. First, overcrowding. Everywhere is full of people – trains, hotels, cafés, parks, theatres, doctors' consulting rooms, beaches. Secondly, this is not just overcrowding; it is intrusion. The crowd has taken possession of places which were created by civilization for the best people. A third consequence is the dictatorship of the mass. The one factor of utmost importance in the current political life of Europe is the accession of the masses to complete social power. This triumph of 'hyperdemocracy' has created the modern state, which Ortega sees as the gravest danger threatening civilization. The masses believe in the state as a machine for obtaining the material pleasures they desire, but it will crush the individual.[3]

Ortega's ideas recall those of Nietzsche, who prefigures many of the developments we shall be concerned with. Nietzsche similarly deplores overpopulation. 'Many too many are born,' his Zarathustra declares, 'and they hang on their branches much too long. I wish a storm would come and shake all this rottenness and worm-eatenness from the tree!' Where the 'rabble' drink, all fountains are poisoned. Zarathustra also denounces the state, which overwhelms the individual. It is 'the coldest of all cold monsters'. In it 'universal slow suicide is called life'. It was invented for the sake of the mass – 'the superfluous'. Nietzsche's message in *The Will to Power* is that a 'declaration of war on the masses by higher men is needed'. The times are critical. 'Everywhere the mediocre are combining in order to make themselves master.' The conclusion of this 'tyranny of the least and the dumbest' will, he warns, be socialism – a 'hopeless and sour affair' which 'negates life'.[4]

We should see Nietzsche, I would suggest, as one of the earliest products of mass culture. That is to say, mass culture generated Nietzsche in opposition to itself, as its antagonist. The immense popularity of his ideas among early twentieth-century intellectuals suggests the panic that the threat of the masses aroused. W. B. Yeats recommended Nietzsche as 'a counteractive to the spread of democratic vulgarity', and George Bernard Shaw nominated *Thus Spake Zarathustra* as 'the first modern book that can be set above the Psalms of David'. True, Nietzsche's acolytes seem often to have read him selectively, in a bid to harmonize his doctrines with socialism, democracy or even feminism. The influential A. R. Orage, for example, editor of the *New Age* (which featured some eighty items relating to Nietzsche between 1907 and 1913), published two studies of Nietzsche which give a very partial idea of their subject. However, Orage's admiration for the 'white heat' of Nietzsche's brain is unstinting, and he reports that Nietzsche is being discussed all over Europe in 'the most intellectual and aristocratically-minded circles'.[5]

Nietzsche's view of the mass was shared or prefigured by most of the founders of modern European culture. Ibsen's *An Enemy of the People* of 1882 showed the isolated, righteous individual as the victim of the corrupt mass. Flaubert wrote in 1871 – a decade before Nietzsche published *Thus Spake Zarathustra* – 'I believe that the mob, the mass, the herd will always be despicable.' One could not, Flaubert asserts, elevate the masses even if one tried.[6] The great Norwegian novelist Knut Hamsun provides an extreme example of this anti-democratic animus. Hamsun's novel *Hunger*, published in 1890, was a seminal modernist text. Thomas Mann, Hermann Hesse and Gide all recorded their debt to Hamsun, and Isaac Bashevis Singer has called him 'the father of the modern school of literature'. Hamsun's Nietzschean view of the mass is epitomized in a speech by his character Ivar Kareno, hero of the *Kareno* trilogy, a young, struggling author of fiercely anti-democratic views:

I believe in the born leader, the natural despot, the master, not the man who is chosen but the man who elects himself to be ruler over the masses. I believe in and hope for one thing, and that is the return of the great terrorist, the living essence of human power, the Caesar.

Hamsun eventually found his great terrorist in Hitler, and he was the only major European intellectual to remain faithful to him to the end. A week after Hitler's suicide he published an admiring obituary in which he celebrates the Führer as 'a warrior for mankind, and a prophet of the gospel of justice for all nations'. 'His fate,' mourns Hamsun, 'was to arise in a time of unparalleled barbarism which finally felled him.'[7]

The 'Revolt of the Masses' which these cultural celebrities deplored was shaped by different factors in each European country. In England, the educational legislation of the last decades of the nineteenth century, which introduced universal elementary education, was crucial.[8] The difference between the nineteenth-century mob and the twentieth-century mass is literacy. For the first time, a huge literate public had come into being, and consequently every aspect of the production and dissemination of the printed text became subject to revolution. 'Never before had there been such reading masses,' remarked H. G. Wells. 'The great gulf that had divided the world hitherto into the readers and the non-reading mass became little more than a slightly perceptible difference in educational level.'[9]

Wells exaggerated. Educational differences remained extreme. But a revolution had taken place, and George Bernard Shaw assessed it with characteristic clarity. In 1879 his novel *Immaturity* was turned down by almost every London publisher. Looking back on this event, and working out the reasons for it, he realized that a radical change had occurred in the reading public. 'The Education Act of 1871,' he explained, 'was producing readers who had never before bought books, nor could have read them if they had.' Publishers were finding that people wanted not George Eliot nor the 'excessively literary' Bernard Shaw, but adventure stories like Stevenson's *Treasure Island* and *Dr Jekyll and Mr Hyde*. In this situation, Shaw concludes, 'I, as a belated intellectual, went under completely.'[10]

Shaw was joking, of course. He did not go under, but he made a conscious decision to write for the millions. By the end of the 1880s he had made himself, as Max Beerbohm acknowledged, 'the most brilliant and remarkable journalist in London'. Newspapers, Shaw conceded, were 'fearfully mischievous' but indispensable, so he resolved to use them for self-publicity.[11]

It was to cater for the post-Education-Act reading public that the popular newspaper came into being. The pioneer was Alfred Harmsworth, later Lord Northcliffe. In 1896 he launched the *Daily Mail*, the paper with the biggest circulation at the start of the twentieth century. Its slogan was 'The Busy Man's Paper' – a hit at the idea of a leisured élite. 'A newspaper,' Northcliffe insisted, 'is to be made to pay. Let it deal with what interests the mass of people.' The principle of his new journalism was 'giving the public what it wants'. To intellectuals, this naturally sounded ominous. Intellectuals believe in giving the public what intellectuals want; that, generally speaking, is what they mean by education.[12]

Furthermore, the popular newspaper presented a threat, because it created an alternative culture which bypassed the intellectual and made him redundant. By adopting sales figures as the sole criterion, journalism circumvented the traditional cultural élite. In an important sense, too, it took over the function of providing the public with fiction, thus dispensing with the need for novelists. This development hinged on the emergence, in the later nineteenth century, of what became known as the human-interest story, a kind of journalism Northcliffe encouraged. In the *Daily Mail*, and its rival, Beaverbrook's *Daily Express*, the concept of 'news' was deliberately extended beyond the traditional areas of business and politics to embrace stories about the everyday life of the ordinary people. As Helen MacGill Hughes points out, this level of journalism supplied for the masses essentially the same aesthetic pleasure that literature gave to the more sophisticated, and commercialized what had previously circulated informally as a component of popular culture – in gossip, ballad and broadsheet. The question 'What are human-interest stories for?' observes Hughes, will have the same answer as the question 'What are novels for?'[13]

Among European intellectuals hostility to newspapers was widespread. The rabble 'vomit their bile, and call it a newspaper', according to Nietzsche. 'We feel contemptuous of every kind of culture that is compatible with reading, not to speak of writing for, newspapers.'[14] Surveying the cultural scene in the *Criterion* in 1938, T. S. Eliot maintained that the effect of daily or Sunday newspapers on their readers was to 'affirm them as a complacent, prejudiced and unthinking mass'.[15] The cultural arbiter F. R. Leavis carried on an extended campaign against newspapers, and the linked evil of advertising, in the pages of *Scrutiny*. The mass media aroused 'the cheapest emotional responses,' he warned; 'Films, newspapers, publicity in all forms, commercially-catered fiction – all offer satisfaction at the lowest level.'[16] *Scrutiny* itself made no bid for the popular market, never printing more than 750 copies per issue in the 1930s.[17] Superciliousness about newspapers was displayed even by writers who were prepared to boost their income by writing for them. Evelyn Waugh, for example, satirized Fleet Street in *Scoop* and in *Vile Bodies*, where Lord Monomark of the *Daily Excess* represents Beaverbrook.

For some male intellectuals, a regrettable aspect of popular newspapers was that they encouraged women. In the Nietzschean tradition the emancipation and education of women were signs of modern shallowness. The man who has depth, Nietzsche pronounces, can think of women only in an 'oriental way'. *Thus Spake Zarathustra* contains the famous advice 'Are you visiting women? Do not forget your whip.'[18] Northcliffe, by contrast, started a new trend among newspaper proprietors by considering women readers worthy of attention. In 1891 he launched a cheap illustrated women's weekly, *Forget-Me-Not*, which achieved a circulation of over 140,000 in three years, and paved the way for the highly successful *Home Chat*. He also insisted on two columns of articles devoted to women's concerns in the *Daily Mail*. As D. L. Le Mahieu has shown in his study of nascent mass media, popular journalism became, however imperfectly, a channel for awareness, independence and self-reliance among women. Male intellectuals reacted predictably. Attacking tabloids (of which Northcliffe's *Daily Mirror*, launched in 1903, was the first), Holbrook Jackson held female readers responsible for the new evil of pictorial journalism. Women habitually think in pictures, he explains, whereas men naturally aspire to abstract concepts. 'When men think pictorially they unsex themselves.'[19]

This contempt among intellectuals for newspapers is not, we should note, shared by the great fictional intellectual of the period, Sherlock Holmes. While the intellectuals were busy inventing alarming versions of the masses for other intellectuals to read, Conan Doyle created, in Holmes, a comforting version of the intellectual for mass consumption – specifically for the middle- and lower-middle-class readers of the *Strand Magazine*, where most of the Holmes stories appeared. Holmes is just as surely a product of mass culture as Nietzsche, his function being to disperse the fears of overwhelming anonymity that the urban mass brought. Holmes's redemptive genius as a detective lies in rescuing individuals from the mass. Characteristically at the start of a story he scrutinizes the nondescript person who has arrived at his Baker Street rooms, observes how they dress, whether their hands are calloused, whether their shoe soles are worn, and amazes them by giving an accurate account, before they have spoken a word, of their jobs, their habits and their individual interests. The appeal of this Holmesian magic and the reassurance it brings to readers are, I would suggest, residually religious, akin to the singling-out of the individual soul, redeemed from the mass, that Christianity promises. The first recorded instance of the Holmes method is, after all, in St John's gospel, Chapter 4, where Christ astounds the woman of Samaria, whom he has met at a well, by telling her she has had five husbands and now lives with a man she is not married to – though whether he deduces this from her shoe soles, or whatever, is not revealed. At all events, newspapers, the bugbear of real-life intellectuals, are one of Holmes's great enthusiasms, and a major resource in his battle against evil. He keeps huge files of newspaper cuttings, and uses the personal columns of newspapers to contact cab-drivers and other chance witnesses who might assist him in his inquiries. The role of the personal column in binding society into a reading group is, admittedly, one of the less likely aspects of the Holmesian *mise-en-scène*, but its function is to combat the isolation and loneliness of mass man. Holmes's passion for newspapers extends to an intimate knowledge of their typefaces, invaluable when confronted with criminals who use cut-up newsprint for their correspondence. Holmes claims in *The Hound of the Baskervilles* that he can identify any newspaper typeface on sight; 'though I confess that once when I was very young I confused the *Leeds Mercury* with the *Western Morning News*'.[20]

Sherlock Holmes's adoption of the newspaper as an ally, when contrasted with the intellectuals' horror of newsprint, marks a fault line along which English culture was dividing. A gulf was opening, on one side of which the intellectual saw the vulgar, trivial working millions, wallowing in newsprint, and on the other side himself and his companions, functionless and ignored, reading Virginia Woolf and the *Criterion* – T. S. Eliot's cultural periodical, the circulation of which was limited, even in its best days, to some 800 subscribers.[21] This view of England on opposite sides of a gulf is the one taken by F. R. Leavis in his first work, *Mass Civilisation and Minority Culture*, published in 1930. Leavis writes in the belief that 'culture is at a crisis' unprecedented in history. The mass media – radio, film, Northcliffe's newspapers – have brought about 'an overthrow of standards'. The small minority capable of a discerning appreciation of art and literature, on whom 'the possibilities of fine living at any time' depend, is beleaguered and 'cut off as never before from the powers that rule the world'. Authority has disappeared and, Leavis observes, an ominous new term, 'highbrow', has come into being to designate deviants like himself. 'The minority is made conscious, not merely of an uncongenial, but of a hostile environment.'[22]

To highbrows, looking across the gulf, it seemed that the masses were not merely degraded and threatening but also not fully alive. A common allegation is that they lack souls. Thomas Hardy writes in 1887:

You may regard a throng of people as containing a certain small minority who have sensitive souls; these, and the aspects of these, being what is worth observing. So you divide them into the mentally unquickened, mechanical, soulless; and the living, throbbing, suffering, vital, in other words into souls and machines, ether and clay.[23]

In *The Waste Land* Eliot associates the crowds of office workers who swarm across London Bridge with the dead in Dante's *Inferno*:

A crowd flowed over London Bridge, so many,
I had not thought death had undone so many.

The implication seems to be that London's crowds are not really alive, and this would correspond to Nietzsche's claim that what is called life in the modern state is really slow suicide. Largely through Eliot's influence, the assumption that most people are dead became, by the 1930s, a standard item in the repertoire of any self-respecting intellectual. Orwell includes it when portraying the conversation of two representative intellectuals in *Keep the Aspidistra Flying*:

My poems are dead because I'm dead. You're dead. We're all dead. Dead people in a dead world . . . life under a decaying capitalism is deathly and meaningless . . . Look at all these bloody houses and the meaningless people inside them! Sometimes I think we're all corpses. Just rotting upright.[24]

The idea that mass existence cannot properly be called life had a strong appeal for D. H. Lawrence, the major English disciple of

Nietzsche, whose works he first came across in Croydon Public Library in 1908. His own inherent superiority to representatives of mass humanity, especially non-white mass humanity, struck Lawrence forcibly. He wrote to Lady Cynthia Asquith from Ceylon, assuring her that the natives were 'in the living sense lower than we are'.[25] When he went to Mexico, it was again apparent to him that a natural ascendancy elevated him above the natives. Only the higher forms of life really live, he argues; the lower merely survive:

> Life is more vivid in the dandelion than in the green fern, or
>   than in the palm tree,
> Life is more vivid in a snake than in a butterfly.
> Life is more vivid in a wren than in an alligator . . .
> Life is more vivid in me, than in the Mexican who drives the
>   wagon for me.[26]

In *Kangaroo*, a character whose experiences closely resemble Lawrence's extends this criticism of inferior life forms to cover the majority of the earth's inhabitants: 'The mass of mankind is soulless . . . Most people are dead, and scurrying and talking in the sleep of death.'[27] If most people are dead already, then their elimination becomes easier to contemplate, since it will not involve any real fatality. In D. H. Lawrence we can see this thought developing. The ending of mankind has evident imaginative allure for him and for leading Lawrentian characters. In *Mornings in Mexico* he feels drawn to the theory that the sun may convulse and 'worlds go out like so many candles': 'I like to think of the whole show going bust, *bang*! – and nothing but bits of chaos flying about.'[28] Dismayed by the war, he suggested to Lady Ottoline Morrell in 1915: 'It would be nice if the Lord sent another flood and drowned the world.'[29] He accepts, in *Fantasia of the Unconscious*, that at certain historical periods men must 'fall into death in millions', and regards this as no more dreadful than the fall of leaves in autumn. Given the condition of modern man, he feels inclined to say, 'Three cheers for the inventors of poison gas.'[30] Hatred of mankind and the wish to exterminate it become associated in Lawrence's mind with the idea of being cleansed and happy: 'To learn plainly to hate mankind, to detest the spawning human-being,' he writes in 1917, 'that is the only cleanliness now.' The thought of the earth 'all *grass* and trees', with no works of man at all, 'just a hare listening to the inaudible – that is Paradise'.[31]

The old, the sick and the suffering suggest themselves as particularly ripe for extermination. Nietzsche affirms that 'the great majority of men have no right to existence, but are a misfortune to higher men'.[32] He blames the corruption of the European races on the preservation of sick and suffering specimens.[33] The breeding of the future master race will entail, he warns, the 'annihilation of millions of failures'.[34] The actual method of annihilation is generally left vague, both in Nietzsche and Lawrence, but Lawrence has a chilling passage in a letter of 1908, in which he explains to Blanche Jennings how he would dispose of society's outcasts:

If I had my way, I would build a lethal chamber as big as the Crystal Palace, with a military band playing softly, and a Cinematograph working brightly; then I'd go out in the back streets and main streets and bring them in, all the sick, the halt, and the maimed; I would lead them gently, and they would smile me a weary thanks; and the band would softly bubble out the 'Hallelujah Chorus'.[35]

What else would softly bubble out in order to make his lethal chamber lethal, Lawrence even here does not specify, but maybe his later interest in poison gas gives a clue to the direction of his imaginings.

It is fair to add that both Nietzsche and Lawrence thirst, at times, for an annihilation that will cancel not only the human race but themselves as well. 'Man,' muses Nietzsche in *The Will to Power*, is 'a little, eccentric species of animal, which – fortunately – has its day . . . the earth itself, like every star, [is] a hiatus between two nothingnesses'.[36] Lawrence, writing to E. M. Forster in 1916, feels gladdened by the prospect that war and violent death will wipe out all the hordes of mankind, and adds: 'I think it would be good to die, because death would be a clean land with no people in it: not even the people of myself.'[37] This ardour for extinction has persisted among the intellectually superior into the nuclear age, at least in a dandified form. Evelyn Waugh told readers of the *Daily Mail* in

1959 that nuclear threat did not worry him, because he could see 'nothing objectionable in the total destruction of the earth'.[38]

A more selective way of eliminating the mass might be found, some intellectuals believed, through the science of eugenics. The term eugenics was coined by Francis Galton in the 1880s, and the Eugenics Education Society, founded in 1907 (the name was shortened to the Eugenics Society in 1926), hoped that by discouraging or preventing the increase of inferior breeds, and by offering incentives to superior people to propagate, the danger of degeneration inherent in the mass might be avoided. W. B. Yeats joined the Society; Shaw and Aldous Huxley were sympathetic. T. S. Eliot's line in 'Gerontion' about the Jew who was 'Spawned in some estaminet of Antwerp' suggests a belief in the importance of good breeding which would have been readily understood in eugenicist circles. As in so much else, Nietzsche was the trendsetter in this area of early twentieth-century progressive thought. In *The Will to Power* he contemplates the establishment of 'international racial unions' whose task will be to rear a master race – a new 'tremendous aristocracy' in which 'the will of philosophical men of power and artist tyrants will be made to endure for millennia'. Meanwhile, there are certain people, such as chronic invalids and neurasthenics, for whom begetting a child should be made a crime. In numerous cases society ought to prevent procreation by the most rigorous means, including, if necessary, sterilization. The prohibition of life to decadents is, Nietzsche urges, vital.[39]

W. B. Yeats developed a keen interest in the beneficial potential of eugenics which was stimulated by his reading of Raymond B. Cattell's *The Fight for Our National Intelligence*, published in 1937. The passing of a Eugenic Sterilization Law in Germany in 1933 had alarmed moderates in the Eugenics Society, but Cattell congratulates the Nazis on being the first government to adopt sterilization of the unfit as a means to racial improvement. Yeats, too, is undeterred by developments in Germany. In *On the Boiler*, published in 1939, he records the conviction of 'well-known specialists' (i.e. Cattell) that the principal European nations are all degenerating in body and mind, though the evidence for this has been hushed up by the newspapers lest it harm circulation. Following Cattell, Yeats reports that innate intelligence can now be measured, especially in children, with great accuracy, and tests prove that it is hereditary. If, for example, you take a group of slum children and give them better food, light and air, it will not increase their intelligence. It follows that education and social reform are hopeless as improvers of the breed. 'Sooner or later we must limit the families of the unintelligent classes.' This is the more urgent, Yeats warns, because these classes are breeding so rapidly: 'Since about 1900 the better stocks have not been replacing their numbers, while the stupider and less healthy have been more than replacing theirs.' The results are already apparent, Yeats suggests, in the degeneration of literature and newspapers and in regrettable benefactions, like Lord Nuffield's ('a self-made man') to Oxford, which 'must gradually substitute applied science for ancient wisdom'. Unfortunately, too, improvements in agriculture and industry are threatening to supply everyone with the necessities of life, and so remove 'the last check upon the multiplication of the ineducable masses'. If this comes about, it

will become the duty of the educated classes to seize and control one or more of these necessities. The drilled and docile masses may submit, but a prolonged civil war seems more likely, with the victory of the skilful, riding their machines as did the feudal knights their armoured horses.

Yeats is cheered to recall that during the Great War Germany had only 400 submarine commanders – and, indeed, 60 per cent of the damage to shipping was the work of just twenty-four men. So the ability of a few educated people to massacre thousands of their fellow mortals should not be underestimated. Indeed, so favourable seem the auguries that Yeats's main fear is that war between the élite and the masses will not break out after all: 'The danger is that there will be no war, that the skilled will attempt nothing, that the European civilization, like those older civilizations that saw the triumph of their gangrel stocks, will accept decay.' Though *On the Boiler* is Yeats's most forthright contribution to the debate, eugenicist prinicples are, of course, readily observable in his poetry – as when he thanks his ancestors for providing him with blood 'That has not passed through any huckster's loin'.[40]

Dreaming of the extermination or sterilization of the mass, or denying that the masses were real people, was, then, an imaginative refuge for early twentieth-century intellectuals. Less drastic, but more practical, was the suggestion that the mass should be prevented from learning to read, so that the intellectual could once more dominate written culture. This idea is already present in Nietzsche, who opposes universal education. Education should remain a privilege, he insists. Great and fine things can never be common. 'That everyone can learn to read will ruin in the long run not only writing, but thinking too.'[41] D. H. Lawrence vigorously develops this theme. 'Let all schools be closed at once,' he exhorts. 'The great mass of humanity should never learn to read and write.' Illiteracy will save them from those 'tissues of leprosy', books and newspapers. Without education the masses will, Lawrence hopes, relapse into purely physical life. Boys will attend craft workshops, and it will be compulsory for them to learn 'primitive modes of fighting and gymnastics'; girls will study domestic science. In this way the dangers of a 'presumptuous, newspaper-reading population may be averted'.[42]

T. S. Eliot is less Utopian than Lawrence, but he regrets, in his essays, the spread of education, prophesying that it will lead to barbarism:

There is no doubt that in our headlong rush to educate everybody, we are lowering our standards . . . destroying our ancient edifices to make ready the ground upon which the barbarian nomads of the future will encamp in their mechanized caravans.

There are, he believes, too many books published. It is one of the evil effects of democracy. Another is the growth of colleges and universities. The numbers receiving higher education in England and America should, Eliot suggests, be cut by two-thirds. Further, there should be a revival of the monastic teaching orders. Students should return to the cloister, where they would be 'uncontaminated by the deluge of barbarism outside'.[43] The intellectual posture struck in these essays contrasts markedly, we should note, with Eliot's actual conduct. In 1916, while he was reading Nietzsche, he was also taking a literature class, made up chiefly of women elementary schoolteachers, under the auspices of London University's Committee for the Higher Education of Working People. He found the class keen and appreciative, and enormously enjoyed it. 'These people,' he told his father, 'are the most hopeful sign in England, to me.'[44] We should hardly guess this from Eliot's essays, which subscribe to restrictive educational ideas of an orthodox intellectual kind, although these ran counter to his own experience.

The intellectuals' response to the spread of education remained pessimistic.

The spectre of famine, of the plague, of war, etc., are mild and gracious symbols compared with that menacing figure, Universal Education, with which we are threatened, which has already eunuched the genius of the last five-and-twenty years of the nineteenth century, and produced a limitless abortion in that of future time,

bleated the Anglo-Irish novelist George Moore. 'Universal education,' jeered Aldous Huxley, 'has created an immense class of what I may call the New Stupid.'[45] Once more, Sherlock Holmes provides a contrast. In Conan Doyle's story 'The Naval Treaty' Holmes and Watson are coming into London by rail past Clapham Junction, and Holmes suddenly remarks: 'Look at those big, isolated clumps of buildings rising up above the slates, like brick islands in a lead-coloured sea.' Watson is surprised: 'The Board schools,' he interjects inquiringly. 'Lighthouses, my boy!' enthuses Holmes. 'Beacons of the future! Capsules, with hundreds of bright little seeds in each, out of which will spring the wiser, better England of the future.' This was not a very realistic prediction of what the Board Schools would achieve, but its optimism was a deliberate counterblast to intellectual denigration.

The intellectuals could not, of course, actually prevent the masses from attaining literacy. But they could prevent them reading literature by making it too difficult for them to understand – and this is what they did. The early twentieth century saw a determined effort, on the part of the European intelligentsia, to exclude the masses from culture. In England this movement has become known as modernism. In other European countries it was given different names, but the ingredients were essentially similar, and they revolutionized the visual arts as well as literature. Realism of the sort that it was assumed the masses appreciated was abandoned. So was logical coherence. Irrationality and obscurity were cultivated. 'Poets in our civilization, as it exists at present, must be difficult,' decreed T. S. Eliot.[46] How deliberate this process of alienating the mass audience was is, of course, problematic and no doubt differed from case to case. But the placing of art beyond the reach of the mass was certainly deliberate at times. As Val Cunningham points out in his *British Writers of the Thirties*, Geoffrey Grigson founded the periodical *New Verse* in 1933 quite explicitly as a reaction against mass values. *New Verse*, Grigson planned, was to be verse rebarbative to the mass. In the first number he deplores the revolt of the masses, as analysed by Ortega y Gasset, and the vulgarization of 'all the arts' that it has occasioned. *New Verse* will provide a forum where writers are free from the limitations of mass intelligence, and can communicate exclusively with one another.[47]

Ortega y Gasset himself, in *The Dehumanization of Art*, reckons that it is the essential function of modern art to divide the public into two classes – those who can understand it and those who cannot. Modern art is not so much unpopular, he argues, as anti-popular. It acts 'like a social agent which segregates from the shapeless mass of the many two different castes of men'. Ortega welcomes this process. For, being aristocratic, modern art compels the masses to recognize themselves for what they are – the 'inert matter of the historical process'. It also helps the élite, the 'privileged minority of the fine senses', to distinguish themselves and one another 'in the drab mass of society'. The time must come, Ortega predicts, when society will reorganize itself into 'two orders or ranks: the illustrious and the vulgar'. Modern art, by demonstrating that men are not equal, brings this historical development nearer.

The means by which modern art antagonizes the masses is, Ortega observes, dehumanization. The masses seek human interest in art. In poetry, for example, they seek 'the passion and pain of the man behind the poet'. They do not want the 'purely aesthetic'. According to Ortega, these preferences prove the inferiority of the mass, because 'grieving and rejoicing at such human destinies as a work of art presents or narrates [is] a very different thing from true artistic pleasure'. Preoccupation with the human content is 'incompatible with aesthetic enjoyment proper'. Needless to say, Ortega's edicts about what is 'proper' and 'true' in art are quite arbitrary, and could not be supported by rational argument. But his view of modern art as essentially excluding the mass has some interest, as a pointer to intellectual motivation.[48]

As an element in the reaction against mass values the intellectuals brought into being the theory of the avant-garde, according to which the mass is, in art and literature, always wrong. What is truly meritorious in art is seen as the prerogative of a minority, the intellectuals, and the significance of this minority is reckoned to be directly proportionate to its ability to outrage and puzzle the mass. Though it usually purports to be progressive, the avant-garde is consequently always reactionary. That is, it seeks to take literacy and culture away from the masses, and so to counteract the progressive intentions of democratic educational reform.

When early twentieth-century writers depict beneficiaries of this reform — representatives of the newly educated masses — they frequently do so with disdain. The effort of the mass to acquire culture is presented as ill-advised and unsuccessful. E. M. Forster, for example, in his novel *Howards End* depicts a lower-class young man called Leonard Bast, who works as a clerk in an insurance office. Leonard lives in a nasty modern flat, eats tinned food and is married to a vulgar young woman called Jacky, who is, Forster tells us, 'bestially stupid'. It would be false to pretend that Forster is wholly unsympathetic to Leonard. His loyalty to Jacky verges on the tragic. But what Forster cannot condone is Leonard's attempt to become cultured. If only his ancestors had stayed in the countryside, he might have made a robust shepherd or ploughboy. But like thousands of others, they were 'sucked into the town', and Leonard strives to educate himself by reading the English literary classics and going to symphony concerts. Despite these efforts, Forster makes it clear, Leonard does not acquire true culture. He has a 'cramped little mind'; he plays the piano 'badly and vulgarly'. There is, Forster assures us, not the least doubt that Leonard is inferior to most rich people. 'He was not as courteous as the average rich man, nor as intelligent, nor as healthy, nor as lovable.' The novel has a cautionary ending, for Leonard's wish to obtain culture proves fatal. Attacked by one of the upper-class characters, he symbolically grabs at a bookcase for support, and it falls over on top of him, so that he dies of a heart attack. Such are the dangers of higher education, we gather, when it is pursued by the wrong people.[49]

Even more unsympathetic is Virginia Woolf's depiction of Doris Kilman in her novel *Mrs Dalloway*. Miss Kilman is employed by the wealthy Dalloways to tutor their daughter Elizabeth. Though she is poor, Miss Kilman is independent, and has gained a degree in history. She is, in other words, just the sort of woman Virginia Woolf, as a campaigning feminist, might be expected to champion. But the social prejudices of an upper-middle-class intellectual prove stronger than feminism, and Miss Kilman is depicted as a monster of spite, envy and unfulfilled desire. She is plain and middle-aged; she wears a cheap green mackintosh; she perspires. She is consumed with bitter impotent hatred of rich people like the Dalloways, and she burns with hopeless lust for their young daughter. Her culture, like Leonard Bast's, is a failure. She plays the violin but, Virginia Woolf tells us 'the sound was excruciating; she had no ear'. Most degrading of all, she seeks comfort in Christianity, forfeiting her intellectual integrity in return for religious emotionalism. Virginia Woolf could scarcely have effected a clearer dissociation of herself from Miss Kilman.[50]

The early twentieth-century fictional character who stands out from these dismal representatives of mass man and mass woman is Leopold Bloom in James Joyce's *Ulysses*. Bloom is not wholly uncultured. 'There's a touch of the artist about old Bloom,' Lenehan concedes. However, Bloom is distinctly not a literary intellectual. The only book we see him buy is called *Sweets of Sin*. His interest in a statue of Venus is the rudimentary one of examining its private parts. We encounter him seated on his outdoor privy, reading the popular newspaper *Tit-Bits*. His job is canvassing advertisements for newspapers like the *Evening Telegraph*, and when we see him at the office Joyce intersperses his account with newspaper headlines.[51] Joyce, then, pointedly embroils Bloom in newsprint and advertising, which were, for intellectuals, among the most odious features of mass culture. Virginia Woolf predictably condemned *Ulysses* in terms that relate to social class and lack of education. It is, she judges, an 'illiterate, underbred book', the product of 'a self-taught working man, and we all know how distressing they are, how egotistic, insistent, raw, striking and ultimately nauseating . . . I'm reminded all the time of some callow board school boy.'[52]

Yet Bloom is not, of course, treated dismissively by Joyce. By the end of the novel, we know him more thoroughly than any character in fiction has ever been known before. We know his secrets, his intimate memories, his half-formed thoughts, his erotic fantasies. We watch him performing bodily functions of a kind strictly excluded from fiction hitherto. We know of his unspoken griefs – over the death of his son; over his father's suicide. We know his height ($5'9\frac{1}{2}''$), his weight (11st 4lb), and the date on which he last had intercourse with his wife (27 November 1893).

Can we say, then, that in *Ulysses* mass man is redeemed? Is Joyce the one intellectual who atones for Nietzschean contempt of the masses, and raises mass man, or a representative of mass man, to the status of epic hero? To a degree, yes. One effect of *Ulysses* is to show that mass man matters, that he has an inner life as complex as an intellectual's, that it is worthwhile to record his personal details on a prodigious scale. And yet it is also true that Bloom himself would never and could never have read *Ulysses* or a book like *Ulysses*. The complexity of the novel, its avant-garde technique, its obscurity, rigorously exclude people like Bloom from its readership. More than almost any other twentieth-century novel, it is for intellectuals only. This means that there is a duplicity in Joyce's masterpiece. The proliferation of sympathetic imagining, which creates the illusion of the reader's solidarity with Bloom, operates in conjunction with a distancing, ironizing momentum which preserves the reader's – and author's – superiority to the created life. The novel embraces mass man but also rejects him. Mass man – Bloom – is expelled from the circle of the intelligentsia, who are incited to contemplate him, and judge him, in a fictional manifestation.

I would suggest, then, that the principle around which modernist literature and culture fashioned themselves was the exclusion of the masses, the defeat of their power, the removal of their literacy, the denial of their humanity. What this intellectual effort failed to acknowledge was that the masses do not exist. The mass, that is to say, is a metaphor for the unknowable and invisible. We cannot see the mass. Crowds can be seen; but the mass is the crowd in its metaphysical aspect – the sum of all possible crowds – and that can take on conceptual form only as metaphor. The metaphor of the mass serves the purposes of individual self-assertion because it turns other people into a conglomerate. It denies them the individuality which we ascribe to ourselves and to people we know.

Being essentially unknowable, the mass acquires definition through the imposition of imagined attributes. The attribute of the newspaper was, as we have seen, a particularly potent aid in imagining the mass for early twentieth-century intellectuals. Another curiously persistent attribute, worth noting in conclusion, is tinned food. We saw that E. M. Forster's Leonard Bast eats tinned food, a practice that is meant to tell us something significant about Leonard, and not to his advantage. The Norwegian Knut Hamsun waged intermittent war in his novels against tinned food, false teeth and other modern nonsense. T. S. Eliot's typist in *The Waste Land* 'lays out food in tins'. John Betjeman deplores the appetite of the masses for 'Tinned fruit, tinned meat, tinned milk, tinned beans'. Tinned salmon is repeatedly a feature of lower-class cuisine in Graham Greene. Greene records that this had a real-life origin. His Nottingham landlady always gave him tinned salmon at high tea, which he would surreptitiously feed to his dog – though it made the dog sick. H. G. Wells's Mr Polly buys, to cheer himself up, 'a ruddily decorated tin of a brightly pink fish-like substance known as "Deep Sea Salmon" ', and the most odious of all Wells's characters, the dastardly forger Mr Lucas Holderness in *Love and Mr Lewisham*, is another tinned-salmon addict. George Orwell, in *The Road to*

Wigan Pier, maintains that the First World War could never have happened if tinned food had not been invented. He blames tinned food for destroying the health of the British people. 'We may find in the long run that tinned food is a deadlier weapon than the machine gun.'

Other instant foods are occasionally attacked by intellectuals. The gentle simple-lifer and sex-maniac Eric Gill, for example, claimed that Bird's Custard Powder was equivalent to blasphemy. But tinned food bore the brunt of the attack, and it is significant in this respect that in the work of an unintellectual or anti-intellectual writer, Jerome K. Jerome, who was designedly catering for the newly literate masses, tinned food should become genial and amusing. One of Jerome K. Jerome's most famous comic scenes in *Three Men in a Boat* is constructed round a tin of pineapple. The *Morning Post* cited Jerome K. Jerome as an example of the sad results to be expected from the over-education of the lower orders.[53]

In the intellectual's conceptual vocabulary tinned food becomes a mass symbol because it offends against what the intellectual designates as nature: it is mechanical and soulless. As a homogenized, mass product it is also an offence against the sacredness of individuality, and can therefore be allowed into art only if satirized and disowned. When Andy Warhol filled the Ferus Gallery, Los Angeles, with paintings of Campbell's Soup Tins in 1962, his controversial impact depended on the intrusion into high art of a mass icon which early twentieth-century intellectuals had successfully outlawed.

right-wing politics and the direction in which his scientific discovery advanced. Horrified by democracy, and obsessed by the notion of swarming invisible multitudes infecting and destroying civilized society, he inaugurated the immensely influential cultural concept of bacteria, which he described in terms analogous to those used to characterize the seething, unclean masses. Once this scientific model had been offered, it could easily be reversed, so that instead of bacteria resembling the masses, the masses resembled bacteria. Inevitably this correspondence was exploited by those wishing to purge or eliminate the mass. Hitler, Bodanis notes, repeatedly alludes to the Jews as a bacterial disease. The Führer applauds Pasteur and also the German Robert Koch, discoverer of the TB bacillus – which, for Germans, acquired a kind of national prestige among bacilli.

The discovery of the Jewish virus is one of the greatest revolutions the world has seen. The struggle in which we are now engaged is similar to the one waged by Pasteur and Koch in the last century. How many diseases must owe their origins to the Jewish virus! Only when we have eliminated the Jews will we regain our health.

Hitler's 'scientific' method of dealing with Jews – herding them into special reception centres, taking away their clothes and leading them either naked or in simple hospital-style gowns to large 'spraying' rooms – followed with a certain logic from the configuration of the problem of the mass as a subject for scientific inquiry and solution.[6]

In the late nineteenth and early twentieth centuries, investigators of the mass invented their own branch of science, or science fiction, of which the pioneer was Gustave Le Bon. Among other accomplishments Le Bon was the first Frenchman to visit Nepal, where he went with a donkey and a pair of calipers to measure the cranial capacity of the Nepalese élite. His book *The Crowd*, published in 1895, went through twenty-six printings in French and sixteen in English before 1925, and was translated into thirteen languages, among them Arabic, Turkish, Hindi and Japanese. It was admired by Sigmund Freud, Ortega y Gasset and, it seems, Adolf Hitler, who probably read it in a German translation.

[2]

Rewriting the Masses

Since the 'mass' is an imaginary construct, displacing the unknowable multiplicity of human life, it can be reshaped at will, in accordance with the wishes of the imaginer. Alternatively, it can be replaced by images, equally arbitrary, of 'typical' mass men or mass women. The tendency among intellectuals to identify particular persons as 'mass' types is recognized and defended by Ortega y Gasset. If we wish to observe the mass, he explains, there is no need for us to wait until an actual mass of people comes along: 'In the presence of one individual we can decide whether he is "mass" or not.'

In Ortega's view, what marks out a mass man is that he is unambitious and 'common'. However, he also refers repeatedly to the 'brutality' of the mass – a difficult idea to square with the humble, nondescript individual he elsewhere imagines the mass comprising.[1] It seems clear that he retains (at least) two distinct and mutually irreconcilable images of mass man, alternating between them as occasion demands. This is normal intellectual practice. Rewriting or reinventing the mass was an enterprise in which early twentieth-century intellectuals invested immense imaginative effort, and it naturally generated a wide variety of identities. The aim of all these rewritings was the same, however: to segregate the intellectuals from the mass, and to acquire the control over the mass that language gives.

The anxiety caused by the mass when it is sensed as a physical presence, as yet unlocated in language, can be illustrated from the notebooks of Thomas Hardy. In the 1880s the Hardys were living in Upper Tooting, and could see across London from their top windows. At night Hardy was persistently kept awake by an eerie feeling of threat. He had a horror of lying down in close proximity to the population of London – 'a monster whose body had four million heads and eight million eyes'. At daybreak he would lurk in an upper back bedroom and peer out as the line of light spread round the horizon. Within that line, he told himself anxiously, 'are the Four Millions'.

When Hardy observed the mass at closer quarters, contempt was able to displace fear. In the British Museum he watched

crowds parading and gaily traipsing round the mummies, thinking today is for ever, and the girls casting sly glances at young men across the swathed dust of Mycerinus. They pass with flippant comments the illuminated manuscripts – the labour of years – and stand under Ramases the Great, joking. Democratic government may be justice to man, but it will probably merge in proletarian, and when these people are our masters, it will lead to more of this contempt, and possibly be the utter ruin of art and literature.[2]

Foreboding remains here, but not fear, because Hardy has been able to locate his general anxiety about the mass in particular beings ('these people'), to whose thoughts he assumes he has access and whom his language, by representing, fictionalizes and controls.

The transition from Hardy nervously watching the populated darkness from his upstairs window to Hardy feeling superior in the British Museum could serve as a paradigm of the modern intellectual's effort to limit and dominate the mass. Creating images that could effect this domination was a major preoccupation of Nietzsche, for whom reimagining the mass seems to have been a vital component of mental stability. Nietzsche's most common image of the mass is as a herd of animals. But he also figures it as a swarm of poisonous flies, or as raindrops and weeds, ruining proud structures.

The essential function of these images is to deprive the mass of human status. Humanity is to be found elsewhere – in the exceptional individuals Nietzsche celebrates. Denial of humanity to the

masses became, in the early twentieth century, an im linguistic project among intellectuals. T. S. Eliot, a community singing in the *Criterion* for June 1927, fears th permitted to spread it will transform the English individua 'the microscopic cheese-mite of the great cheese of the William Inge tells *Evening Standard* readers in 1928, 'Th cratic man is a species of ape.' Trying to imagine what she ca anonymous monster the Man in the Street', Virginia Woo herself visualizing 'a vast, featureless, almost shapeless human stuff . . . occasionally wobbling this way or that instinct of hate, revenge, or admiration bubbles up beneath Ezra Pound, humanity, apart from artists, is merely a 'mass c a 'rabble', representing 'the waste and the manure' from grows 'the tree of the arts'. In Pound's *Cantos* the 'multitud their leaders transmogrify into a torrent of human excre 'Democracies electing their sewage'. This vision of 'the gre hole' was meant, Pound explained, as a portrait of conten England.[4]

Eliminating the humanity of the masses can also be effe converting them into scientific specimens. This was the en undertaken in the 1930s by Mass Observation. Tom Harris founder of the project, was a naturalist and anthropologist w been a keen bird-watcher at Harrow. He and his team of class observers based themselves in Bolton ('Worktown' ir Observation code) and mingled with the natives, collecting local customs such as the cult of the aspidistra, football pool jokes, armpit hygiene and the proportion of males wearing hats in pubs. Observers were instructed to use an imp notation when identifying human specimens. The formula 'M for example, meant a man of about forty-five who loo sounded unskilled working class (Category D).[5]

Amateurish and innocent as Mass Observation now see employment of a scientific model for the purpose of segregati degrading the mass had a sinister counterpart in the assimila the masses to bacteria and bacilli. David Bodanis has suggest there was, indeed, a causal connection between Pasteur's e

A confusion essential to Le Bon's argument is that of the crowd with the mass. His method is to build up a picture of anarchic crowd behaviour, with allusions to the massacres perpetrated by crowds during the French Revolution, and to suggest that people in the mass behave in a comparable way, even when they are not members of an actual crowd but only of a 'psychological' crowd, such as a democratic electorate. A crowd need not, Le Bon stresses, be gathered in one place. Thousands of isolated individuals, or even a whole nation, may constitute a psychological crowd.

According to Le Bon, crowds are mentally inferior and intent on destruction. They act like microbes, which hasten the dissolution of dead bodies. They are extremely suggestible, impulsive, irrational, exaggeratedly emotional, inconstant, irritable and capable of thinking only in images – in short, just like women. 'Crowds are everywhere distinguished by feminine characteristics.' They also resemble children and savages. Merely by joining a crowd a man descends several rungs in the ladder of civilization, becomes a 'barbarian', acts by instinct, and is seized by violence and ferocity. Crowds are intolerant and dictatorial. But they also respond to force, not kindness, and admire the 'Caesar-type' – again, like women.

The modern era has, in Le Bon's estimation, been taken over by crowds. 'The voice of the masses has become predominant.' Their aim is to destroy civilization and return to the primitive communism which was the normal condition for all human groups before civil society began. Further, they will succeed. Civilization as we know it, created by a 'small intellectual aristocracy', will, Le Bon predicts, be extinguished and give way to a 'barbarian phase'. The optimistic liberal idea that the masses can be educated is false. Statistics show that criminality actually increases with the spread of education. Schooling transforms people into 'enemies of society', makes young people dissatisfied with honest toil and recruits numerous disciples for 'the worst forms of socialism'.[7]

A treatise even more prone to fantasy than Le Bon's was Wilfred Trotter's *Instincts of the Herd in Peace and War*, published in 1916. Some of the confusion of this work stems from its having been composed at two distinct periods – the first part in 1905, the rest under pressure of the Great War. As a medical man Trotter is strongly attracted to scientific models, and unlike Le Bon he rather favours the herd, arguing that 'socialized gregariousness' is, biologically speaking, the most probable destiny for mankind. However, the herd will need a 'directing intelligence or group of intelligences' of a bold, experimental type to save it from its own irrationality and prejudice. Further, not all herds are good. Some correspond to useful creatures, such as the bee, but others resemble wolves. The Germans and their allies, in particular, are 'barbarous peoples of the lupine type', and must be given a 'sound thrashing', like a dog (biologically, Trotter points out, akin to a wolf), to show them who is master. The English, on the other hand, being by nature superior to sabre-rattling foreigners and obeying a mysterious 'communal mind', will, Trotter prophesies, follow the 'inevitable trend of Nature' towards an ideal beehive state. They will grow to despise war and will 'sail their ships into the gulfs of the ether, and lay tribute upon the sun and stars'. That these activities are not much like those of bees does not deter Trotter. Nor does he anticipate that there will have to be any upsetting redistribution of material wealth in the Utopian English beehive of the future.

The fact that it is difficult to persuade a man with 30 shillings a week that he has as much to lose by the loss of national independence as a man with 30 thousand a year is merely evidence that the imagination of the former is somewhat restricted by his type of education, and that we habitually attach an absurd moral significance to material advantages.

This being so, it should be possible to attain a 'very fair approximation' to moral equality among English bees, Trotter reckons, without any undue disturbance of existing material inequalities.[8]

Freud's *Group Psychology and the Analysis of the Ego*, published in 1921, praises Trotter's 'thoughtful book' but is even more impressed by the 'brilliant psychological character-sketch of the group mind' provided by Le Bon. The original German title of Freud's work was *Massenpsychologie und Ich-Analyse*, and he uses *Masse* throughout to translate Le Bon's *foule*. He agrees with Le Bon that the individual in the mass becomes a barbarian, ferocious and violent, and also childlike and credulous. What happens, Freud explains, is that the individual, on becoming a mass man, throws off the repressions of his unconscious instincts: 'The apparently new characteristics he then displays are in fact the manifestations of this unconscious, in which all that is evil in the human mind is contained as a predisposition.' Freud then proceeds to weave his own fantasy (or 'scientific myth', as he calls it) around the idea of the mass. According to this, the mass represents the 'primal horde', which was the primitive form of human society. Composed of sons, persecuted and dominated by their 'primal father' or pack leader, the horde united against the father and killed him, thus conforming to Freudian expectations, and giving the murderous propensities of the mass a sound basis in psychological theory.[9] Freud's association of the mass with 'evil', unconscious desires justifies the political suppression of the mass. Those entitled to suppress it will be, according to Freud, the élite, who have already suppressed the promptings of the mass-unconscious within their own psyches: 'Our mind . . . is no peacefully self-contained unity. It is rather to be compared with a modern State in which a mob, eager for enjoyment and destruction, has to be held down forcibly by a prudent superior class.' It is impossible, Freud stresses, to conceive of civilization without the control of the mass by a minority, and that control will inevitably involve coercion: 'For masses are lazy and unintelligent; they have no love for instinctual renunciation, and they are not to be convinced by argument of its inevitability.'[10]

Elias Canetti, generally cited as the most profound modern commentator on the mass, stands at the end of the 'scientific' tradition stretching from Le Bon to Freud, and inherits its fantasies and confusions. His attitude to crowd psychology was complicated by his personal history. During his student days in Vienna, in July 1927 he had found himself caught up in a crowd which marched on the Palace of Justice and set it alight. The excitement of this occasion, and the feeling of being absorbed, remained with him: 'I became part of the crowd. I dissolved into it fully.' But as a Jewish refugee from Nazi Germany, he was also conscious of the crowd as a mindless persecuting agent, obedient to the voice of its Führer.

It is presumably this dual awareness that accounts for the ambivalence that runs through Canetti's *Masse und Macht*, and disturbs its intellectual coherence. On the one hand his approach is self-consciously detached and 'scientific', intent upon seeing the crowd in its 'biological state'. From this viewpoint the crowd is subhuman, resembling in part an inert substance (Canetti refers to groups round which crowds gather as 'crowd crystals') and in part an animal. Its 'first and supreme attribute' is its will to grow indefinitely. It hungers to seize and engulf everything within reach. It wants to 'experience for itself the strongest possible feeling of its animal force and passion'. It is naturally destructive, enjoying the demolition of homes and objects apparently as an end in itself.

In these respects Canetti's crowd is virtually identical with Le Bon's. Yet Canetti also envisages the crowd as the salvation of mankind. In a crowd, he argues, the individual escapes the burden of distance from his fellow beings, and escapes, too, from commands, from the imperatives of superiors, which Canetti sees as the origin of all evil. Within the crowd no one has the right to give commands to anyone else, and in this lies its redeeming power.

So in Canetti's logic the crowd is both a subhuman monster and a community offering human fellowship and resistance to tyranny. It is noticeable that despite the second of these alternatives, orthodox intellectual contempt for the crowd, and confusion of the crowd with the mass, colour Canetti's account, inclining him to disparage familiar intellectual bugbears, such as newspaper-readers. He argues that the old 'baiting crowd', of a kind that provided the audience at public executions, survives in the newspaper-reading public. 'Today everyone takes part in public executions through the newspapers.' This is, moreover, the 'most despicable' form of such a crowd, since it gloats over the details of death in complete security. It does not even have to assemble: the multitudinous newspaper-readers remain dispersed in their own homes.

Canetti's superiority, as an intellectual, to the mass – to 'everyone' gloating over newsprint – is apparent in this passage. Yet it is precisely that sense of superiority, in great generals, kings and despots, that he identifies as the curse and doom of mankind.[11]

A persistent intellectual tradition, running alongside the 'scientific' equation of the mass with savages, women, children, bacilli or animals, was the image of the mass as exclusively preoccupied with fact and mundane realism. As intellectuals saw it, it was the dogged literalism of the masses that unfitted them for the appreciation of art, and banished them from the higher aesthetic reaches. When T. S. Eliot writes in 'Preludes' of

. . . short square fingers stuffing pipes,
And evening newspapers, and eyes
Assured of certain certainties,

he is drawing on a set of customary intellectual reactions which attribute to the masses an obtusely factual outlook and gullibility with regard to newsprint (as well as insensitive hands – Virginia Woolf similarly regards the hands as indices of cultural level when writing of Septimus Warren Smith in *Mrs Dalloway*: 'To look at, he might have been a clerk, but of the better sort; for he wore brown boots; his hands were educated').[12]

A modern invention implicated in the fact-fixation of the masses was the camera. The emergence of the post-Education Act reading public coincided with the appearance of widely available, mass-produced hand cameras – most notably the Kodak, invented by George Eastman in New York, which was introduced in 1888 and brought photography, Eastman declared, 'within reach of every human being'. Its very name was an affront to traditional culture. Eastman coined the name 'Kodak' as an arbitrary combination of letters, not derived from any existing word, which could not be misspelled so as to destroy its identity even by the semi-literate.[13]

For many intellectuals, the camera epitomized mass man's lack of imagination. Baudelaire condemned photography as a 'sacrilege' which allowed 'the vile multitude' to 'contemplate its own trivial image'.[14] 'The mere multitude is everywhere with its empty photographic eyes,' complained Yeats.[15] Explaining the popularity of photography, Lady Eastlake observed that the desire for art belonged to a small minority 'but the craving for cheap, prompt and correct facts resides in the public at large'.[16] The camera was early identified as the art substitute favoured by clerks, suburban dwellers and similar philistine types. The suburban ideal in art, shuddered George Moore, is 'the degrading naturalism of the colour photograph'. In Gissing's *The Whirlpool*, published in 1897, Cecil Morphew opens a camera shop on Westminster Bridge Road, observing that the 'swarms' of men who go back and forth along it morning and evening are just the sort that take up photography – 'the better kind of clerk and the man of business who lives in the south suburbs'.[17]

The role of the camera in changing the direction of art and literature was charted by Walter Benjamin in his essay 'The Work of Art in the Age of Mechanical Reproduction', published in 1936.

With the advent of the first truly revolutionary means of reproduction, photography, simultaneously with the rise of socialism, art sensed the approaching crisis . . . Art reacted with the doctrine of *l'art pour l'art*, that is, with a theology of art. This gave rise to . . . 'pure' art, which not only denied any social function of art but also any categorizing by subject matter.[18]

The culmination of this process was abstract art, but an early sign of the elimination of subject matter was the new importance of fog, especially in paintings of London. Whereas, as John House has noted, earlier artists like Doré had seen London fog as gloomy and threatening, Whistler, Monet and Pissarro all valued the indistinctness of fog because it expunged fact and realism. Monet said that what he liked most of all in London was the 'mysterious cloak' of fog, and this appreciation of fog's effect on London went back to Gautier, whose 1842 essay 'A Day in London' praised the 'mystery and vagueness' fog brought, and the way it softened the 'barrenness' and 'vulgarity' of civilization.[19]

In literature, the counterpart of this foggy elimination of subject matter is to be found (as Benjamin suggests) in the Symbolists, and also in T. S. Eliot, who sets against the 'certain certainties' of the mass the vague, private areas in which the individual soul has its being. 'It is impossible to say just what I mean!' exclaims J. Alfred Prufrock, encircled by the city fog. Only in vagueness can Prufrock survive ('Oh, do not ask, "What is it?" '), and the poetic style Eliot evolves to convey Prufrock is suffused with vagueness, like the fog-

identified as the art substitute favoured by clerks, suburban dwellers and similar philistine types. The suburban ideal in art, shuddered George Moore, is 'the degrading naturalism of the colour photograph'. In Gissing's *The Whirlpool*, published in 1897, Cecil Morphew opens a camera shop on Westminster Bridge Road, observing that the 'swarms' of men who go back and forth along it morning and evening are just the sort that take up photography – 'the better kind of clerk and the man of business who lives in the south suburbs'.[17]

The role of the camera in changing the direction of art and literature was charted by Walter Benjamin in his essay 'The Work of Art in the Age of Mechanical Reproduction', published in 1936.

With the advent of the first truly revolutionary means of reproduction, photography, simultaneously with the rise of socialism, art sensed the approaching crisis . . . Art reacted with the doctrine of *l'art pour l'art*, that is, with a theology of art. This gave rise to . . . 'pure' art, which not only denied any social function of art but also any categorizing by subject matter.[18]

The culmination of this process was abstract art, but an early sign of the elimination of subject matter was the new importance of fog, especially in paintings of London. Whereas, as John House has noted, earlier artists like Doré had seen London fog as gloomy and threatening, Whistler, Monet and Pissarro all valued the indistinctness of fog because it expunged fact and realism. Monet said that what he liked most of all in London was the 'mysterious cloak' of fog, and this appreciation of fog's effect on London went back to Gautier, whose 1842 essay 'A Day in London' praised the 'mystery and vagueness' fog brought, and the way it softened the 'barrenness' and 'vulgarity' of civilization.[19]

In literature, the counterpart of this foggy elimination of subject matter is to be found (as Benjamin suggests) in the Symbolists, and also in T. S. Eliot, who sets against the 'certain certainties' of the mass the vague, private areas in which the individual soul has its being. 'It is impossible to say just what I mean!' exclaims J. Alfred Prufrock, encircled by the city fog. Only in vagueness can Prufrock survive ('Oh, do not ask, "What is it?" '), and the poetic style Eliot evolves to convey Prufrock is suffused with vagueness, like the fog-

A persistent intellectual tradition, running alongside the 'scientific' equation of the mass with savages, women, children, bacilli or animals, was the image of the mass as exclusively preoccupied with fact and mundane realism. As intellectuals saw it, it was the dogged literalism of the masses that unfitted them for the appreciation of art, and banished them from the higher aesthetic reaches. When T. S. Eliot writes in 'Preludes' of

> . . . short square fingers stuffing pipes,
> And evening newspapers, and eyes
> Assured of certain certainties,

he is drawing on a set of customary intellectual reactions which attribute to the masses an obtusely factual outlook and gullibility with regard to newsprint (as well as insensitive hands – Virginia Woolf similarly regards the hands as indices of cultural level when writing of Septimus Warren Smith in *Mrs Dalloway*: 'To look at, he might have been a clerk, but of the better sort; for he wore brown boots; his hands were educated').[12]

A modern invention implicated in the fact-fixation of the masses was the camera. The emergence of the post-Education Act reading public coincided with the appearance of widely available, mass-produced hand cameras – most notably the Kodak, invented by George Eastman in New York, which was introduced in 1888 and brought photography, Eastman declared, 'within reach of every human being'. Its very name was an affront to traditional culture. Eastman coined the name 'Kodak' as an arbitrary combination of letters, not derived from any existing word, which could not be misspelled so as to destroy its identity even by the semi-literate.[13]

For many intellectuals, the camera epitomized mass man's lack of imagination. Baudelaire condemned photography as a 'sacrilege' which allowed 'the vile multitude' to 'contemplate its own trivial image'.[14] 'The mere multitude is everywhere with its empty photographic eyes,' complained Yeats.[15] Explaining the popularity of photography, Lady Eastlake observed that the desire for art belonged to a small minority 'but the craving for cheap, prompt and correct facts resides in the public at large'.[16] The camera was early

It is presumably this dual awareness that accounts for the ambivalence that runs through Canetti's *Masse und Macht*, and disturbs its intellectual coherence. On the one hand his approach is self-consciously detached and 'scientific', intent upon seeing the crowd in its 'biological state'. From this viewpoint the crowd is subhuman, resembling in part an inert substance (Canetti refers to groups round which crowds gather as 'crowd crystals') and in part an animal. Its 'first and supreme attribute' is its will to grow indefinitely. It hungers to seize and engulf everything within reach. It wants to 'experience for itself the strongest possible feeling of its animal force and passion'. It is naturally destructive, enjoying the demolition of homes and objects apparently as an end in itself.

In these respects Canetti's crowd is virtually identical with Le Bon's. Yet Canetti also envisages the crowd as the salvation of mankind. In a crowd, he argues, the individual escapes the burden of distance from his fellow beings, and escapes, too, from commands, from the imperatives of superiors, which Canetti sees as the origin of all evil. Within the crowd no one has the right to give commands to anyone else, and in this lies its redeeming power.

So in Canetti's logic the crowd is both a subhuman monster and a community offering human fellowship and resistance to tyranny. It is noticeable that despite the second of these alternatives, orthodox intellectual contempt for the crowd, and confusion of the crowd with the mass, colour Canetti's account, inclining him to disparage familiar intellectual bugbears, such as newspaper-readers. He argues that the old 'baiting crowd', of a kind that provided the audience at public executions, survives in the newspaper-reading public. 'Today everyone takes part in public executions through the newspapers.' This is, moreover, the 'most despicable' form of such a crowd, since it gloats over the details of death in complete security. It does not even have to assemble: the multitudinous newspaper-readers remain dispersed in their own homes.

Canetti's superiority, as an intellectual, to the mass – to 'everyone' gloating over newsprint – is apparent in this passage. Yet it is precisely that sense of superiority, in great generals, kings and despots, that he identifies as the curse and doom of mankind.[11]

violent, and also childlike and credulous. What happens, Freud explains, is that the individual, on becoming a mass man, throws off the repressions of his unconscious instincts: 'The apparently new characteristics he then displays are in fact the manifestations of this unconscious, in which all that is evil in the human mind is contained as a predisposition.' Freud then proceeds to weave his own fantasy (or 'scientific myth', as he calls it) around the idea of the mass. According to this, the mass represents the 'primal horde', which was the primitive form of human society. Composed of sons, persecuted and dominated by their 'primal father' or pack leader, the horde united against the father and killed him, thus conforming to Freudian expectations, and giving the murderous propensities of the mass a sound basis in psychological theory.[9] Freud's association of the mass with 'evil', unconscious desires justifies the political suppression of the mass. Those entitled to suppress it will be, according to Freud, the élite, who have already suppressed the promptings of the mass-unconscious within their own psyches: 'Our mind . . . is no peacefully self-contained unity. It is rather to be compared with a modern State in which a mob, eager for enjoyment and destruction, has to be held down forcibly by a prudent superior class.' It is impossible, Freud stresses, to conceive of civilization without the control of the mass by a minority, and that control will inevitably involve coercion: 'For masses are lazy and unintelligent; they have no love for instinctual renunciation, and they are not to be convinced by argument of its inevitability.'[10]

Elias Canetti, generally cited as the most profound modern commentator on the mass, stands at the end of the 'scientific' tradition stretching from Le Bon to Freud, and inherits its fantasies and confusions. His attitude to crowd psychology was complicated by his personal history. During his student days in Vienna, in July 1927 he had found himself caught up in a crowd which marched on the Palace of Justice and set it alight. The excitement of this occasion, and the feeling of being absorbed, remained with him: 'I became part of the crowd. I dissolved into it fully.' But as a Jewish refugee from Nazi Germany, he was also conscious of the crowd as a mindless persecuting agent, obedient to the voice of its Führer.

composed at two distinct periods – the first part in 1905, the rest under pressure of the Great War. As a medical man Trotter is strongly attracted to scientific models, and unlike Le Bon he rather favours the herd, arguing that 'socialized gregariousness' is, biologically speaking, the most probable destiny for mankind. However, the herd will need a 'directing intelligence or group of intelligences' of a bold, experimental type to save it from its own irrationality and prejudice. Further, not all herds are good. Some correspond to useful creatures, such as the bee, but others resemble wolves. The Germans and their allies, in particular, are 'barbarous peoples of the lupine type', and must be given a 'sound thrashing', like a dog (biologically, Trotter points out, akin to a wolf), to show them who is master. The English, on the other hand, being by nature superior to sabre-rattling foreigners and obeying a mysterious 'communal mind', will, Trotter prophesies, follow the 'inevitable trend of Nature' towards an ideal beehive state. They will grow to despise war and will 'sail their ships into the gulfs of the ether, and lay tribute upon the sun and stars'. That these activities are not much like those of bees does not deter Trotter. Nor does he anticipate that there will have to be any upsetting redistribution of material wealth in the Utopian English beehive of the future.

The fact that it is difficult to persuade a man with 30 shillings a week that he has as much to lose by the loss of national independence as a man with 30 thousand a year is merely evidence that the imagination of the former is somewhat restricted by his type of education, and that we habitually attach an absurd moral significance to material advantages.

This being so, it should be possible to attain a 'very fair approximation' to moral equality among English bees, Trotter reckons, without any undue disturbance of existing material inequalities.[8]

Freud's *Group Psychology and the Analysis of the Ego*, published in 1921, praises Trotter's 'thoughtful book' but is even more impressed by the 'brilliant psychological character-sketch of the group mind' provided by Le Bon. The original German title of Freud's work was *Massenpsychologie und Ich-Analyse*, and he uses *Masse* throughout to translate Le Bon's *foule*. He agrees with Le Bon that the individual in the mass becomes a barbarian, ferocious and

A confusion essential to Le Bon's argument is that of the crowd with the mass. His method is to build up a picture of anarchic crowd behaviour, with allusions to the massacres perpetrated by crowds during the French Revolution, and to suggest that people in the mass behave in a comparable way, even when they are not members of an actual crowd but only of a 'psychological' crowd, such as a democratic electorate. A crowd need not, Le Bon stresses, be gathered in one place. Thousands of isolated individuals, or even a whole nation, may constitute a psychological crowd.

According to Le Bon, crowds are mentally inferior and intent on destruction. They act like microbes, which hasten the dissolution of dead bodies. They are extremely suggestible, impulsive, irrational, exaggeratedly emotional, inconstant, irritable and capable of thinking only in images – in short, just like women. 'Crowds are everywhere distinguished by feminine characteristics.' They also resemble children and savages. Merely by joining a crowd a man descends several rungs in the ladder of civilization, becomes a 'barbarian', acts by instinct, and is seized by violence and ferocity. Crowds are intolerant and dictatorial. But they also respond to force, not kindness, and admire the 'Caesar-type' – again, like women.

The modern era has, in Le Bon's estimation, been taken over by crowds. 'The voice of the masses has become predominant.' Their aim is to destroy civilization and return to the primitive communism which was the normal condition for all human groups before civil society began. Further, they will succeed. Civilization as we know it, created by a 'small intellectual aristocracy', will, Le Bon predicts, be extinguished and give way to a 'barbarian phase'. The optimistic liberal idea that the masses can be educated is false. Statistics show that criminality actually increases with the spread of education. Schooling transforms people into 'enemies of society', makes young people dissatisfied with honest toil and recruits numerous disciples for 'the worst forms of socialism'.[7]

A treatise even more prone to fantasy than Le Bon's was Wilfred Trotter's *Instincts of the Herd in Peace and War*, published in 1916. Some of the confusion of this work stems from its having been

masses became, in the early twentieth century, an important linguistic project among intellectuals. T. S. Eliot, attacking community singing in the *Criterion* for June 1927, fears that if it is permitted to spread it will transform the English individualist into 'the microscopic cheese-mite of the great cheese of the future'. William Inge tells *Evening Standard* readers in 1928, 'The democratic man is a species of ape.' Trying to imagine what she calls 'that anonymous monster the Man in the Street', Virginia Woolf finds herself visualizing 'a vast, featureless, almost shapeless jelly of human stuff . . . occasionally wobbling this way or that as some instinct of hate, revenge, or admiration bubbles up beneath it'.[3] For Ezra Pound, humanity, apart from artists, is merely a 'mass of dolts', a 'rabble', representing 'the waste and the manure' from which grows 'the tree of the arts'. In Pound's *Cantos* the 'multitudes' and their leaders transmogrify into a torrent of human excrement – 'Democracies electing their sewage'. This vision of 'the great arsehole' was meant, Pound explained, as a portrait of contemporary England.[4]

Eliminating the humanity of the masses can also be effected by converting them into scientific specimens. This was the enterprise undertaken in the 1930s by Mass Observation. Tom Harrisson, cofounder of the project, was a naturalist and anthropologist who had been a keen bird-watcher at Harrow. He and his team of middle-class observers based themselves in Bolton ('Worktown' in Mass-Observation code) and mingled with the natives, collecting data on local customs such as the cult of the aspidistra, football pools, dirty jokes, armpit hygiene and the proportion of males wearing bowler hats in pubs. Observers were instructed to use an impersonal notation when identifying human specimens. The formula 'M 45 D', for example, meant a man of about forty-five who looked or sounded unskilled working class (Category D).[5]

Amateurish and innocent as Mass Observation now seems, its employment of a scientific model for the purpose of segregating and degrading the mass had a sinister counterpart in the assimilation of the masses to bacteria and bacilli. David Bodanis has suggested that there was, indeed, a causal connection between Pasteur's extreme right-wing politics and the direction in which his scientific discovery advanced. Horrified by democracy, and obsessed by the notion of swarming invisible multitudes infecting and destroying civilized society, he inaugurated the immensely influential cultural concept of bacteria, which he described in terms analogous to those used to characterize the seething, unclean masses. Once this scientific model had been offered, it could easily be reversed, so that instead of bacteria resembling the masses, the masses resembled bacteria. Inevitably this correspondence was exploited by those wishing to purge or eliminate the mass. Hitler, Bodanis notes, repeatedly alludes to the Jews as a bacterial disease. The Führer applauds Pasteur and also the German Robert Koch, discoverer of the TB bacillus – which, for Germans, acquired a kind of national prestige among bacilli.

The discovery of the Jewish virus is one of the greatest revolutions the world has seen. The struggle in which we are now engaged is similar to the one waged by Pasteur and Koch in the last century. How many diseases must owe their origins to the Jewish virus! Only when we have eliminated the Jews will we regain our health.

Hitler's 'scientific' method of dealing with Jews – herding them into special reception centres, taking away their clothes and leading them either naked or in simple hospital-style gowns to large 'spraying' rooms – followed with a certain logic from the configuration of the problem of the mass as a subject for scientific inquiry and solution.[6]

In the late nineteenth and early twentieth centuries, investigators of the mass invented their own branch of science, or science fiction, of which the pioneer was Gustave Le Bon. Among other accomplishments Le Bon was the first Frenchman to visit Nepal, where he went with a donkey and a pair of calipers to measure the cranial capacity of the Nepalese élite. His book *The Crowd*, published in 1895, went through twenty-six printings in French and sixteen in English before 1925, and was translated into thirteen languages, among them Arabic, Turkish, Hindi and Japanese. It was admired by Sigmund Freud, Ortega y Gasset and, it seems, Adolf Hitler, who probably read it in a German translation.

Rewriting the Masses

Since the 'mass' is an imaginary construct, displacing the unknowable multiplicity of human life, it can be reshaped at will, in accordance with the wishes of the imaginer. Alternatively, it can be replaced by images, equally arbitrary, of 'typical' mass men or mass women. The tendency among intellectuals to identify particular persons as 'mass' types is recognized and defended by Ortega y Gasset. If we wish to observe the mass, he explains, there is no need for us to wait until an actual mass of people comes along: 'In the presence of one individual we can decide whether he is "mass" or not.'

In Ortega's view, what marks out a mass man is that he is unambitious and 'common'. However, he also refers repeatedly to the 'brutality' of the mass – a difficult idea to square with the humble, nondescript individual he elsewhere imagines the mass comprising.[1] It seems clear that he retains (at least) two distinct and mutually irreconcilable images of mass man, alternating between them as occasion demands. This is normal intellectual practice. Rewriting or reinventing the mass was an enterprise in which early twentieth-century intellectuals invested immense imaginative effort, and it naturally generated a wide variety of identities. The aim of all these rewritings was the same, however: to segregate the intellectuals from the mass, and to acquire the control over the mass that language gives.

The anxiety caused by the mass when it is sensed as a physical presence, as yet unlocated in language, can be illustrated from the notebooks of Thomas Hardy. In the 1880s the Hardys were living in Upper Tooting, and could see across London from their top windows. At night Hardy was persistently kept awake by an eerie feeling of threat. He had a horror of lying down in close proximity to the population of London – 'a monster whose body had four million heads and eight million eyes'. At daybreak he would lurk in an upper back bedroom and peer out as the line of light spread round the horizon. Within that line, he told himself anxiously, 'are the Four Millions'.

When Hardy observed the mass at closer quarters, contempt was able to displace fear. In the British Museum he watched

crowds parading and gaily traipsing round the mummies, thinking today is for ever, and the girls casting sly glances at young men across the swathed dust of Mycerinus. They pass with flippant comments the illuminated manuscripts – the labour of years – and stand under Ramases the Great, joking. Democratic government may be justice to man, but it will probably merge in proletarian, and when these people are our masters, it will lead to more of this contempt, and possibly be the utter ruin of art and literature.[2]

Foreboding remains here, but not fear, because Hardy has been able to locate his general anxiety about the mass in particular beings ('these people'), to whose thoughts he assumes he has access and whom his language, by representing, fictionalizes and controls.

The transition from Hardy nervously watching the populated darkness from his upstairs window to Hardy feeling superior in the British Museum could serve as a paradigm of the modern intellectual's effort to limit and dominate the mass. Creating images that could effect this domination was a major preoccupation of Nietzsche, for whom reimagining the mass seems to have been a vital component of mental stability. Nietzsche's most common image of the mass is as a herd of animals. But he also figures it as a swarm of poisonous flies, or as raindrops and weeds, ruining proud structures.

The essential function of these images is to deprive the mass of human status. Humanity is to be found elsewhere – in the exceptional individuals Nietzsche celebrates. Denial of humanity to the

smudged cityscapes of Whistler or Monet. We cannot tell what happens in 'The Love Song of J. Alfred Prufrock'. The shapes are blurred. Who are the 'you' and 'I' at the poem's start ('Let us go then, you and I')? Are they Prufrock's two selves? And which two selves? Is he looking at his reflection in a mirror before going out? Does he ever get to the room where the mysterious women come and go, talking of Michelangelo? These famous unanswerable questions about the poem have generated so much debate only because they have been mistaken for answerable questions, which is like supposing that a Monet is really a Canaletto that has been accidentally smudged. The questions are unanswerable because the poem designedly withholds the information needed to answer them. It withdraws itself into indefiniteness, eluding the fact-hungry masses. The fact that we cannot be sure what it is about is essential to what it is about. Its syntax is veiled. For example:

> In the room the women come and go
> Talking of Michelangelo.

'In' is odd with 'come and go'. You would expect people to come and go to and from a room. What is meant by coming and going *in* is not clear, and cannot, of course, be clarified. The poetic enterprise is successfully evasive, embodying Prufrock's evasiveness. Instead of facts, it offers a phantom meaning which dissolves when the reader tries to isolate it.

The invented identities for mass man that we have met with so far – from bacillus to camera-toting fact-addict – have all been derogatory, providing the intellectual with a defence against the unidentifiable Other. However, intellectual mythology also yields cosmetic versions of the mass – that is, versions fabricated to make the mass more acceptable to intellectuals. A large subgroup of these function by turning the mass into a kind of pastoral. Ezra Pound's 'In a Station of the Metro' provides a conveniently brief example:

> The apparition of these faces in the crowd:
> Petals on a wet, black bough.

Pound later explained how he came to write this poem. He got out of the metro at Concorde, and in the jostle saw several beautiful faces. He tried for weeks to write a poem about this. Then he thought of using the ancient Japanese haiku form, because it struck him that in Japan 'or in some other very old, very quiet civilization, some one else might understand the significance'.

His restriction of the poem's length can itself be seen as a protest against the numerousness of the crowd. In Japan, he comments, 'a work of art is not estimated by its acreage, and sixteen syllables are counted enough for a poem if you arrange and punctuate them properly'. The poem subjects the modern Parisian crowd to a double displacement: it transforms it into a bough with blossoms – a pastoral accessory, with no vestiges of human life; and it assimilates it to the foreign, ancient, colourfully aesthetic culture of old Japan.[20]

This fusion of pastoral and historical pageant to provide a cosmetic version of the mass becomes the dominant motive in the fiction of E. M. Forster. Repelled by what he saw as the coldness of the English middle classes, and especially by their coldness to homosexuals, Forster looked southwards to Italy for more congenial life forms. In *Where Angels Fear to Tread* and *A Room with a View*, the narrow propriety of English visitors to Italy collides with the vigour and sensuality of 'ordinary' Italians. The exemplary warm-bloodedness of the Italian masses links them, in Forster's fantasy, with the pagan deities and with the European high culture of the past. When the Italian cab-driver in *A Room with a View* gives his girl a lift, Forster interposes: 'It was Phaethon who drove them to Fiesole . . . a youth all irresponsibility and fire . . . And it was Persephone whom he asked leave to pick up on the way.' The scene earlier in the novel where one Italian stabs another in a street brawl, and blood splashes on to Lucy Honeychurch's picture postcards, is designed to tell us that the world of passion and casual violence in which the Italian masses live was the world that produced the great artworks that Lucy buys her emasculated photographic replicas of. The splash of lower-class blood gives them back their authenticity.[21]

When he went to India Forster found a mass that was even more primitive and colourful than the Italians. It has often been pointed out that he did not know India very well. As a Maharajah's secretary, his contact with the common people was minimal, and he did not even need to seek lower-class lovers, as he did in England and Egypt, because the Maharajah supplied him with a reliable concubine from among the hereditary palace servants.[22] Consequently, the Indian people remained for Forster a spectacle he could endow with whatever imaginative attributes he chose. He invented an India in which the masses, unlike those of industrialized Europe, are surrounded by a romantic aura of primitivism and naturalness. The famous punkah-wallah in the courtroom in *A Passage to India* illustrates this:

Almost naked, and splendidly formed . . . he had the strength and beauty that sometimes come to flower in Indians of low birth. When that strange race nears the dust and is condemned as untouchable, then nature remembers the physical perfection that she accomplished elsewhere, and throws out a god . . . This man would have been notable anywhere; among the thin-hammed, flat-chested mediocrities of Chandrapore he stood out as divine, yet he was of the city, its garbage had nourished him, he would end on its rubbish heaps. Pulling the rope towards him . . . he seemed apart from human destinies, a male fate, a winnower of souls.[23]

Forster's mythical fantasizing floats above social problems such as the caste system and urban destitution. As a 'god' and a nursling of 'nature' the punkah-wallah belongs to a scheme of things more ancient and lasting than politics. He provides a pastoral (and winningly subservient) alternative to the troublesome, literate European masses. Discoursing upon Leonard Bast in *Howards End*, Forster had remarked: 'Had he lived some centuries ago, in the brightly coloured civilizations of the past, he would have had a definite status . . . But in his day the angel of Democracy had arisen, enshadowing the classes with leathern wings.'[24] The punkah-wallah is quite unshadowed by democracy, and he does, in effect, live in a brightly coloured past civilization. Though his 'definite status' might seem rather limiting, there is no question but that Forster prefers him to Leonard as a representative of mass man.

All D. H. Lawrence's later life could be seen as a quest for an

35

unspoiled mass of this kind. Reading his letters from about 1920 onwards we find him becoming disappointed with one nation or racial group after another as they fail to meet his standards of simplicity and primitivism – first the Italians, then the Sardinians, then the Indians, whom Lawrence, unlike Forster, finds disgusting ('silly dark people' with 'temples like decked-up pigsties'), then the Australians ('almost imbecile'), then the South Sea Islanders, who stink of coconut oil, and finally the Mexican Indians, who fill Lawrence with hope when he first hears of them, because they are said to be unspoiled sun-worshippers and rain-makers, but who turn out to be Americanized like everyone else and to have, Lawrence decides, 'no inside life throb' left in them at all.[25]

Forster's and Lawrence's quest for a mass untouched by modern industrial civilization was an offshoot of the widespread intellectual cult of the peasant. As representatives of simple, healthy, organic life, peasants had been popular with William Morris, with the Arts and Crafts movement, with Eric Gill and with early Fabians, as well as with Paul Gauguin and the Pont-Aven school. Nietzsche endorsed this fanciful pastoralism, selecting in *Thus Spake Zarathustra* 'a sound peasant, coarse, artful, obstinate, and enduring' as 'the noblest type'.[26] Irish writers, notably W. B. Yeats and J. M. Synge also found admirable simplicity and folk wisdom in peasants. Unlike Germany and Ireland, England had no peasants left at the end of the nineteenth century, so English writers seeking a pastoral version of the mass had to invent them, or, like Eric Gill and other simple-lifers, pretend to be peasants themselves. Gill wore an adaptation of peasant costume, consisting of a drab, colourless, belted smock and, in winter, loose scarlet-silk under-drawers. He was, it is worth noting, a keen disciple of Nietzsche as well as an enemy of mass culture. He thought it 'extremely doubtful' that everybody should be taught to read, and hoped that a bomb would fall on Selfridge's.[27]

A striking example of peasant-invention occurs in Virginia Woolf's *Mrs Dalloway* when an old woman, holding out her hand for coppers, sings a song on the pavement outside Regent's Park Tube Station. The woman is said to resemble a wind-beaten tree:

for ever barren of leaves which lets the wind run up and down its branches singing

> ee um fah un so
> foo swee too eem oo

and rocks and creaks and moans in the eternal breeze.

Through all ages – when the pavement was grass, when it was swamp, through the age of tusk and mammoth, through the age of silent sunrise – the battered woman – for she wore a skirt – with her right hand exposed, her left clutching her side, stood singing of love – love which has lasted a million years, she sang, love which prevails.[28]

These curious thoughts are not presented as occurring to any distinct character in the novel. They are offered, apparently, as a poetic reverie on a member of the mass singing a song, and they go on for several paragraphs in a sort of transcendent dreaminess. The old woman merges with the soil. Her mouth – 'so rude a mouth' – is 'a mere hole in the earth, muddy too, matted with root fibres and tangled grasses', and its 'old bubbling' song streams away in rivulets down the Marylebone Road.

Virginia Woolf's flight of fancy here is a way not of describing but of eliminating old women who beg outside Regent's Park Tube Station. By converting her into a peasant or super-peasant, timeless, immemorial, mixed up with soil and tree roots, Woolf deprives the woman of the distasteful social reality which she would possess as a member of the mass asking for money. The beggar disappears in a primitivist cosmetic haze.

An alternative to promoting the masses to peasanthood is to blame them for not being peasants, or point out how much more attractive they would have been had they remained peasants. J. B. Priestley, watching the coronation crowds in 1937, felt disillusioned with the English people. They had lost the natural life of woods and fields. 'Most probably,' he lamented, 'they did not know how to make love or even to eat and drink properly.'[29] Priestley does not divulge what alerts him to this curious possibility. But his implication is clearly that proper love-making, eating and drinking are what used to go on in the woods and fields, and many intellectuals of his day would have agreed with him. Though he had started out as a novelist for the masses, disdained by highbrows like Graham Greene (who ridiculed him as Mr Savory in *Stamboul Train*), Priestley, by the 1930s, had become a vehement critic of mass culture. He coined the term 'Admass' for the system of advertising, material welfare and mass communication which created 'the mass mind, the mass man'. At Blackpool during Illuminations Week in 1938, he deplores the 'empty idiocy' of the commercial amusements and the low quality of holidaymaker: 'mostly small, rather mis-shapen, toothless men and women, harmless enough, but very unattractive in the mass'.[30]

The demand among intellectuals for a cosmetic version of the mass, which prompted the quest for peasants and primitives in pastoral settings, also sanctioned political rewritings of the mass, whether as stalwart workers or as the downtrodden and the oppressed. These fictions were readily available for rhetorical purposes even to writers who neither knew nor desired to know any workers. Graham Greene, writing to his future wife from Nottingham early in 1926, admits to finding the place 'ghastly': 'One sees absolutely no one here of one's own class. In the street, in the cafés, anywhere. It destroys democratic feelings at birth.' However, in a spare moment he writes a poem about Nottingham which contains the lines:

> . . . I only see
> Out in the streets where there's always rain
> With cracked harmoniums the unemployed.

The unemployed are here singled out from the general ghastliness of Nottingham's inhabitants as recipients of Greene's caring concern. Mention of them attests his proper leftist sympathies. Their function is, in effect, to vouch for the intellectual who observes them. This is a common role for the mass (and synonyms for the mass) in leftist rhetoric. Such usages imply a democratic solidarity which may, of course, be fictitious. Greene's real attitude to the unemployed is indicated by the fact that when the General Strike occurred, a few weeks later, he automatically sided with his class against the workers, enrolled as a Special Constable and enjoyed the fun of strike-breaking. The atmosphere, he recalls, was like that of a rugger match played against a team from a rough council school.[31]

Leftist intellectuals were not all as transparent as Greene. But their rewriting of mankind as mass inevitably segregated them, as intellectuals, from the non-intellectual majority – though it was intended to have quite the opposite effect. This development belonged particularly to the 1930s, when, as Martin Green has chronicled in *Children of the Sun*, the dandies and aesthetes of the 1920s turned left and became honorary proletarians.[32] Reporting from Paris in the first number of *New Writing*, John Lehmann enthuses about the 'new revolutionary unity of the workers', and about the 'masses [who] swarm over the surrounding hills and the factory suburbs'. To share the spirit of the masses, it was not necessary, it seems, even for Lehmann to get up from his chair: 'To the poet, who sits in one corner and lifts his head from his paper to watch the incessant flow of faces before the door . . . all these masses,' he recounts, seem 'suddenly to be transformed by the confidence of victory'.[33] Though Lehmann's purpose is the contrary of Nietzsche's, his images of flood and swarm are the same, and serve as effectively to distance the intellectual from those he observes. Edwin Muir complained of this effect in leftist writing when corresponding with Stephen Spender in 1937. The whole impulse of left literature, Muir observes, is:

in danger of being dehumanized, formalized, throttled by an automatic ideology, which denies humanity except in great bulk, so huge that it has no immediate relation to our lives: the 'masses', for instance, not as a collection of men and women, but as an instrument, dehumanized as an army.[34]

The spokesman of the left who was most suspicious of such rhetoric was George Orwell. His case is worth pausing over not only because of his attractiveness as man and writer but also because of the tangles he gets into in trying to confront the problem of the mass. Basically the trouble was that he identified the masses both with freedom and with dirt. He believed in freedom, but dirt repelled him. He reflected this quandary when he wrote that 'the thinking person' is usually left-wing by intellect but right-wing by temperament.

According to his own account of his upbringing, he was about six before he became aware of class distinctions. Before that his heroes were working-class people such as the farm-hands, who used to let him ride on the drill when they were sowing turnips, and builder's labourers, and the plumber's children, with whom he went bird's-nesting. Soon, though, he was forbidden to play with these children because they were 'common'. He does not especially blame his family for this – it was typical middle-class snobbishness. But it meant that for him the working class ceased to be 'a race of friendly and wonderful beings' and became enemies – 'almost subhuman' and 'brutal'. It was dinned into him that they were dirty and smelt. Thanks to this indoctrination, he developed a dread of working-class bodies, imagining their 'nests and layers of greasy rags' and their 'bacon-like reek'. On one dreadful occasion when he was thirteen he found himself in a third-class railway compartment with shepherds and pig-men coming back from market and was almost sick, when a bottle of beer was passed round, at the thought of having to drink from it 'after all those lower-class male mouths'. In Burma, with the Indian Police, the smell of a marching column of soldiers would make his stomach turn: 'All I knew was that it was *lower-class* sweat that I was smelling, and the thought of it made me sick.'

Though Orwell protests that all this was 'pure prejudice', he does not in fact deny that the working classes are dirty or smell. He praises Somerset Maugham for lack of 'humbug' in insisting that the working man 'stinks'. It is not the working class's fault, Orwell concedes – often they do not have bathrooms. But they are undeniably on the whole 'dirtier than the upper classes'. This seriously limits the extent to which one can be intimate or affectionate with them. 'You can have an affection for a murderer or a sodomite, but you cannot have an affection for a man whose breath stinks.' Hence 'the chiasmic, impassable quality of class-distinctions'. Whatever we may pretend, it is not possible to be 'really intimate' with the working class.

Orwell's difficulty is clear. He claims that those who brought him up brainwashed him on the matter of the working class's dirt. Yet he insists that their dirt is a fact, attested by his own experience. This contradiction leads to further muddles. On the one hand, he reprimands those who idealize the working class, and who pretend their 'dirtiness is somehow meritorious in itself'. On the other hand, he proclaims (on behalf of some slum-dwellers who have objected to being deloused), 'I sometimes think that the price of liberty is not so much eternal vigilance as eternal dirt.' Fighting alongside the POUM Anarchist militia in Spain, he encountered the same dilemma. The militiamen used churches as latrines, and habitually defecated in their own trench. This, Orwell reports, was 'a disgusting thing when one had to walk round it in the darkness'. Astonishingly, though, he goes on without a pause: 'But the dirt never worried me. Dirt is a thing people make too much fuss about.' The contradiction is glaring. How can dirt be disgusting, yet never worry Orwell? His phobia about lower-class dirt collides head-on with his determination to invest dirt with political value, as the price of liberty.[35]

It was the political significance of dirt that drove him to disguise himself as a tramp and mingle with down-and-outs. Confronting dirt in common lodging houses was a self-imposed penance – an expiation of the guilt he felt at having allied himself with oppression as an Indian Police officer. It is dirt that he dwells on in his descriptions of tramps and destitutes – the sweat and spittle and bedbugs, the strange swirls of grime, like marble-top tables, on the skin of his fellow lodgers, the awful filth of the communal bathwater. Those he mingled with were not so much people to him as representatives of dirt. They might as well, from this viewpoint, have been rats as people – and he admits that the first time he entered a common lodging house it was like going into 'a sewer full of rats'. Dirt, in these circumstances, acquires an almost sacramental value. The first cup of tea Orwell drank in a common lodging house was 'a kind of baptism'. It atoned for that bottle of beer he did not share with the pig-men and shepherds. Dirt, if sufficient of it got on him, could make up for his past career as an imperialist oppressor.[36]

Doublethink over dirt persists in Orwell. Among the tramps dirt is meritorious and redeeming. But the plentiful supply of dirt he finds in his digs over a tripe shop in Wigan strikes him as simply repellent.

41

Presumably this was because the landlord and his wife (whom he calls the Brookers) were lower middle class rather than working class, so that sharing their dirt could serve no redemptive purpose. The images of squalor Orwell evokes – Mr Brooker's sickening antics with the chamber pot; his wife's soggy, catarrh-soaked balls of newspaper – are among the most nauseous in his writing. He evidently agrees with the verdict of a fellow lodger, a southerner like himself: 'The filthy bloody bastards!'

Moreover, Orwell treats the Brookers not as isolated horrors but as representatives of mass man:

People like the Brookers . . . exist in tens and hundreds of thousands; they are one of the characteristic by-products of the modern world . . . This is part at least of what industrialism has done for us . . . This is where it all led – to labyrinthine slums and dark back kitchens with sickly, ageing people creeping round and round them like blackbeetles.[37]

There is a clear connection between the Brookers and the masses who invade George Bowling's childhood paradise in Orwell's last pre-war novel, *Coming Up for Air*. Bowling is a henpecked insurance agent who wins some money on a horse and decides to treat himself to a secret holiday in the idyllic Thames Valley village where he spent his childhood. When he gets there, it is unrecognizable. There are no fields any more, just rows and rows of red-brick houses, obliterating the old village. The river bank, secluded once, is black with people and lined with penny-in-the-slot machines and tea-kiosks. Paper bags and cigarette cartons choke the water; the air pulses with the din of gramophones. Bowling learns that 20,000 new inhabitants have been rehoused from Lancashire on a slum-clearance scheme. It is their provenance – Lancashire – that links them with the Brookers. The blackbeetles have been rescued, rehoused and provided with gramophones and other symbols of consumer prosperity. But this has turned them into pollution. Spread over the Thames Valley countryside, they have destroyed it. Bowling puts the twentieth-century predicament succinctly: 'The dustbin that we're in reaches up to the stratosphere.'[38]

Orwell's ambivalence over the dirtiness of the masses reaches a climax in *Nineteen Eighty-Four*. Here the masses, renamed the proles, live in dirt, among rats and bedbugs. But it is meritorious dirt – *Down and Out* dirt as opposed to Brooker dirt – signifying the proles' human decency and their freedom from the Party. In a bid to emulate these qualities Winston hires a room in a prole house, swarming with vermin. 'If there is hope,' he writes in his secret diary, 'it lies in the proles.'

However, as Winston well knows, the proles are stupid, ignorant and gullible. They receive no education. Rubbishy entertainment and spurious news, collectively called Prolefeed, are manufactured for their consumption, as is pornography, which issues from the Pornosec section of the Ministry of Truth. How, then, can anything be hoped of the proles? Winston spells out the dilemma in his diary: 'Until they become conscious they will never rebel, and until after they have rebelled they cannot become conscious.'[39]

Although Orwell had apparently not read, or at least never mentions, Theodor Adorno, Max Horkheimer and their colleagues in the Frankfurt Institute for Social Research, the impasse at which Winston arrives was essentially the same as theirs. The Frankfurt theorists (except Benjamin) shared the view that mass culture and the mass media, as developed under capitalism, had degraded civilization in the twentieth century. They blamed radio, cinema, newspapers and cheap books for 'the disappearance of the inner life'. Like Winston, they wished to believe in the revolutionary potential of the proletariat. But they regarded the masses as dupes, seduced by capitalism's equivalent of Prolefeed. Happily gobbling down the products of the commercialized 'culture industry', the masses had developed a 'false consciousness', so that they no longer saw things as the Frankfurt theorists wished. Consequently, Horkheimer reports, 'truth has sought refuge among small groups of admirable men', and 'the general intellectual level of the masses is rapidly declining'. Following this line, Marcuse preaches the confessedly 'élitist' doctrine that genuine art must be inaccessible to the masses. Only the individual can appreciate 'high' culture – and mass civilization threatens to obliterate the individual. 'The picture of freedom against society,' Adorno proclaims, 'lives in the crushed, abused individual's features alone.' This is not so very different from

O'Brien's warning to Winston: 'If you want a picture of the future, imagine a boot stamping on a human face – for ever.'[40]

To the Frankfurt School as to Orwell's Winston, then, the masses are a disappointment. Wallowing in consumer pleasures, they refuse to take on the revolutionary role the intellectual ascribes to them. Towards the end of *Nineteen Eighty-Four*, though, another, more optimistic, identity is suggested for the masses. Winston and Julia listen to a prole woman singing as she pegs nappies on a line, and Orwell surrounds her with images of countryside and farmyard. She is like a mare, with powerful buttocks, and like the rose hip that follows the rose, and like a turnip (linking her, perhaps, with the friendly turnip-sowing farm-hands little Orwell knew). She must, Winston thinks, have had many children – swelling like a fertilized fruit. She evokes a 'mystical reverence' in him. She has, he realizes, no mind, only strong arms, a warm heart and a fertile belly. But it is people like her who are 'storing up in their hearts and bellies and muscles' the power that will one day overturn the world. The proles, Winston feels, are like birds, passing on from body to body the vitality that the intellectuals of the Party do not share and cannot kill.[41]

We can recognize here Orwell's urge to repudiate his intellectual isolation and enter into fellowship with those 'friendly and wonderful beings' he admired as a child. But present too is a cosmetic version of the masses as pastoral. They are transposed to an innocent, pre-industrial existence – an existence prior to that in which they pollute George Bowling's village with their swarming thousands. The eruption of countryside images – birds, trees and song – shows Orwell rewriting the mass, rather as Yeats had done in 'Sailing to Byzantium'.

> The young
> In one another's arms, birds in the trees,
> – Those dying generations – at their song,
> The salmon-falls, the mackerel-crowded seas,
> Fish, flesh or fowl, commend all summer long
> Whatever is begotten, born, and dies.

Caught in that sensual music all neglect
Monuments of unageing intellect.

Yeats's swarming masses, though unintellectual, are made innocent by association with the self-regulating populations of birds and fish ('dying generations'). They are identified with the natural plenty, which, in reality, they consume. Likewise Orwell (or Winston) merges the masses back into a pastoral world of birds and wild roses, which redeems them but also eliminates them. For that pastoral world predated the revolt of the masses.

3

The Suburbs and the Clerks

The imaginative project of rewriting the masses, which intellectuals undertook, was coloured by various historical factors. Prominent among these were the growth of suburbs and the enormous increase in the numbers of white-collar workers, collectively designated clerks. The two factors were linked, since it was in the suburbs that the clerks lived. This chapter will consider each, and intellectual reaction to each. First, the suburbs.

The spread of suburbs around major population centres was already considerable before 1900 and was accelerated by developments in transport, such as electric trams and cheaper rail fares, which facilitated commuterism. These improvements encouraged a major building boom around the turn of the century which was especially vigorous in the London area. The number of houses in outer west London (Acton, Chiswick, Ealing, Hanwell), for example, rose from fewer than 3,000 in 1851 to over 33,000 in 1911. Alarm at the loss of countryside was strongly voiced. To surround London with acres of suburbia, warned *The Times* in 1904,

is to produce a district of appalling monotony, ugliness and dullness. And every suburban extension makes existing suburbs less desirable. Fifty years ago Brixton and Clapham were on the edge of the country; a walk could take one into lanes and meadows. Now London stretches to Croydon. It is no longer possible to escape from the dull suburbs into unspoiled country.

It was in response to consternation of this kind that the ideal of the garden suburb came into being, and over sixty garden-city estates were started before the First World War. But between the wars this impetus faltered. With the arrival of motor transport, and the appearance in the 1930s of large-scale building firms capable of completing a semi in three days, suburbia flung its tentacles along the bus routes, and no attempt was made to check it until the passing of the 1935 Restriction of Ribbon Development Act – by which time it was, many felt, too late. Housebuilding in England and Wales rose from 91,653 in 1923 to 202,060 in 1930. The new housing, and intellectual distaste for it, were not confined to Britain. Nietzsche's Zarathustra sees rows of new houses and demands: 'What do these houses mean? Truly, no great soul put them up as its image! Did a silly child perhaps take them out of its toy-box?'[1]

A concomitant of suburban growth that caused additional dismay in Britain was 'the spoiling of the suburbs'. This was the process by which established and largely green middle-class suburbs were engulfed by new development, with rows of houses being fitted on to adjacent meadow land, and the gardens of old mansions being bought by speculative builders. The periodical *Building News* complained in 1896: 'Every suburb is being spoiled by the hand of the jerry builder and the greed of landowners. Instead of swelling hills and green pastures we see serrated lines of house tops and slated roofs.' Awareness that this process was causing irreparable damage was widespread by the turn of the century in the provinces as well as London. It was, for example, a frequent topic of regret in Manchester and Sheffield newspapers.[2]

Since English writers in this period were recruited, generally speaking, from the educated and comfortably-off, many of them grew up in old-style green outer suburbs, which were later spoiled by housing development. The ruined childhood paradise becomes a familiar refrain in writers' biographies and autobiographies. Graham Greene, for example, tells how the crawling mediocrity of suburbia destroyed his uncle's big house, The Hall, in Berkhamsted:

No stone of it now remains, a building estate has swallowed all – the lawns, the trees, the stables, and the meadows, which were to be the scenery of my calf-love. When I see a performance of *The Cherry Orchard* today, it is on that estate I hear the axes falling.[3]

47

A similar despoilment features in the biography of Evelyn Waugh. When he was a child, his father moved the family out of London to a house on the edge of Hampstead Heath, called 'Underhill' after a lane in his native Midsomer Norton. The elder Waugh wrote ecstatically of the meadow he could see from his book-room. Soon, however, other houses were built, the tube railway arrived and the area was swallowed up by the suburb of Golders Green. 'The whole place,' Evelyn reports, 'volleys and thunders with traffic.' He pronounced his verdict on suburban England in *Vile Bodies*, published in 1930, in the scene where Ginger and Nina leave on their honeymoon by aeroplane. While Ginger stumblingly tries to recall Shakespeare's lines about 'This precious stone set in a silver sea', Nina surveys the reality:

Nina looked down and saw inclined at an odd angle a horizon of straggling red suburb; arterial roads dotted with little cars; factories, some of them working, others empty and decaying; a disused canal; some distant hills sown with bungalows; wireless masts and overhead power cables; men and women were indiscernible except as tiny spots; they were marrying and shopping and making money and having children. The scene lurched and tilted as the aeroplane struck a current of air.

'I think I'm going to be sick', said Nina.[4]

The house where E. M. Forster spent his happiest childhood days, Rooksnest, near Stevenage, was also threatened. In *Howards End* Helena Schlegel points from the eponymous house, which is really Rooksnest, over the meadows towards a 'red rust' on the horizon. It is houses. 'London's creeping,' she warns. Rooksnest and the Purbeck Downs are doomed. 'The melting-pot,' Forster rightly predicts, 'was being prepared for them.'[5]

Even the relatively plebeian George Bernard Shaw had a tale of ruinous suburban spread to tell, affecting his own family. His uncle Walter, a doctor, had settled and prospered in Leyton, until

London spread and swallowed up Leyton. The country houses of his patients were demolished and replaced by rows of little brick boxes inhabited by clerks, supporting families on incomes scaling down to fifteen shillings a week. This ruined him.[6]

The ugliness of suburban sprawl is a persistent theme in Edith Nesbit, whose children's books helped fashion the minds of several generations in the early twentieth century. Her story *Fortunatus Rex and Co.* decries the activities of speculative builders, who buy 'all the pretty woods and fields', grub up the grass and trees, and 'put streets there and lamp-posts and ugly little yellow brick houses'. Everything, Edith feels, 'is getting uglier and uglier. And no one seems to care.' When E. M. Forster stayed with the Nesbits he was surprised to find that at sundown a strange little ceremony took place in the garden. Edith produced models of factories and suburban villas, made of cardboard and brown paper, and everyone ritually set light to these effigies of urban encroachment.[7]

When the Nesbits bought their house in Eltham in 1899, it stood among fields at the end of a country lane with hawthorns and chestnut and lilacs. But cheap housing had gradually spread up to the garden walls, and trams rattled along the main road beyond the gates. Edith and her husband Hubert Bland were both leading Fabians, and a friend once pointed out that as Socialists they ought to be in favour of cheap housing instead of deploring it. This criticism pinpointed the quandary in which the intellectuals were placed. They rightly saw that housing the masses caused irreparable damage, yet they could not ignore the social reasons that demanded it. E. M. Forster in 'The Challenge of Our Time' faces this dilemma. He aknowledges that slums must be cleared and people housed, but he also feels that with each new housing development a piece of England has been destroyed as surely as if a bomb had hit it. 'I cannot,' he concludes, 'equate the problem. It is a collision of loyalties.'[8]

It was the speed of the disaster that appalled. Within two or three decades farms, fields and woods that had stood unchanged for centuries were lost for ever. English writers born in the last decades of the nineteenth century witnessed ecological catastrophe on a scale no previous generation had experienced. In *The Horrors of the Countryside*, published in 1931, C. E. M. Joad catalogues the desecrations of the last twenty years: the 'drab and squalid' suburbs to the south of London, the 'scurf of villas and bungalows' that has polluted practically the whole coast of Kent and Sussex, the 'purulent beastliness' of Worthing. Short of a change in public opinion, of which there is no sign, nothing, he predicts, can prevent the total disappearance of rural England.[9]

The uglification of England drove young writers abroad, preferably to wild and remote locales, producing an Indian Summer of English travel-writing between the wars. Evelyn Waugh went to East Africa, Graham Greene to West; Robert Byron to India, Tibet, Persia, Siberia and China, as well as the remoter parts of Greece. It is clear from Byron's letters home that a prime motive behind his travels is escape from the crush and ugliness of modern England – only to discover that tourist spots abroad are equally defiled. In Venice at the Lido the water is 'like hot saliva – cigar ends floating into one's mouth'. The pyramids and the Sphinx 'lie in a suburb surrounded by advertisement hoardings'. Tokyo 'is simply *Ealing* . . . The genius of Marks and Spencer's and Lyons Corner House presides.' The so-called 'country' in up-state New York is nothing but a vast suburb, and flying over it Byron reacts like Waugh's Nina:

I can't tell you how loathesome [*sic*], how inconceivably disgusting, the landscape is here. Even from the air it almost made me feel sick . . . Everything is under snow, which adds to the squalor of the millions of little detached houses sitting by themselves.

He seeks emptiness, and eventually finds it amid the snows of Tibet and on the Central Asian steppe: 'the most lovely thing you ever saw, an endless sea of lush green, wild barley and wild oats, full of flowers, irises, poppies, etc., with larks trilling in a spring sky'.[10]

But the effects of suburban spread went far beyond travel-writing. The massive expansion of suburbia, and the antagonisms, divisions and sense of irrecoverable loss it generated, were major shaping factors in twentieth-century English culture. They exacerbated the intellectual's feeling of isolation from what he conceived of as philistine hordes, variously designated the middle classes or the bourgeoisie, whose dullness and small-mindedness the intellectual delights in portraying (that is, inventing). Hostility to the suburbs as ecologically destructive quickly fused with contempt for those who lived in them. The supposed low quality of life encouraged by suburban conditions became a favourite theme for intellectual ridicule or censure. Mrs Leavis in *Fiction and the Reading Public* stigmatized the 'emptiness and meaningless iteration of suburban life', as well as the 'inflexible and brutal' idiom of suburban people, ascribable to newspapers and radio. Life for the suburban dweller is, she reported, 'a series of frivolous stimuli'. Cyril Connolly in *The Unquiet Grave* considered suburbs worse than slums. 'Slums may well be breeding-grounds of crime, but the middle-class suburbs are incubators of apathy and delirium.' Graham Greene in *The Lawless Roads* described suburbia as 'a sinless, empty, graceless chromium world'.[11]

One of the empty, graceless things Greene connects it with is cremation. The first crematorium in England had been built at Woking in 1885, and the 1902 Cremation Act laid down regulations for this modern and efficient way of disposing of the dead. Most literary intellectuals, like Greene, found cremation repellent, and blamed the masses – reasonably, in a sense, since it was the overcrowding of cemeteries by the masses that had made the practice necessary. The masses had, it seemed, reduced even death to conveyor-belt level. Greene attended his first cremation – his mother-in-law's – at Golders Green in 1933. Fictional cremations, based on this, appear in several novels, with the suburban connection spelt out. In *Brighton Rock*, Ida sees the last of Fred Hale issuing from the crematorium's twin towers: 'People passing up the flowery suburban road looked up and noted the smoke . . . Fred dropped in indistinguishable grey ash on the pink blossoms.' In *The End of the Affair*, Bendrix turns up too late at Golders Green for Sarah's cremation: 'The crematorium tower was smoking, and the water lay in half-frozen puddles on the gravel walks . . . As we reached the chapel everyone was leaving . . . I thought dully, so it was her smoke that was blowing over the suburban gardens.'[12]

Though intellectuals agreed that suburbia was dreadful, their fantasy versions of it vary widely. Greene's suburbia is dull and soulless, but the mystical ruralist Arthur Machen (a member, like W. B. Yeats, of the Order of the Golden Dawn) believed suburbs to be seething with religious zealotry and illicit sex. In *The Secret Glory*, published in 1922, Machen becomes heated about the irregular goings-on which, he feels sure, suburban 'swine' indulge in behind their decent net curtains. His saintly hero Ambrose Meyrick explains that it is not so much suburban vice ('child torture, secret drinking, and low amours with oily commercial travellers') that offend him, as suburban pretences to virtue: 'I suppose that, by nature, these people would not be so very much more depraved than the ordinary African black fellow. Their essential hideousness comes, I take it, from their essential and abominable hypocrisy.'[13]

The meaning of 'suburban', as a term of disparagement, likewise fluctuates. Sometimes it registers no more than social snobbery. When the fop and poseur Brian Howard was working for MI5 during the war, and was overheard discussing military secrets loudly in a pub, a policeman came up and asked for his name and address. 'I am Brian Howard and I live in Mayfair,' he replied. 'No doubt *you* come from some dreary suburb.' T. S. Eliot, when announcing the aims of his new periodical the *Criterion*, explains that it is directed against 'suburban democracy', presumably referring to the cult of the common man which he took to characterize suburban life. Ezra Pound, discussing his anti-Semitism with the Jewish Allen Ginsberg in 1967, regretted that he had been led astray by a 'stupid, suburban prejudice' – a bid to offload his guilt on to the suburbs that drew on the intellectual's image of suburbia as narrow-minded and conservative.[14]

There was a tendency among intellectuals to identify the suburbs as the site not just of triviality but of specifically female triviality. Louis MacNeice, surveying West End theatre audiences in 1938, reports that they consist chiefly

of people – mainly women – who use the theatre as an uncritical escape from their daily lives. Suburb-dwellers, spinsters, schoolteachers, women secretaries, proprietresses of teashops, all these, whether bored with jobs or idleness, go to the theatre for their regular dream-hour off. The same instinct leads them which makes many hospital nurses spend all their savings on cosmetics, cigarettes and expensive underclothes.[15]

MacNeice's snobbish outburst, like his airy familiarity with nurses' underclothes, does not seem to be grounded in any very rigorous research. But it reflects a prejudice against female suburbia that was shared by other intellectuals, as we shall see.

Intellectuals were, of course, in no position to generalize about the suburbs, since the subject was too various for categorization. Like 'masses', the work 'suburban' is a sign for the unknowable. But 'suburban' is distinctive in combining topographical with intellectual disdain. It relates human worth to habitat. The history of the word shows how a development in human geography that caused widespread dismay came to dictate the intellectuals' reading of twentieth-century culture.

Whether the suburbs were in fact anti-cultural can already be felt as a controversial issue in the early years of the twentieth century. G. K. Chesterton's novel *The Man Who Was Thursday*, published in 1908, is set in a suburb called Saffron Park which is consciously unlike the suburbs vilified by intellectuals. Saffron Park, Chesterton conveys, is beautiful – 'as red and ragged as a cloud of sunset'. It had been the fanciful brainchild of a speculative builder, and 'although its pretensions to be an intellectual centre were a little vague, its pretensions to be a pleasant place were quite indisputable'. It has an odd, fantastic air, especially at night, when 'the extravagant roofs were dark against the afterglow . . . the little gardens were often illuminated, and the big Chinese lanterns glowed in the dwarfish trees like some fierce and monstrous fruit'.

Chesterton is intent on making us see the poetry of the suburbs, and two poets, with diametrically opposed aesthetic theories, live in Saffron Park. One, Lucian Gregory, is an intellectual and an anarchist. He believes in art for art's sake, and in blowing up policemen. 'The man who throws a bomb is an artist,' he claims. 'He sees how much more valuable is one burst of blazing light, one peal of perfect thunder, than the mere common bodies of a few shapeless policemen.' Gregory represents the urge to annihilate inherent in post-Nietzschean intellectualism. 'I would destroy the world if I could,' he acknowledges. The other poet, Gabriel Syme, stands for law, order and respectability, and taunts Gregory by assuring him that the underground railway is the most poetical thing in the world. By profession, Gabriel is a police detective, and Chesterton is clearly on his side. His name confers a kind of archangelic status, just as Lucian's name suggests Lucifer.

The love and loyalty inspired by suburbs was the theme, too, of Chesterton's first novel, *The Napoleon of Notting Hill*, published in 1904, a futurist fantasy which ends with an apocalyptic battle fought in Kensington Gardens between the armies of various London districts. Nor, we are instructed, is such partisanship absurd. Men who laugh at Notting Hill, and celebrate Athens and Jerusalem, forget that Athens and Jerusalem were once 'silly suburbs' like Notting Hill. 'The earth itself is a suburb' in God's eyes. Chesterton's political creed, Distributism, meant giving everyone a plot of land to cultivate, and would, rigorously pursued, have turned the whole of Britain into a garden suburb.[16]

Against the pro-suburban Chesterton could be set H. H. Munro ('Saki'), whose story 'The Mappined Life' likens the tame, uneventful life of suburban man to that of the animals cooped up and cut off from nature on the Mappin Terraces at London Zoo. Munro specializes in wit which is glittering, hard and cruel, and which functions implicitly to elevate him above the vulgar humanity of the masses. It is no coincidence that his short stories regularly have an upper-class setting, where the wit is wielded by duchesses, baronesses and the like. For Saki's readers this offered a social as well as a literary pleasure, elevating them into a position of passionless superiority. This kind of cruel, aloof wit, which can be matched in Oscar Wilde, and later in Evelyn Waugh, who greatly admired Saki, was a new departure in English literature, and it represented a response to a new pressure – the encroaching mass, with its demands for common human sympathy.

To escape from the world as zoo – safe, smelly and cramped – Munro planned to go and farm in Siberia, though he never actually got there. Paganism was another imaginative escape for him. Savage and alluring woodland deities, one of them a wolf-boy who eats children, appear in his stories. They kill women as well as children, as in 'The Music on the Hill', where a brown, beautiful boy with 'unutterably evil eyes' turns out to be the god Pan. Homosexual and repressed, Munro loved to imagine boys as wild, lordly killers. 'Nearly every red-blooded human boy,' he affirmed, 'has had war, in some shape or form, for his first love.' This craving for violence and wildness was representative of the period. Adventure stories about the wild found a new popularity, producing celebrity authors like Jack London. Paganism appealed to writers as diverse as Rupert Brooke and D. H. Lawrence. (Nietzsche led the way here, too, extolling the 'affirmation of life' in paganism, which he associated with the 'bright, glittering, mysterious' South). The First World War was welcomed by many as an opportunity for heroism and adventure which the tame, suburban world denied. 'I have always looked forward to the romance of a European war,' wrote Munro in 1914. Two years later he was killed on the Western Front.[17]

Anti-suburban aesthetes were attracted by Nietzschean postures. They liked to claim that art was essentially undemocratic, and that what nourished it were bloodshed, slavery and the wild ways of the old pagan world. George Moore's *Confessions of a Young Man*, published in 1888, is an early statement of this case, reminding us of Eliot's later objection to 'suburban democracy':

Democratic art! Art is the direct antithesis to democracy . . . Athens! a few thousand citizens who owned many thousand slaves, call that democracy! No! what I am speaking of is modern democracy – the mass. The mass can only appreciate simple and naive emotions, puerile prettiness, above all conventionalities.

Since the life Moore describes himself as living is that of an effete dandy, hanging around cafés and studios in Paris, he might not seem best suited to survival in a barbaric environment. However, this does not deter him from presenting himself as a thoroughly desperate type:

Pity, that most vile of all vile virtues, has never been known to me. The great pagan world I love knew it not. Now the world proposes to interrupt the terrible austere laws of nature which ordain that the weak shall be trampled upon, shall be ground into death and dust.

To the pitilessly pagan Moore the 'suburban ideal' is anathema. He argues not merely that slaughter and human suffering are requisite for great art to flourish but that they add an indispensable piquancy for the connoisseur.

Injustice we worship; all that lifts us out of the misery of life is the sublime fruit of injustice. Every immortal deed was an act of fearful injustice . . . What care I that some millions of wretched Israelites died under Pharaoh's lash or Egypt's sun? It was well that they died that I might have the pyramids to look on. Is there one amongst us who would exchange them for the lives of the ignominious slaves that died? What care I that the virtue of some sixteen-year-old maiden was the price paid for Ingres' *La Source*? . . . Nay more, the knowledge that a wrong was done – that millions of Israelites died in torments, that a girl, or a thousand girls, died in hospital for that one virginal thing, is an added pleasure which I could not afford to spare. Oh for the silence of marble courts, for the shadow of great pillars, for gold, for reticulated canopies of lilies; to see the great gladiators pass, to hear them cry the famous 'Ave Caesar', to hold the thumb down, to see the blood flow, to fill the languid hours with the agonies of poisoned slaves! Oh, for excess, for crime! I would give many lives to save one sonnet by Baudelaire; for the hymn, '*A la très-chère, à la très-belle, qui remplit mon cœur de clarté*', let the first-born in every house in Europe be slain; and in all sincerity I profess my readiness to decapitate all the Japanese in Japan and elsewhere, to save from destruction one drawing by Hokee. Again I say that all we deem sublime in the world's history are acts of injustice; and it is certain that if man does not relinquish at once, and for ever, his vain, mad and fatal dream of justice, the world will lapse into barbarism . . . But the old world of heroes is over now. The skies above us are dark with sentimentalism . . . nothing remains for us to worship but the Mass, the blind, inchoate, insatiate Mass; fog and fenland before us, we shall founder in putrefying mud, creatures of ooze and rushes about us.[18]

We need to remind ourselves, reading this, that Moore was not (or not merely) a crackpot and pervert, but the friend and collaborator of W. B. Yeats, and a leading figure in the Irish literary renaissance. Puerile and disgusting though the passage admittedly is, it is of interest because of what has aroused it. Behind Moore's half-baked social Darwinism and Wardour Street classicism can be detected anger, defiance and a wish to shock, and the cause of these is a dimly apprehended threat, variously designated the 'mass', or the 'sub-

urban ideal', or 'democracy', which he senses as antagonistic to people like himself.

One of the most sustained intellectual attacks on the suburbs was T. W. H. Crosland's *The Suburbans*, published in 1905. Crosland was a minor poet of deeply conservative stripe who penned jingoistic war verses and vitriolic attacks on suffragettes. His poetry seems to have been taken seriously by some, however. Arnold Bennett, writing in 1908, expresses incredulity that Crosland ('the slanger of suburbs') should be compared to Yeats.[19] *The Suburbans* sneers relentlessly at every aspect of suburban life, and it is hard to pin down why Crosland hates it so much. It seems partly snobbishness, partly fear of the new, partly resentment at what he sees as a self-assured, ambitious, materialistic middle class.

Crosland's suburbans are 'soulless' and 'stingy' and eat tinned salmon. Though they are 'a low, inferior species', young suburbans have been taught to grip you hard by the hand and look you straight in the eye, which Crosland finds impudent and offensive. He derides both the suburbans' lack of education and their attempts to acquire it. They frequent 'hideous Board Schools' and 'idiotic free libraries', and buy cheap reprints of the classics: 'The rush for low-priced classics has been a mean, discreditable suburban rush.'

Although Crosland presents the suburbans as hamstrung by respectability, he also blames them for all the daring new ideas in circulation. Socialism, women's rights, disillusion with marriage, disbelief in God and most other 'morbid movements' of the last half-century arose, Crosland insists, in suburbia. Further, women are to blame. The female suburban shapes the male, and is the 'principal agent' of change. Among other modern heresies, 'the grand principle of female independence' had its rise in suburbia.

The muddle and anger of Crosland's book are themselves instructive, because they show the target he tries to attack expanding beyond his focus. He interprets his term suburbans so widely that it includes at one extreme families living in three rooms for 14 shillings a week rent, and at the other professional people – solicitors, civil servants, journalists. His suburbans manage to be simultaneously socialists, penny-pinching drudges and rapacious businessmen. In

other words, he seems to be talking about a whole society, with many gradations, and his conclusion admits that the present social system is 'almost entirely suburban'. The category he tries vainly to get into his sights accounts for virtually the whole population, excluding manual workers. It is the same notional mass, conceived of as literate but hostile to the intellectual, which Marxist intellectuals of the 1930s would designate the bourgeoisie.[20]

The name for them in the early twentieth century, however, and the name Crosland uses, was 'the clerks'. In sensing that they had virtually come to constitute society, Crosland was responding to a quantifiable social development. Betweeen 1860 and 1910 the section of the middle and lower-middle class employed in commerce, banks, insurance and real estate increased markedly in all Western European countries, as a result of the emergence of the imperialist and international economy of the late nineteenth century. In England by 1911 the clerical profession, including 124,000 women, was one of the most rapidly expanding occupational groups. The educational level of the clerks was relatively low, because education for the majority in Britain did not extend much beyond basic skills. At the turn of the century the authorities were still allowing 40 per cent of all children to leave school earlier than the statutory age of fourteen. In 1926, of over half a million children who left elementary school each year, only 9.5 per cent went on to secondary schools. Admission to universities depended on money and privilege rather than ability. In 1921 over 2,000 candidates qualified for the 200 available State Scholarships, while approximately 75 per cent of the annual entry to university passed in without any scholarship at all.[21]

As these figures suggest, the clerks were hardly equipped to appreciate 'high' culture, which is why an alternative culture was created for them. Northcliffe aimed the *Daily Mail* specifically at clerks. The whole paper, said one intellectual critic, 'reeks of the concerns of villadom', with its cycling column, its fashion section and its home hints. The periodicals *Tit-Bits* and *Answers*, and the department store Selfridge's, were likewise seen as components of clerk culture. Writers recognized as catering for the clerks included

the three picked out by Crosland as favourite suburban authors: Shaw, Wells and Jerome K. Jerome. Each of these had actually worked as a clerk himself, as had P. G. Wodehouse, a slightly later favourite with the same readership. Reviewers denouncing the 'vulgarity' of Jerome K. Jerome's *Three Men in a Boat* pointed out that it was written in 'colloquial clerk's English'.

Clerk's slang annoyed intellectuals partly because it was flippant and philistine and trivialized 'serious' subjects. It was also resented on class grounds as being over-familiar. Graham Greene, in Nottingham with the British-American Tobacco Co., was disgusted to find a young bank clerk among his fellow management trainees who talked about 'johnnies' and 'pals' and said 'your label' for 'your name'. 'I want to kick him,' Greene confessed. The idiolect P. G. Wodehouse evolved for Bertie Wooster in the Jeeves books may be seen as an elaborate development of clerk's slang, in that it consists essentially of jaunty and defiantly un-highbrow circumlocutions. In Wodehouse's letters, where the idiolect is less fully worked out, the vestiges of clerk's slang ('old cake', 'sound egg', 'largely banana oil', etc.) can easily be spotted.[22]

There were clearly defined 'clerks' suburbs' around the major cities. These included, around London, Clapham, Forest Gate, Walthamstow, Kilburn and Peckham. Crosland seems to be right in tracing the development of new ideas to the clerks and the suburbs, and this is hardly surprising, since with tertiary education virtually restricted to the wealthy, the clerks must have accounted for a large proportion of the nation's unexploited intelligence. A study of the Manchester suburbs in the first decade of the twentieth century shows that a new culture of socialism, cycling, free thinking and the flouting of respectable norms was flourishing among clerks, teachers, shop assistants, telegraphists and other white-collar youth. Cycling was important in extending the clerks' experience and interests. It is by cycling that H. G. Wells's Mr Polly escapes from his clerkly background.

The rebellion of the younger clerks against their fathers' respectability seems to have begun in 1890s, and is already reflected in George and Weedon Grossmith's *Diary of a Nobody*, published in

1892, where Lupin Pooter openly flouts the humble obedience Mr Pooter cherishes. This would fit in with Crosland's complaint that by 1905 the new generation of suburbans are offensively self-assured, having been taught to speak up and look you straight in the eye. This assurance, unpleasing to the intellectual, is noted also by T. S. Eliot when depicting his house agent's clerk in *The Waste Land*. This spotty ('carbuncular') young man with his 'one bold stare' is:

> One of the low, on whom assurance sits
> Like a silk hat on a Bradford millionaire.

In the manuscript Eliot's (and the readers') superiority to the young man is reinforced by other unpalatable details: 'His hair is thick with grease and thick with scurf', he spits, urinates, drops cigarette ash, etc. The young man's occupation also helps to incriminate him. By dint of working for a house agent he is implicated in the destruction of nature and the spread of the suburbs. At the end of H. G. Wells's *The War in the Air*, when civilization has been destroyed and the survivors of 'suburban parisitism' are reduced to subsistence agriculture, they take a brief respite from their toil in order to lynch and drown a house agent.[23]

That the life-style and behaviour of clerks had become topical issues can be gathered from Shan F. Bullock's novel *Robert Thorne: The Story of a London Clerk*, published in 1907. This is a wholly sympathetic treatment of clerkdom – an answer, as it were, to Crosland's *Suburbans*. Robert Thorne is a Devonshire boy who goes up to London, wins a place in the Civil Service and works in the tax office at a starting salary of £80 a year. In the course of the novel he marries and brings up a family, first in the upper flat of a two-storey cottage in Dulwich, later in a jerry-built house owned by a retired milkman near Denmark Hill, which has the standard suburban accoutrements:

In front was a privet hedge behind an oak fence, and a tiny flower bed under the parlour bay window; at the back, within brick walls, was a small garden having a grass plot, two beds with a subsoil of sardine tins and brickbats, a poplar at the bottom, and a lilac tree near the scullery window. The hall door had its brass knocker and letter box.

Before she marries, Thorne's wife, Nell, earns 15 shillings a week in a mining agency – half what Robert gets, because, as she pointedly says, 'I happened to be born a girl.'

A progressive feature of the novel is that the clerk's daily life and financial difficulties are treated as matters of serious concern. Thorne earns 36 shillings a week by the time he marries. Seven shillings goes on rent; Nell manages on 15 shillings' housekeeping. On Saturdays Thorne hurries home to a 3 o'clock dinner (steak and kidney pie usually) and in the evening he and Nell go to Rye Lane to shop: 'Our business was to get the utmost value for every penny, the best half leg of mutton in the market, the largest bunch of watercress, the most tempting smoked haddock for our Sunday morning breakfast.' This is just the kind of penny-pinching that aroused Crosland's fury, but in Bullock it is seen from the inside. The lid is taken off the suburbans. We learn the precise layout of the Thorne flat, exactly what the furniture cost (£28 15s. 6d.), and the dimension of the bedroom (9ft by 10ft).

The extreme care with which Thorne's life is charted does not prevent Bullock seeing how easily he merges into the mass: 'There are thousands like him. There they go, hurrying for the bridges, each in his cheap black coat, each with his pale face and uneven shoulders: thousands of them. Slaves of the desk. Twopenny clerks.' But it is Bullock's point that in this sameness individuality survives: 'He has a soul, this figure that I see in the crowd.'

Thorne makes strenuous attempts at self-education. He vows to read a good book each month and to spend Saturday afternoons in the National Gallery or the British Museum. Nell encourages this and shares in his reading. The Thornes' books include Scott, Dickens, Dumas and Jane Austen, all in the sixpenny editions disparaged by Crosland. To satisfy 'more intellectual cravings' Thorne and Nell plod through Carlyle, Shakespeare and Tennyson, and Thorne wrestles with *Paradise Lost* and Bacon's *Essays* over his supper of cocoa and bread and cheese. Clearly what Bullock means to show us is an undirected but eager mind trying to acquaint itself with what it takes to be the components of culture. Thorne, who had only Board School education, retains intellectual curiosity and a thirst for self-improvement despite his daily grind at the office. So he obliquely indicts a higher-education system closed to people like himself. In all these respects he resembles Forster's Leonard Bast in *Howards End*, published three years later, though he is seen with more sympathy and intelligence.

Though Bullock is on the side of Thorne and clerks, he is also depressed by them and makes Thorne voice his depression: 'What is life but heroic pretence? Our houses are jerry-built, our clothes shoddy, our food adulterated, ourselves not what we are. It is the penalty of civilization.' Civilization also stunts Thorne's body. He has a narrow chest and one shoulder higher than the other, and he fears that clerks are not real men. He envies bricklayers and navvies, and daydreams about joining his brother, who has emigrated to New Zealand. He imagines himself outside a log cabin, stripped to the shirt, tucking into a big meal of bacon and beans. Towards the end of the novel the call of the wild proves irresistible. Thorne makes his big decision, buys tickets for New Zealand and heads for 'freedom, life, the open air'. He wants his children to have 'a chance of being something better than typists and clerks'.[24]

The image of the clerk as stunted was standard in intellectual portrayals. Leonard Bast has a 'spine that might have been straight' and a 'chest that might have broadened' – might have, it is explained, had his forebears stayed in the country, allowing him to become a shepherd or ploughboy.[25] Another substandard clerk features in George Bernard Shaw's *Misalliance* of 1910. Shaw's irreverence and novelty attracted the clerkly readership, as Crosland noted, but his cult of personal dynamism involved a degree of contempt for dogsbodies of the clerkly kind. Essentially he was a sentimental pseudo-Nietzschean who disparaged the democratic electorate ('the promiscuously bred masses') and universal education, which, he predicted, could never 'raise the mass above its own level'. He was even capable of asserting that 'the majority of men at present in Europe have no business to be alive' (compare Nietzsche:

'The great majority of men have no right to existence, but are a misfortune to higher men.') In the Preface to *On the Rocks* he rejects the doctrine of the sacredness of human life, insisting:

Extermination must be put on a scientific basis if it is ever to be carried out humanely and apologetically as well as thoroughly . . . if we desire a certain type of civilization and culture, we must exterminate the sort of people who do not fit into it.

Despite these Nietzschean noises, all Shaw actually subscribed to was woolly-headed socialist mysticism of a perfectly harmless variety, according to which a benevolent power called variously the 'Life Force' or 'Nature' was at work in the universe, struggling to evolve a higher type of human being (Superman) who would be more intellectual and less obsessed by sex than the current model – in fact, remarkably like Shaw himself. It was the duty of humans, Shaw preached, to aid the efforts of the Life Force by practising eugenics, which would 'eliminate the Yahoo'. The scientific and socio-legal details of this elimination, Shaw left vague. In practice his 'Vitalism' amounted to no more than admiration for forceful people and genial scorn for weaklings and failures. The clerk, Julius Baker, who bursts in on the wealthy Tarletons' country-house weekend in *Misalliance* belongs to both of the last two categories. His mother was seduced years ago by the elder Tarleton, and he has come armed with a revolver to seek revenge. He gives Tarleton a lecture on the miseries of clerking – 'the most damnable waste of human life that was ever invented' – and announces he is going to shoot him because, 'Ive had enough of being talked down to by hogs like you, and wearing my life out for a salary that wouldnt keep you in cigars.' However, Baker is easily disarmed by one of the women guests – 'Thats a clerk all over', he wails. 'Beaten by a female.' – and the male Tarletons bully him into signing a confession, though he snivels that if he had eaten their food ('grub' in clerk's slang) and had their lessons in boxing he would be able to withstand them. In the event his hand is shaking too much for him to sign anyway. By these means Shaw identifies Baker as lacking in the Life Force.[26]

Clerks could not be expected to welcome the portrayal of clerks as feeble and ineffective, and other authors who wrote for clerkly readers replaced the weakling in the threadbare black coat with a more manly figure. In Conan Doyle's 'The Stockbroker's Clerk' Sherlock Holmes's client is a Mr Hall Pycroft, who talks in clerk's slang – 'ripping', 'chaps', 'screw' for 'salary' – and whose credentials are established with obtrusive care. 'The man whom I found myself facing', reports Watson,

was a well-built fresh-complexioned young fellow with a frank honest face and a slight, crisp, yellow moustache. He wore a very shiny top hat and a neat suit of sober black, which made him look what he was – a smart young City man, of the class who have been labelled Cockneys, but who give us our crack Volunteer regiments, and who turn out more fine athletes and sportsmen than any body of men in these islands.

Read in its social context, this flattering portrait is unmistakably partisan. Pycroft's athletic build has nothing to do with the story, and the puff about the patriotism and military virtues of clerks is quite gratuitous. Conan Doyle is not, at this point, composing a detective story but redrawing the English cultural map along anti-intellectual, pro-clerk lines. His boast that clerks enlisted in volunteer regiments was, incidentally, true. Richard Price, studying middle-class jingoism in the late nineteenth century, has found that there was a disproportionate number of clerks among volunteers for the Boer War.[27] Hall-Pycroft-type clerks, designed to cheer clerkly readers, also feature in H. G. Wells's *The History of Mr Polly*, where the fearsome Uncle Jim is vanquished and ducked in the Thames by 'hilarious, strong young stockbrokers' clerks', who are identified as 'Territorials and seasoned boating men'.[28]

A subtler vindication of a clerk is Kipling's 'The Finest Story in the World', which Robert Crawford has shown to be a source of Eliot's *The Waste Land*. Kipling's story is about the encounter of an intellectual and a clerk. The narrator, a man of letters, befriends a twenty-year-old bank clerk called Charlie Mears. Charlie has literary aspirations, and tells the narrator an idea he has for a story. As Charlie talks it becomes clear to the narrator, though Charlie never realizes it, that he is remembering his previous incarnations –

as a Greek galley slave and as a Viking. In the grip of his vision, Charlie even jots down some strange characters which a British Museum expert later identifies as demotic Greek. This idea of 'a confused tangle of other voices' speaking through Charlie, 'like the mutter and hum through a city telephone', was what Eliot used in his poem.

On the surface the story's view of Charlie is disparaging. He talks in clerk's slang – 'awful rot', 'by gum' – and has 'the curious nasal drawl of the underbred city man'. He writes second-rate poetry; is naïve and bigoted, referring to an Indian friend of the narrator as a 'big black brute'; reads *Tit-Bits*, and hopes to win its guinea essay prize; and has narrow shoulders and a hairless face.

But the story's subtext is more to Charlie's advantage. The narrator meets him on London Bridge one day with a 'bill-book chained to his waist'. This reminds us that Charlie is still a slave, as when chained to his oar in the galley – though such a realization never occurs to the supercilious narrator. Also, we are allowed to see that Charlie is a young man crying out for education. With the £5 the narrator gives him for his story, he buys poetry (in three-and-sixpenny Bohn volumes) and grows wild with enthusiasm reading Byron and Longfellow. The narrator views this with patronizing impatience, particularly as it stops Charlie talking about his previous lives. But the starved delight with which Charlie devours books carries a clear message about the lack of educational opportunity in Kipling's England. The British Museum expert who examines Charlie's scrawl identifies it as 'an attempt to write extremely corrupt Greek on the part . . . of an extremely illiterate – ah – person'. This is richly ironic, for we know that the 'illiterate' Charlie and the galley slave who wrote 'corrupt' Greek were the same being, and both were shut out from the citadels of their culture. The British Museum expert occupies those citadels, yet his erudition allows him only to decipher, rather uncertainly, what Charlie, in his previous incarnation, wrote. Charlie has *been* the slave – and still is. He knows at first hand what the scholar can only reconstruct. The scholar devotes his whole life to trying to find out about Charlie, the galley slave, and about what that galley slave knew. Yet he dismisses the real, present-day Charlie as an illiterate person. Kipling, standing above and behind the scholar and the narrator, satirizes the intellectual's attitude to the masses, observing that the masses must pass into history before they become suitable for intellectual contemplation.[29]

The rejection by intellectuals of the clerks and the suburbs meant that writers intent on finding an eccentric voice could do so by colonizing this abandoned territory. The two writers who did so were John Betjeman and Stevie Smith. Betjeman, as Bevis Hillier has noticed, was aware of a submerged tradition of suburban verse, which had begun with Frederick Locker-Lampson's *London Lyrics*, published in 1857, and included Hugh Owen Meredith's *Week-Day Poems*, 1911, Douglas Goldring's *Streets and Other Verses*, 1920, and F. O. Mann's *London and Suburban*, 1925. Clerks are central figures in this tradition, varying in fortune from Mann's 'bald-headed old fool', besotted with a young typist at the office, to Goldring's woeful wage-slave, trying to grow strawberries on his suburban patch as a treat for his child.[30]

What makes Betjeman distinctive, though, is the emotional intensity with which he invests the suburbs. This takes the form of love or hatred, according to the age of the suburb concerned. The older suburbs, and the even older countryside they replaced, shimmer in a nostalgic haze, where the steam and gaslight of early railway waiting rooms mingle with sepia views of leafy lanes in Pinner, and glimpses of white, weather-boarded mills in Edwardian Essex. Back beyond these tear-dimmed vistas lie the lost, paradisaical days when Perivale was still a 'parish of enormous hayfields', and Greenford was market gardens. The ghosts of old-world clerks roam these Edens – Murray Poshes and Lupin Pooters who now lie silent under soot and stone in Kensal Green or Highgate.

Modern suburbs, on the other hand, are monstrous, 'Bathed in the yellow vomit' of sodium lamps, and harbouring the mixed bag of atrocities with which Betjeman associates progress – radios, cars, advertisements, labour-saving homes, peroxide blondes, crooked businessmen, litter, painted toenails and people who wear public-school ties to which they are not entitled. The contrast between old and new justifies Betjeman's hatred of planners and bureaucrats, gleefully expressed at the scene of a fatal car crash, where the 'first-class brains of a senior civil servant' become 'sweetbread on the road'.

Betjeman is so emotionally involved because he assimilates suburbia into his personal history. He associates the old, leafy suburbs with his parents, whom he disappointed as a young man by refusing to go into the family furniture-making business and by idling at Oxford. The old suburbs he imagines in his poems are free from this sorrow and guilt. They belong to the time of his parents' youth ('These were the streets my parents knew when they loved and won'), and they express Betjeman's yearning for, as Philip Larkin phrased it in an admiring appraisal of Betjeman, 'a world unburdened by himself'. The rage that modern life stirs in him is inextricable from a feeling that it has killed his parents and desecrated their haunts:

> The trees are down. An Odeon flashes fire
> Where stood their villa by the murmuring fir.

The cinema, like the angels with fiery swords who drive Adam and Eve from Eden in *Paradise Lost*, marks a historical frontier, on the far side of which lies Betjeman's unfallen world.[31]

For Stevie Smith, suburbs do not need to be embalmed in nostalgia in order to make them poetically acceptable. Her taste for suburban sensations is keen and immediate. The suburb where she spent virtually all her life, Palmers Green, had been a village till the end of the nineteenth century. But in 1902 Captain J. V. Taylor of Grovelands sold large tracts of his land for development and, as more and more land came on the market, suburbia spread. When Stevie arrived as a child in 1906, the fields and country lanes were fast diminishing with the spread of bricks and mortar. In the period from 1901 to 1911 the population of Southgate, which includes Palmers Green, rose from 15,000 to 33,000. These changes might well have endowed Stevie with a standard intellectual lost-paradise angst, but in fact her response to Palmers Green was rapt. She especially liked Winchmore Hill woods, which, says her biographer

Frances Spalding, bred her lifelong love of trees and water, and Grovelands, the public park created in 1911 when Southgate Urban District Council bought 94 acres of Captain Taylor's estate that had failed to reach the reserve price at auction. Grovelands, according to Spalding, is really a 'very average park', dull and dreary in bad weather. But Stevie, who associated its 'loamish landscape' with the poetry of Tennyson and Thomas Hood, liked it best when it was raining, and the only other people there were anglers.

When the wind blows east and ruffles the water of the lake, driving the rain before it, the Egyptian geese rise with a squawk, and the rhododendron trees, shaken by the gusts, drip the raindrops from the blades of their green-black leaves. The empty park, in the winter rain, has a staunch and inviolate melancholy that is refreshing.

She admits to finding the brightness and busyness of suburban life, 'the kiddycars on the pavement and the dogs', intolerable at times, and she hates the narrowness of well-off suburbans, who, she alleges, unite in a 'mass of littleness to oppose every great idea that is at all difficult to understand'. But the beauty far outweighs these drawbacks.

In the high-flying outer northern suburb the wind blows fresh and keen, the clouds drive swiftly before it, the pink almond blossom blows away. When the sun is going down in stormy red clouds the whole suburb is pink, the light is a pink light, high brick walls that are still left standing where once the old estates were hold the pink light and throw it back. The laburnum flowers on the pavement and trees are yellow, so there is this pink and yellow colour, and the blue-grey of the roadway, that are special to this suburb. The slim stems of the garden trees make a dark line against the delicate colours. There is also the mauve and white lilac.

As this suggests, getting away from people was a special suburban pleasure for Stevie. Her poem 'Suburb' values the same release.

> How nice it is to slink the streets at night
> And taste the slight
> Flavour of acrity that comes
> From pavements throwing off the dross
> Of human tread.

But she also valued the human reliability of the suburb – the 'briskness, shrewdness, neighbourliness' – and her taste for the wild and hostile depended, she reckoned, on the underlying security the suburb gave: 'Only those who have the luxury of a beautiful kindly bustling suburb . . . can indulge themselves in these antagonistic forest-thoughts.'[32]

There is a parallel to be drawn between suburban experience and the features that distinguish Stevie Smith's poetic voice. She evolved a model of female writing that avoids and undercuts the kinds of dignity and authority that males have appropriated. Her poems are unnerving and uncategorizable, wavering between joke and pain. They have the unpretentiousness and irreverence of the suburbs, and are constructed of ordinary well-worn materials – fairy-tales, nonsense verse, conversational turns of phrase. They achieve cultural significance because they are entirely careless of cultural significance. Emerging from a notional area (suburban woman) that has been ridiculed and contemned, they invite ridicule and contempt. In this way they occupy the territory – or part of it – left vacant by anti-suburban disdain.

If we ask what has happened to the antagonism between the intellectuals and the suburbs, the answer is, of course, that it still persists. When critics – generally young male critics – attack Anita Brookner for being middlebrow and unexperimental, and for not being South American, they parrot all the old intellectual prejudices. Brookner is unashamedly a suburban novelist. In *Lewis Percy* her unheroic hero sighs, 'I'm suburban man . . . I am what I am, a poor clerk. I'll never be anything different.' It could be Bullock's Robert Thorne talking. And Brookner puts into Percy's mind a defence, typically low-key, of suburban life:

He felt that to be suburban was almost a calling in itself, involving steadiness, a certain humility in the face of temptation, social or otherwise, and a loving, almost painful attachment to home. The stamp of a suburban childhood, he reflected, probably marked one for life . . . There was for him a sweetness in the absence of excitement that such a condition implied, or perhaps imposed.[33]

Those are sentiments we can imagine Philip Larkin echoing, and it is worth remembering that when, in 1957, Charles Tomlinson attacked Larkin and the Movement poets, it was specifically 'the suburban mental ratio they impose on experience' that he deplored.[34]

4

Natural Aristocrats

In response to the revolt of the masses, intellectuals generated the idea of a natural aristocracy, consisting of intellectuals. On the question of precisely what makes natural aristocrats aristocratic, there was some disagreement. One suggestion was that there was, or ought to be, a secret kind of knowledge which only intellectuals could possess – a 'body of esoteric doctrine, defended from the herd', as D. H. Lawrence put it.[1] W. B. Yeats agreed. When he joined the Hermetic Students of the Golden Dawn in 1890, it was part of a widespread revival of occultism, centred on Paris, which answered intellectual craving for a source of distinction and power that the masses could not touch. Yeats also felt that the intellectual aristocrat had natural links with titled people – the old aristocracy of birth – who would constitute his patrons and audience. He announced in 1916 that he had invented a new kind of drama: 'distinguished, indirect, and symbolic, and having no need of mob or Press to pay its way – an aristocratic form'.[2]

Other intellectuals attributed their distinction to the supposedly timeless values of which they were transmitters and guardians. It was part of T. S. Eliot's aesthetic theory that the true artist's works transcend time, unlike the products of ephemeral commercial culture.[3] This view easily merged with the belief that art was sacred, 'a religion', as Clive Bell proclaimed in 1914. The artist need not bother about the fate of humanity, Bell stipulated, for 'aesthetic rapture' was self-justifying.[4] This notion of artists and intellectuals soaring above mere human concerns also attracted Ezra Pound, though he gave it a more despotic turn, warning that artists were natural rulers, 'born to the purple', and would shortly take over the world:

The artist has no longer any belief or suspicion that the mass, the half-educated simpering general . . . can in any way share his delights . . . The aristocracy of the arts is ready again for its service. Modern civilization has bred a race with brains like those of rabbits, and we who are the heirs of the witch-doctor and the voodoo, we artists who have been so long the despised are about to take over control.[5]

Pound later acclaimed Mussolini as his ideal artist-dictator. Behind all these recipes for supremacy we can observe the pressure of mass culture, driving intellectuals to invent new proof of their distinction in a world which increasingly found them redundant. The awkward question was, how could the superiority of the intellectual or artist be demonstrated, and in what, precisely, did it consist? In considering how intellectuals tackled this problem we must start with Nietzsche, because his answers represent intellectual aspiration in its most extreme form.

Men, Nietzsche decrees, are not, equal. The mistaken belief that they are is to blame for the degeneracy of Europe. Benevolence, public spirit and consideration for others are despicable herd virtues. The truly noble man is egotistic. He despises pity, which is unhealthy and is valued only by slaves. The warrior is a type of the finest man. War and courage have achieved greater things than charity. Men should be trained for war, and women for the recreation of the warrior. The belief that women are equal, or merit education, is a sign of shallowness. They should be treated as property, slaves or domestic animals. This item in Nietzsche's programme has proved particularly congenial. The early twentieth-century intellectual aristocrat is an almost exclusively male fantasy. By comparison women, children and family life are regarded as secondary concerns.[6]

Nietzsche's beliefs were not, of course, compatible with Christianity. 'I abhor Christianity with a deadly hatred,' he explained. Nothing had done more to undermine the old aristocratic outlook than the poisonous Christian doctrine that all souls were equal before God. It was this that had bred the modern European: 'a shrunken, almost ludicrous species, a herd animal . . . full of good will, sickly and mediocre'. For Nietzsche, Christianity represented 'the revolt of everything that crawls along the ground against that which is elevated', and it stank of the rabble. 'One does well,' he cautioned, 'to put gloves on when reading the New Testament. The proximity of so much uncleanliness almost forces one to do so.' The only figure in the Gospels he admires is Pontius Pilate, because Pilate could not persuade himself to take a Jewish affair seriously: 'One Jew more or less, what does it matter?' Since Christianity had outlawed all great human qualities and called them evil, it must, Nietzsche reasoned, be the aim of the higher type of man to become more and more evil. 'All great human beings have been criminals.'[7]

In abandoning Christianity Nietzsche also abandoned the fixed value system that it offered. To forsake Christianity but cling to Christian morality was, he believed, an absurd English peculiarity, observable in 'little bluestockings à la George Eliot'. He ridicules, in *Beyond Good and Evil* and *Twilight of the Idols*, the very concept of moral judgement. Nothing is inherently moral or immoral, he argues. 'Moral judgement . . . never contains anything but non-sense.' It has no truth value. Clearly this conclusion strikes at the very basis of his own position, for his writings consist largely of a series of vehemently expressed moral judgements. If such judgements are illusory, then it is meaningless for Nietzsche to claim that the warrior is better than the slave, or cruelty than pity, and so on.[8]

Conscious of this difficulty, Nietzsche occasionally makes a bid to ground his beliefs in something firmer than mere personal preference – namely, biology. Life is essentially and biologically, he argues, the overpowering of the weak by the strong, so to forbid exploitation would be like forbidding an organic function. Likewise it is 'anti-biological', in Nietzsche's terms, to prefer peace to war, because life consists in war. However, argument from biology was unpropitious for Nietzsche, because the swarming multitudes of inferior men, who were overwhelming the superior, were clearly the product of biology. Nietzsche, contradicting Darwin, declared that humanity as a species was not progressing but degenerating. This meant that biology could not be trusted to produce the right answer after all.[9]

Nietzsche developed, in response to these perplexities, not so much a philosophy as a rhetoric. He licensed a way of feeling, rather than a system of thought, which depended on metaphors, fantasies and pictorial projections. An imaginary landscape of forests and mountain peaks, with the intellectual striding alone through the high, cold air, was vital to his meaning. 'In the pages of Nietzsche,' enthused Arthur Symons, 'are the intoxication of mountain air, the solitude of Alps, a steadfast glitter, almost dazzling, like that of frozen snow.' Zarathustra is a wanderer and a mountain climber, who hates cities and the green plains where the rabble lead their soft lives. 'Let us live above them like strong winds,' he urges, 'neighbours of the eagles, neighbours of the snow, neighbours of the sun. Their bodies and their spirits would call our happiness a cave of ice.' This language, and the figure of the mountain-scaling visionary, were borrowed from romantic poetry, but Nietzsche gave them a new anti-democratic thrust. The cult of mountaineering and alpine holidays among English intellectuals like Leslie Stephen seems to have been encouraged by Nietzschean images of supremacy. Climbing a mountain gave, as it were, objective expression to the intellectual's sense of superiority and high endeavour, which otherwise remained rather notional.[10]

Spatial metaphors of 'high' and 'low' culture are logically meaningless, of course. When Oscar Wilde, for example, pronounces that 'Aesthetics are higher than ethics', it does not actually mean anything, any more than it would mean anything to claim that aesthetics were 2 feet to the left or the right of ethics. However, all systems of cultural hierarchy depend on believing that such metaphors do mean something, hence the attractiveness for intellectuals of Nietzsche's mountain scenery, which fixed the empty metaphors back into a convincing terrain. So we find, for example, Clive Bell hymning 'the austere and thrilling raptures of those who have climbed the cold, white peaks of art', and contrasting them with the herd who frequent the 'snug foothills of warm humanity'.[11] Bell's language figures himself and fellow aesthetes as engaged upon dangerous and energetic pursuits, when in fact they are merely looking at pictures or reading books. That might make the Nietzschean rhetoric seem somewhat fatuous. Nevertheless, its appeal to aesthetes remained strong.

Before leaving Nietzsche we should note, briefly, two more consequences of his difficulties in the area of logical demonstration. One was that he renounced logic. The laws of logic are universal and reduce everyone to the same level, so they are, Nietzsche decides, just a stratagem of the rabble for getting on top of and humiliating the truly superior man. To obey one's instincts is noble, but to obey logic is to give way to the mob. Logic destroys the real, sensual world and substitutes for it an unreal grey world of mental concepts. Nietzsche's second answer to logic leads on from this, and is that the body is wiser than the mind. 'Listen,' he instructs, 'to the voice of the healthy body.' We should, he advises in *Ecce Homo*, trust only thoughts which have come to us in the open air, while using our muscles. This health-and-fitness fetish, so powerful in Nietzsche, and so important to his Nazi followers, contrasts pathetically, as has often been pointed out, with his own chronic ill-health, nervous prostration, myopia, ghastly digestive disorders and so on.[12]

The same contrast between ill-health and worship of the healthy body is apparent in D. H. Lawrence, Nietzsche's major English disciple. All Lawrence's central concepts are derived from Nietzsche. 'My great religion,' he wrote in a famous letter of January 1913, 'is a belief in the blood, the flesh, as being wiser than the intellect. We can go wrong in our minds. But what our blood feels and believes and says, is always true.' This could be a summary of Nietzschean doctrine, and its key word, 'blood', is from Nietzsche, who wrote in *The Will to Power* that the only nobility is of blood. Nietzsche explains that he does not mean by this aristocratic lineage. Precisely what he did mean – and what Lawrence means – is hard to define. However, 'blood' for both of them evidently includes instinct, bodily sensations and masculine sexual urges. It is in these that real wisdom inheres.[13]

It is noticeable, though, that 'blood' in the sense of lineage is not discounted. 'Breeding' is an important word for Nietzsche and for

Lawrence. In combating the mongrel vulgarity of the masses, good family and pure blood are advantages, we gather. Nietzsche declares that one has a right to be a philosopher only by virtue of one's origin. One's ancestors, one's blood, are the decisive factors. The philosopher's lofty glance that looks down on the mob and its 'duties' and 'virtues' takes generations of good breeding to produce. 'Breeding' is always a term of approval in Lawrence. Alvina, in Lawrence's *The Lost Girl*, is said to have 'a certain breeding and inherent culture', which give her a deep 'ancient sapience'; and Connie Chatterley is relieved to see that Mellors, though a gamekeeper, is a gentleman: 'She saw at once, he could go anywhere. He had a native breeding.'[14]

Lawrence follows Nietzsche, too, in discrediting logic and rationality. Ideas, which are the components of mental consciousness, are not real, he emphasizes. They are like dead husks or spectral abstractions. They are 'thrown off from life, as leaves are shed from a tree, or as feathers fall from a bird', and form a 'dry, unliving, insentient' insulation between us and the universe. Further, they are mechanical. The mind prints off like a telegraph instrument the grey representations which we call ideas. In his essay 'Democracy', Lawrence develops the case against ideas in order to devalue Christian humanism. The real enemy today, he maintains, is idealism, which seeks to instil love of humanity and the public good. These notions are, in Lawrence's terms 'a trick of the devil', because they deprive life of its reality, substituting mere abstractions for the warm, felt pressures of which life is actually composed.[15]

Both Lawrence and Nietzsche are in an awkward position when discrediting ideas, since they are, of course, expressing ideas themselves. Their arguments reflect their frustration, and their urge to escape the limiting conditions of their merely human state. As supermen they can expose the inbuilt fallacy which disqualifies all human thinking, but they can do so only by human thinking. Reason, said Nietzsche, 'is a mere idiosyncrasy of a certain species of animal', and does not relate to any reality. Nevertheless, reason was all he had to use.

Lawrence's dissatisfaction with logic, like Nietzsche's, arose, too, from a suspicion that logic would not warrant his conviction that he was a natural aristocrat. This conviction always intensified when he came into contact with what he regarded as particularly unwholesome outbreaks of democracy, such as trades unions or the United States of America. 'I don't believe either in liberty or democracy,' he wrote when planning a trip to America in 1921. 'I believe in actual, sacred, inspired authority: divine right of natural kings: I believe in the divine right of natural aristocracy, the right, the sacred duty to wield undisputed authority.' 'Divine' is obviously a questionable term for Lawrence to use, since he did not, in any clear sense, believe in a divinity. His belligerent repetitions reflect his feeling of impotence in confrontation with the mass – 'the monster with a million worm-like heads'. He tells himself that he will gradually call together 'a choice minority, more fierce and aristocratic in spirit', and that when labour troubles have led to revolution, then he will take over: 'then I shall come into my own'. But the unlikelihood of such a political development was humiliatingly clear, and there was also the nagging consciousness that claims to natural aristocracy ran counter to his own deep poetic awareness of the singularity and uniqueness of every created thing. For if everything is unique, then it cannot be compared with other things, nor pronounced superior or inferior, and with this realization claims to natural aristocracy dissolve.[17]

Lawrence faces this perplexity in two essays, 'Reflections on the Death of a Porcupine' and 'Democracy'. In the first he uses a dandelion as an emblem of individuality. The dandelion in full flower, 'a little sun bristling with sun-rays on the green earth', is 'incomparable and unique'. It occupies its own space, fulfils its own being. You cannot subject it to comparisons without infringing its uniqueness. The 'Democracy' essay applies this understanding to human beings.

Each human self is single, incommutable, and unique. This is its *first* reality. Each self is unique, and therefore incomparable. It is a single well-head of creation, unquestionable: it cannot be compared with another self, another well-head, because, in its prime or creative reality, it can never be comprehended by any other self.

77

But when Lawrence proclaims that life is more vivid in him than in the Mexican who drives his wagon, or when he distinguishes himself and other aristocratic spirits from the monster with a million worm-like heads, he is engaging in precisely the act of comparison which his 'Democracy' essay forbids. He felt this contradiction with angry acuteness, but did not know how to resolve it. In 'Reflections on the Death of a Porcupine' he simply juxtaposes the two irreconcilable positions. It is nonsense, he asserts, to declare there are no higher and lower beings. We simply know there are. We know, for instance – or Lawrence says he knows – that the dandelion belongs to a 'higher cycle of existence' than the hart's-tongue fern. Higher means 'more vividly alive'.

It is all very well saying that they are both alive in two different ways, and therefore they are incomparable, incommensurable. This is also true.

But one truth does not displace another. Even apparently contradictory truths do not displace one another. Logic is far too coarse to make the subtle distinctions life demands.

The fictional counterpart to this dismissal of logic, and acceptance of self-contradiction, comes at the end of *Aaron's Rod*, where a character called Lilly, who closely resembles the Lawrence of the letters, announces that he is sick of ideals like the brotherhood of man and the sanctity of human life. They are 'putrid' and 'stinking'. What he wants is the reintroduction of a 'proper and healthy and energetic slavery', plus a programme of extermination so that the lower orders can be persuaded to hand over power to the higher. Levison, the character Lilly is talking to, has just decided Lilly ought to be in a lunatic asylum when Lilly, with a 'peculiar, gay, whimsical smile', explains that he would say the 'blank opposite' to everything he has been proposing 'with just as much fervour', and goes on to profess that he thinks every person 'a sacred and holy individual, *never* to be violated'.[18]

It might seem that Lawrence's – and Lilly's – rejection of logic permits them to keep hold of both the natural-aristocrat idea and the idea of human beings as incomparable and unique. But strictly it is just another affirmation of natural aristocracy. For since logic, as

Nietzsche pointed out, is social and contractual, with communally agreed rules, it follows that if the individual can override it on the grounds that it is too coarse to contain his subtleties, then he remains superior to the community and its procedures. Lawrence seems to have taken the notion of logic's coarseness from Nietzsche, who maintains in *The Will to Power* that only when we see things 'coarsely' can we use logic, and that the axioms of logic are not adequate to reality, because they wrongly disallow self-contradiction.[19]

It must be stressed that Lawrence, for all his Nietzschean debts, was not like Nietzsche. The range and subtlety of his imagination went far beyond Nietzsche's. The Nietzschean warrior ideal, and countenancing of cruelty, could only have seemed disgusting to Lawrence, who turns his characters not into warriors but into flowers. This tendency is already apparent in the early novel *The Trespasser*, where Siegmund's hands hang 'like two scarlet flowers' in the firelight, and as Helena kneels by him, 'One of the flowers awoke and spread towards her'. In *The Virgin and the Gipsy*, Yvette responds to the gipsy's dark potency by becoming a snowdrop: 'The waking sleep of her full-opened virginity, entranced like a snowdrop in the sunshine, was upon her.' To cite such passages – and there are hundreds of them in Lawrence – and to contemplate the impossibility of Nietzsche having written them, is not just to emphasize that Lawrence was a poet and that Nietzsche was in some respects a desperately restricted and unfulfilled human being. It is also to contend that, for Lawrence, the stance of natural aristocrat, with its presuppositions of isolation and alienation, was adverse to all the promptings of his sympathetic imagination, which taught him to fuse and integrate. In *St Mawr*, when Lou Witt and her mother are discussing men, Lou's mother says she seems to want a caveman who would come and hit her on the head with his club – a variant, as it were, of Nietzschean man with his whip. Lou at once contradicts her. A caveman, she points out, would be a brute and a degenerate. But a 'pure animal man' would be an amalgam of all different animals:

As lovely as a deer or a leopard, burning like a flame fed straight from underneath. And he'd be part of the unseen, like a mouse is, even. And he'd never cease to wonder, he'd breathe silence and unseen wonder, as the partridges do, running in the stubble. He'd be all the animals in turn, instead of one, fixed, automatic thing.

This protean and elusive creature, transforming into other creatures and feeling with them, is incompatible with the separateness of the natural aristocrat. But it is true to Lawrence's poetic intelligence, as that idea was not.[20]

Bound up with the question of how you recognize natural aristocrats is the question of what privileges they should enjoy. Both problems engage Clive Bell in *Civilization*, a work on which, Bell's dedicatory letter tells us, Virginia Woolf acted as consultant. Civilization depends, according to Bell, on the existence of a small group of people of exquisite sensibility, who know how to respond to works of art, and who also have a refined appreciation of sensory delights such as food and wine. Without this 'civilizing élite', standards are bound to fall. Signs of decay are already apparent. 'There are now,' Bell regrets, 'but two or three restaurants in London where it is an unqualified pleasure to dine.'[21]

What distinguishes these rare and gifted beings is their ability to detect 'pure form' in works of art. They pay no attention to the human interests or emotions which artworks might seem to arouse. Though these are what people incapable of aesthetic emotion look for in art, they are actually 'sentimental irrelevancies'. True art does not consist in 'what the grocer thinks he sees', but in the 'sense of ultimate reality' the artwork yields to 'educated persons of extraordinary sensibility'. No artist, Bell feels sure, has ever believed in human equality. 'All artists are aristocrats.' And by the same token true appreciators of art must always be few and superior. 'The mass of mankind will never be capable of making delicate aesthetic judgements.'[22]

It follows that, if society wants to be civilized, it must establish conditions favourable to the preservation of the gifted few. Connoisseurs of pure form cannot be expected to earn their own living, for 'almost all kinds of money-making are detrimental to the subtler and more intense states of mind' required for artistic appreciation. Consequently, people of taste and discernment must be supported by public funds. They alone will be fully educated, and the state will make them a regular and ample allowance throughout their lives. It will also take responsibility for their children should they have any. Bell admits that this arrangement entails a degree of inequality, but all civilizations, he argues, have been built on inequality. Civilization requires the existence of a leisured class, and a leisured class requires the existence of slaves. Besides, the leavening effect of the civilized élite will, or may, percolate through to the slaves. The 'barbarian' in his 'suburban slum' may notice that the élite scorn gross pleasures ('football, cinemas'), such as he wallows in, and this may entice him to sample refined artistic pleasure himself. A flaw in Bell's scheme is that the barbarian, even if he develops artistic tastes, will not be able to indulge them, as he will remain deprived of the leisure obligatory for civilized life. This is not a complication Bell pursues, but he seems to anticipate some discontent on the part of the slaves, for he stipulates that his civilization will need an efficient police force.[23]

Since for Bell what makes a civilization civilized is the presence of people able to view artworks in the approved way, such details as the form of government remain subsidiary. There is absolutely no reason, according to Bell, why tyrannical and despotic regimes should not be perfectly civilized. 'To discredit a civilization it is not enough to show that it is based on slavery and injustice; you must show that liberty and justice would produce something better.' 'Better', in this context, means, we note, more adapted to supporting people like Bell. This is the vital criterion. Liberty and justice are not good in themselves.[24]

Bell accords with the general intellectual consensus in recognizing that civilizing women presents special difficulties. It is impossible, he decides, for a housewife to be civilized, for home and children blunt her intelligence and sensibility. But single women ('old maids' in Bell-speak) cannot be civilized either, for women must make love to men before the 'exquisite' is available to them, and before the 'subtlest and most impalpable things of the spirit' can float into their

81

minds. In ancient Athens the sensitive and intelligent women were mistresses or prostitutes (*hetairae*), and so, Bell proposes, they should be in his civilization. Only a mistress, with a wide choice of 'delightful lovers', can overcome the drawbacks of her sex and attain civilized status.[25]

Any theory of natural aristocracy must attribute the aristocrat's superiority either to intrinsic qualities (secret knowledge, better artistic taste, superior vitality, etc.) or to some kind of supernatural selection. The theories we have considered so far, including Bell's, opt for the first alternative. But Bell also inclines to the second, though rather mistily. By contemplating 'pure form' in artworks, his civilized élite will become aware of 'the God in everything', and taste the 'ecstasy' of the mystics, which is unavailable to the 'vulgar'. Other intellectuals gave a more specifically Christian turn to such speculations. Middleton Murry, like Bell, holds that the 'highest' and 'truest' art offers a breakthrough to 'ultimate reality'. According to Murry, this means that the great writer is 'like Jesus'. He 'drops the seed of the Word into the earth of our being' as the 'prophet and priest of God'. This redemptive effect is available, though, only to intellectuals. The large numbers of people who seek in literature 'a reflection of their idle selves and a satisfaction of their frivolous appetites' will naturally shun great literature 'as a dead soul is bound to shrink from contact with a live one'.[26]

This bid to re-establish links between high culture and religion reflects intellectual reaction against 'soulless' God-forsaking suburbia, which cuts its lawns and listens to the radio on Sundays. The interwar years saw a 'stampede', as Stevie Smith archly puts it, of sensitive and intellectual persons away from the 'vulgarities of the secular world'. Roman Catholicism offered an attractive haven, with its ancient tradition and Latin liturgy. By comparison with the Church of England, it seemed culturally pure. Hilaire Belloc advised fellow Catholics to 'spread the mood that we are the bosses, the chic, and that the man who does not accept the Faith writes himself down as suburban'. For refugees from mass culture, the Roman Church was also winningly authoritarian and anti-democratic. Evelyn Waugh seems frequently to confuse Catholicism with social distinction, as has been noted by, among others, Conor Cruise O'Brien. Analysing the social messages behind *Brideshead Revisited*, O'Brien remarks that in Catholic countries Catholicism is not invariably associated with big houses or the fate of the aristocracy. Waugh, however, was romantically enthralled by the idea of the 'Catholic squires of England', who were doomed to die 'so that things might be safe for the travelling salesman, with his polygonal pince-nez, his fat wet hand-shake, his grinning dentures'. These icons of class hatred might seem to have little to do with religion, but clearly that is not Waugh's view. By becoming a Catholic he implicitly spurned dentures and travelling salesmen and joined the persecuted nobility.[27]

Graham Greene, another Catholic convert, constructed his masterpiece, *Brighton Rock*, around the idea that by comparison with Catholics ordinary mass mankind does not truly exist at all. Loathing of what the masses have done to England reverberates throughout the novel. Around Brighton the suburbs spread – bungalows, half-made roads, hoardings, advertisements for Mazawattee Tea. It is a scarred, shabby terrain, littered with empty corned-beef tins. On the day Greene's novel opens, 50,000 trippers are cramming into the town. Bank-holiday trains leave Victoria every five minutes, carrying 'clerks, shop girls, hairdressers'. It is a world in the grip of newspapers and advertisements. Fred Hale, the novel's first murderee, has surrendered his identify for a newspaper's publicity stunt, and mingles with the holiday crowds as Kolly Kibber of the *Messenger* (based on real-life Lobby Lud of the *News Chronicle*). An aeroplane, advertising patent medicine, does skywriting overhead.

The figure in the novel on whom Greene's distaste for mass civilization focuses is Ida, an ageing belle who brings the vicious juvenile murderer Pinkie to justice, and so saves the life of his young wife, Rose, whom he was going to kill. Ida belongs, Greene tells us, to 'the great middle law-abiding class'. 'I believe in right and wrong,' she announces firmly. To the ordinary reader, she might seem the heroine of the novel. But Greene's point is that Pinkie, being a Catholic, and evil, is more real than Ida, and spiritually her superior.

As a child he was destined for the priesthood. When Cubitt denies knowledge of him, Greene alludes to Peter's denial of Christ ('a courtyard, a sewing wench beside the fire, the cock crowing'). Pinkie belongs to the realm of good and evil, compared with which Ida's right and wrong are, Greene implies, as trivial as a slot-machine. Pinkie and Rose, from their position of Catholic superiority, despise Ida. 'She doesn't know what a mortal sin is,' objects Rose. 'She's just nothing,' sneers Pinkie. Greene seems to agree. Pinkie and Rose inhabit a different reality from Ida's: 'She was as far from either of them as she was from Hell – or Heaven.' She does not exist within a spiritual dimension. Her fleshliness is emphasized with disgust – her 'big breasts', her 'thin vulgar summer dress', her 'port-winy laugh', her soft, friendly 'cow-like' eyes, her 'carnal' face. An air of compassion accompanies her 'like a rank cheap perfume'. She is sentimental, likes cheap drama and pathos, and cries in cinemas. She reads best-sellers – Warwick Deeping; Priestley's *The Good Companions*. She is also a woman – a disadvantage in Greene's world of hard-bitten masculine spirituality: 'You thought of sucking babies when you looked at her.'[28]

By his treatment of Ida and Pinkie, Greene offered a calculated affront to non-Catholic readers. His proposition that a murderer is essentially more real than a good-hearted, law-abiding woman is a gesture of intellectual defiance, aimed at the complacent, materialistic masses. George Orwell, reviewing Greene's *The Heart of the Matter*, detected in that book too the implication that it is better to be an erring Catholic than a virtuous pagan, and registered his affront. Such an idea carries, Orwell objects,

the fairly sinister suggestion that ordinary human decency is of no value . . . In addition it is impossible not to feel a sort of snobbishness in Mr Greene's attitude . . . He appears to share the idea, which has been floating around ever since Baudelaire, that there is something rather *distingué* in being damned; Hell is a sort of high-class nightclub, entry to which is reserved for Catholics only, since the others, the non-Catholics, are too ignorant to be held guilty, like the beasts that perish.[29]

Orwell's reference to Baudelaire is apposite, for Norman Sherry has shown that a source for *Brighton Rock* was T. S. Eliot's essay on

Baudelaire, which makes out essentially the same case for Baudelaire as Greene makes for Pinkie. Baudelaire, Eliot concedes, may have been evil, but at least he was 'man enough for damnation'. In a world consisting of 'electoral reform, plebiscites, sex reform', even damnation, Eliot suggests, is a kind of salvation, since it redeems one from 'the ennui of modern life'. Baudelaire hated women and thought love evil, but 'he was at least able to understand that the sexual act as evil is more dignified, less boring, than as the natural, "life-giving", cheery automatism of the modern world'. What an unboring, dignified sexual act would be like, Eliot does not divulge, but he makes it clear that it would be superior to anything available in contemporary secular life. 'It is better,' he concludes, 'in a paradoxical way, to do evil than to do nothing: at least we exist.' This appalling sentence leaves out of account, we notice, the effect of evil on its victims. A murderer, like Greene's Pinkie, could hardly be said to make things 'better' for those he kills, even if he enhances his own spiritual reality. Eliot disregards such side issues, because he is intent upon the spiritual aristocrat, apart from and superior to the mass. Nietzsche, in the same vein, declared that the criminal 'has this advantage over many other men, that he is not mediocre'.[30]

The image of the Catholic that attracts Greene is never that of a church member subsumed into a body of believers, for that would reduce the convert to a mere recruit. When he went to Mexico in 1938, it was in the hope of finding evidence of Catholics being persecuted, and though he was disappointingly too late for any real atrocities, his artistic fascination with victims and outsiders remained a powerful element in his Catholicism. As a fugitive, hunted down by the pack, or as a rebel, cast out by God, the Catholic acquires the glamour of singularity – a glamour not available to mere faithful sheep. This meant that Greene had to seek an accommodation with Catholicism which would give him the special status of renegade. He made no secret of the fact that he was not convinced of God's existence, which placed him on the perimeter of Catholic Church membership, and in his later years he discontinued going to confession or mass.[31] So, despite his Catholicism he remained 'On the dangerous edge of things' – like a Nietzschean solitary on his mountain peak, except that in Greene's version there would be gunmen among the pine trees, closing in.

Even among intellectuals who have not entered a recognized church, we can observe a tendency to invoke God when they are driven to justify belief in the superiority of intellectuals and the artworks they prefer. A crucial example is Aldous Huxley, whose *Brave New World* is the classic denunciation of mass culture in the interwar years. With Huxley, as with Clive Bell, cultural élitism, antagonism to the mass and mystic breakthrough to 'ultimate reality' hang together. Despite democracy's wish to do away with the concept of the elect, Huxley contends, grace and reprobation are 'observable facts'. Appreciation of the higher things in life is limited to the chosen few. 'For the great majority of men and women, there obviously *is* nothing in culture.' On these grounds Huxley denounces universal education, which has, he believes, greatly extended the domain of stupidity and ignorance. For whereas under the old privileged system those who could benefit from education did, 'on the whole', get it, universal education turns out enormous numbers of people who feel qualified to sneer at culture because they have brushed against it and realize it has nothing to offer them. Meanwhile, the press, cinema and radio have hastened the descent into mindlessness, purveying 'stale balderdash' to the 'interminable democracies of the world'.[32]

For the initiate, the way out of this dismaying situation lies through contemplation and mystic ecstasy, which offer direct experience of 'divine immanence'. A convenient access to this higher realm was provided, Huxley discovered, by mescalin ('almost completely innocuous,' he assured would-be acolytes). Under its influence he made contact (in May 1953) with 'the divine source of all experience'. Looking at reproductions of paintings (by Botticelli, Vermeer, etc.) while under the influence of mescalin, he realized that the divine region he was glimpsing was that which great artists are 'congenitally equipped to see all the time'. The connection between 'high' art and the divine was thus effectively demonstrated.[33]

These discoveries still lay in the future, of course, when Huxley wrote *Brave New World*. But the novel is similarly intent on

Shakespeare, a copy of which he happened to find on the reserve. When Lenina takes him to the feelies, he declares them base and ignoble. When she tries to get him into bed, he is aghast at her shamelessness and drives her away with cries of 'whore' and 'strumpet'. He opts to live like a hermit in the countryside, growing his own food, and praying.

That a savage who had grown up on an Indian reservation among practitioners of fertility cults should emerge, as John does, with the inhibitions and cultural preferences of a late nineteenth-century public schoolboy could not be called a realistic development. Huxley later admitted it was a flaw in his design, and said he had done it for dramatic effect.[38] But the purpose it actually serves, within the novel's argument, is to show that the savage's decency, uprightness, contempt for mass values and love of Shakespeare are not just preferable but natural. They have the endorsement of uncorrupted Nature.

Religious belief is shown to be natural in the same way. 'God,' John proclaims in his final showdown with the Controller, 'is the reason for everything noble and fine and heroic.' Even the Controller, the supremo of Brave New World, admits that he believes in God.[39] Christianity has been eliminated not because it is untrue, but because it is incompatible with the social model the rulers want to impose. For all Huxley's modern and cynical brilliance, what he is finally driven to hold against Brave New World is that it is Godless.

The intellectual's stratagem of appealing to God to justify the pre-eminence of intellectuals did not, of course, stop with Huxley. George Steiner's recent book *Real Presences* shows the same inclination. It is in part an onslaught on mass culture, conveying the intellectual's customary disdain for journalism, gadgetry and the empty lives most people lead. Like all Steiner's books, it is a dazzling display of erudition. The index lists some 300 artists, musicians, philosophers, poets and cultural notables, ranging from Theodor Adorno to Gioseffo Zarlino, the Renaissance music theorist. Throughout Steiner firmly and persistently distinguishes what he calls worthwhile or significant or serious art and literature from the trash and kitsch most people prefer. Given a free vote the bulk of humankind would, he feels sure, choose football or bingo rather than Aeschylus. Further, they cannot be proved wrong. The truth or falsehood of literary and artistic judgements is not, he concedes, verifiable.

So how can the intellectual's preferences be vindicated? How can the natural aristocrat establish his aristocracy? At this point Steiner, like Huxley, invites God to step in. All great art and literature, he declares, is 'touched by the fire and the ice of God'.[40] Some of it, he admits, may have been produced by non-believers, but they must have been non-believers who felt God's absence as an 'overwhelming weight'. The analogy is with Graham Greene's kind of Catholic, who is unsure God exists but remains, by implication, as serious and spiritually distinguished as a believer, if not more so.

Steiner, then, forcibly recruits God as a cultural adjudicator, whose job is to vouch for those examples of art that intellectuals prize. What art, if any, God might like, Steiner does not inquire, and has no means of knowing (though if it is the biblical God he has in mind, the divine prejudice against graven images suggests artistic priorities incompatible with those of Western intellectuals like Steiner). The question of God's likes and dislikes is irrelevant, though, to Steiner's case, for God's role in the transaction is not to make choices but to sanction the intellectual's – that is, Steiner's – judgements. This means that God is reduced to a convenient fiction, and in this respect He has the same utility, within intellectual discourse, as the 'masses'. Like the masses He must conform to the intellectual's imaginings; like the masses He must ratify the intellectual's distinction.

PART II

Case Studies

5

George Gissing and the Ineducable Masses

Writing to his friend Eduard Bertz in 1892, George Gissing gives a devastating summary of the cultural evils he sees around him. It is impossible to take up a newspaper without noting the 'extending and deepening Vulgarity' of the great mass of people. This is partly due to American influence, he fears, but the ground is prepared for it 'by the pretence of education afforded by our School-board system'. Society is being 'levelled down'. Democracy appeals only to base, material motives. 'Thus, I am convinced, the gulf between the really refined and the masses grows and will grow constantly wider.' Before long we shall have 'an Aristocracy of mind and manners' more distinct from the vast majority of the population than aristocracy has ever been before.[1]

Intellectuals were to go on repeating these forebodings for decades. Precisely the same fears and loathings activated F. R. Leavis and his Scrutineers in their quest for superior 'sensibility', and they dominate his wife Q. D. Leavis's anatomy of popular culture in *Fiction and the Reading Public*. Gissing's anxiety about 'levelling down' is still echoed by intellectuals today, and the modern intellectual habit of contrasting English 'philistinism' with the allegedly richer culture to be found in France, Italy, or other countries where intellectuals spend their holidays, is also prefigured in Gissing, who fancied that he discerned in Italians an 'innate respect for things of the mind' lacking in 'the typical Englishman'.[2] Gissing seems, in fact, to have been the earliest English writer to formulate the intellectuals' case against mass culture, and he formulated it so thoroughly that nothing essential has been added to it since. The case has not been developed or advanced; it has simply been repeated. One reason for reading Gissing is that he allows us to watch the superstitions that dominate our idea of 'culture' taking shape.

Foremost among these superstitions is belief in an entity called 'the masses', which is by definition uneducated. Whether the masses could ever conceivably be educated or not is, for Gissing, a question of prime importance. It is noticeable that when he introduces a new character in a novel, he has two standard procedures. He concentrates either on the character's facial features or on the character's bookcase. The facial features yield, under Gissing's scrutiny, extraordinarily detailed information about intellect and personality. From the nose, the chin, the curve of the lips or eyebrows even the most fugitive weaknesses of moral and mental make-up can with confidence be diagnosed.[3] The contents of the bookcase invariably corroborate the evidence of physiognomy, and are divisible into two categories. Shelves which contain poetry, literature, history and no natural science belong to sensitive, imaginative, intelligent characters. Shelves which contain politics, social science, technology and modern thought of virtually any description brand their owner indelibly as at best semi-educated and at worst cruel, coarse and dishonest.[4]

These two standard devices for typing people suggest mutually antagonistic ways of accounting for human behaviour. Physiognomy, revealing the individual's innate qualities, implies determinism. 'I am a determinist,' Gissing announced bleakly in a letter.[5] But books imply – or ought to imply – a capacity for change and enlightenment. They seem to hold out the possibility that, through education, inherent inclinations may be schooled or redirected. Why, otherwise, should Gissing have spent his life writing them?[6]

But books, in Gissing, do not educate. They belong to those who are already educated; those who are not are beyond help.[7] Pondering the brutishness of the masses, Gissing concludes that their 'fatal defect' is lack of imagination – which can be acquired only by 'intellectual training', specifically the reading of literature and poetry. Lacking this, the masses are bound to be crude and vicious – though, fortunately for them, their coarse sensibilities exempt them from the sufferings finer natures feel. Stella Westlake in *Demos* fails to understand this. 'When she spoke of the toiling multitude, she saw them in a kind of exalted vision; she beheld them glorious in their woe, ennobled by the tyranny under which they groaned.' Her illusion indicates that she has seen little of 'the representative proletarian'. But her friend Adela, who has the misfortune to be married to one, knows 'the monstrous gulf between men of that kind and cultured human beings'. She knows, too, that Stella's pity is misdirected. Only readers of poetry are truly capable of suffering. The masses 'have not those feelings you attribute to them. Such suffering as you picture them enduring comes only of the poetry-fed soul at issue with fate.'[8]

If this is so, then teaching the masses poetry would seem a needful educational step. Gissing's tendency, however, was to ridicule those who attempted it. May Tomalin, a modern young woman in *Our Friend the Charlatan*, is keen to extend civilization among the ignorant and, having studied early English Literature herself, she feels 'it would be so good if our working classes could be brought to read Chaucer, Langland and Wyclif and so on'. It would give them 'the philological training, which has such an excellent effect on the mind'. May reports that she has visited a poor family, living in two rooms, who have promised to give an hour every Sunday to studying *Piers Plowman*, and as a reward she has made them a present of the Clarendon Press edition, 'which has excellent notes'. May and her friends plan musical concerts for the poor. These will contain nothing popular: 'It isn't our object to *amuse* people . . . We want to train their intelligence.' So the programmes will consist of Bach, Beethoven and other classics. It is true, May concedes, that the audience may be weary and discontented. 'But they must be made to understand that their weariness and discontent is *wrong*. We have to show them how bad and poor their taste is, that they may strive to develop a higher and nobler.'[9]

This is unusually broad humour for Gissing. May's foolish chatter exposes not only the absurdity of giving the lower classes middle-class culture but also the degree to which May's own acquisition of culture has eroded her common sense. Less preposterous but similarly deluded is the idealistic Walter Egremont in *Thyrza*, who gives lectures on English Literature to selected working men in Lambeth. If he can only get them to understand what is meant by 'the love of literature pure and simple', Walter feels, 'without a thought of cash profit', then social reform must surely follow. He chooses the Elizabethan period as his topic, and reads his audience Sidney's *Defence of Poetry*, which, not surprisingly, leaves them cold. Gissing clearly thinks the enterprise absurd – he intended it as a critical allusion to F. D. Maurice's pioneer experiment in adult education, the Working Men's College.[10] It also reflects personal disillusionment, for Gissing, in his brief socialist phase, had himself lectured in working men's clubs.[11] Significantly, in *Thyrza* he blames the audience, not Egremont, for the failure of the lecture. It does not occur to him, any more than to Egremont, to ask why grown men with a living to earn should waste their time with Sidney's *Defence of Poetry*. Sidney's essay was officially designated culture, and therefore from Gissing's profoundly conservative viewpoint it qualified to be digested by culture-seekers. The audience's lack of enthusiasm shows, in his view, that they have no sense of 'intellectual beauty'. As for poetry, it is really hopeless putting it before them. They read the 'loveliest lyric' as if it were 'a paragraph from a daily newspaper'.[12] In these strictures, Gissing resembles his own May Tomalin, blaming the lower classes for their poor taste, and for being discontented when missionaries from the middle class try to improve it.

Egremont's experience suggests that, in teaching the masses poetry, the proper strategy might be to instruct them before newspapers have contaminated their minds. However, when Gissing depicts a lower-class child learning poetry, there is no mistaking the scorn and repulsion that animate his account. In *Born in Exile* the intellectual Godwin Peak is distressed by the unexpected arrival at his lodgings of his cockney Uncle Arthur, a café proprietor, and his little son Joey. To impress his educated nephew, Arthur encourages Joey to recite:

'Jowey, jest sye a few verses of poitry; them as you learnt larst. E's good at poitry, is Jowey.'

The boy broke into fearsome recitation:

> The silly buckits *on* the deck
> That 'ed so long rem'ined,
> I dreamt as they was filled with jew,
> End when I awowk, it r'ined.

Half a dozen verses were thus massacred, and the reciter stopped with the sudden jerk of a machine.[13]

Gissing's scorn is undisguised. Though committed in theory to a belief in the civilizing power of poetry, he did not think the masses could or should be civilized by it. To make poetry available to them would pollute the culture for which he himself had sacrificed so much. He hated lower-middle-class pretensions to education because they were a vulgar travesty of the refinement he held dear. Education is to blame for the abomination Joey commits. Untaught, he could not have perpetrated it. This goes, too, for *In the Year of Jubilee*'s piano dealer, Samuel Barmby. When he reads *Paradise Lost* to his daughters on Sunday afternoons, it comes out like this:

> Ail, orrors, ail! and thou profoundest Ell,
> Receive thy new possessor . . . [14]

The performance, Gissing makes clear, has no redeeming effect on either Samuel or his daughters. Even when the masses have advanced to the stage where they read *Paradise Lost* for pleasure, they cannot conceal 'the depth of the gulf which lies between the educated and the uneducated'.[15]

Authoritative characters in Gissing voice the belief that it will take generations of education to redeem the labouring classes from their 'hoggish slough'.[16] No impact can be made in a single generation. Even so, it is hard to see how the process can begin if the efforts of aspirants like Joey and Samuel Barmby are to be ridiculed. The truth is that, observing the lower classes, Gissing could not for a moment conceive that they would ever be capable of what he understood by education. In *The Private Papers of Henry Ryecroft* he deplores 'the host of the half-educated, characteristic and peril of our time'. But he does not hold out any hope that they could ever become wholly educated. 'Education is a thing of which only the few are capable.'[17]

Where women were concerned his scepticism redoubled. The most hideous examples of sham culture in his novels are all female. Women's education is to blame for generating 'the filth and insolence of a draggle-tailed, novelette-reading feminine democracy' – as Harvey Rolfe laments in *The Whirlpool*.[18] Lower-middle-class women seemed to Gissing the worst. *In the Year of Jubilee* presents Beatrice, Ada and Fanny, daughters of a Camberwell builder, who have had a pretentious private education at a young ladies' academy. They can all play the piano, after a fashion; they 'have done' political economy and 'been through' chemistry and botany. However, their minds and characters have remained proof against every educational influence. By rights they belong below-stairs with their 'spiritual kindred', the servants. Only money has hoisted them above that level. Ada is a vicious slattern who reads only illustrated magazines; Fanny is a worthless, feather-brained flirt. Beatrice alone displays any ability. Though uninterested in culture, she starts a fashion business – the South London Fashionable Dress Supply Association – marketing cut-price *haute couture*, and incorporating a club room and refreshment bar. Though successful, the enterprise illustrates for Gissing only the 'folly and greed' of women in general, and in particular 'the ineptitude of uneducated English women in all that relates to their attire'. A fight that breaks out between Ada and Beatrice gives Gissing a chance to moralize about their bogus veneer of culture: 'Now indeed the last rag of pseudo-civilization was rent off these young women.' Vilifying each other like 'the female spawn of Whitechapel', they uncover the bestial natures which 'the mill of education is supposed to convert into middle-class ladyhood'.[19]

Female education in this instance is merely futile, but it can be worse. It can, Gissing discloses, bring about physical and mental breakdown if pursued with unfeminine zeal. An acquaintance of Beatrice and Ada's, Jessica Morgan, aims to become a graduate of London University. Jessica has never been much to look at – 'a dolorous image of frustrate sex', with 'hysteric determination' glaring from her face. But as she labours for her matriculation, her appearance deteriorates alarmingly. Her complexion is ruined; her hair falls out. What she gains, moreover, is not genuine knowledge. Her head fills up with a 'thrice-boiled essence of history' and 'ragged scraps of science'. The examinations, when they arrive, prove too much for her. She collapses on the last day with an overtaxed brain and is carried out delirious. She never really recovers. The last we see of her is as a recruit to the Salvation Army, her face half-hidden by a 'hideous bonnet', her eyes fixed in a 'stare of weak-minded fanaticism'.[20]

In portraying Jessica's plight Gissing had modern scientific thought on his side. An article by the Darwinian George Romanes, on which he had made notes, pointed out that since a woman's brain weighs on average 5 ounces less than a man's, the intellectual inferiority of women, and their lack of creative originality, is biologically inevitable. It will, Romanes argues, take centuries of education for them to catch up, and attempts to hasten the process may be dangerous, since the physique of young women cannot stand the strain of severe study.[21]

Nor is it only women who are at risk. The next generation is imperilled too. Cecily Doran in Gissing's *The Emancipated* is a highly educated 'new' woman, and a great beauty. Her education is her ruin, however, for she considers herself above conventions, refuses to take the advice of her elders and elopes with arrogant, dissipated Reuben Elgar. Inevitably, he abandons her, but not before their little boy, Clarence, has died. Gissing clearly implies that his death is to be attributed to the mother's educational accomplishment. It is not just that Cecily attended cultural gatherings instead of minding the baby – though she did. Rather, her physical chemistry was mysteriously changed by her intellectual pursuits, in a manner fatal to her child: 'Education had made her an individuality; she was nurtured into the disease of thought. This child of hers showed in the frail tenure on which it held its breath how unfit the mother was for fulfilling her natural functions.'[22] Here, too, Gissing might have invoked contemporary science. As David Grylls points out, Herbert Spencer's *Principles of Biology* had suggested that overtaxing a woman's brain with intellectual work might unfit her for maternity and make her less fertile.[23]

Educated women who do not lose their babies, hair or reason are still suspect, in Gissing's view, on a number of counts. However learned they are, they remain helpless against the onset of passion. Lust for some desirable male will quickly reduce them to extremes of cunning and malice of which even their uneducated sisters might feel ashamed. The blue-stocking Mrs Wade in *Denzil Quarrier*, who counts a mastery of Greek among her accomplishments, effectively murders Denzil's mistress, Lilian, by explaining to her that her illicit relationship with him may prejudice his political career. Depressed by this thought, Lilian goes out into the night and drowns herself in a convenient pool. Mrs Wade follows at a distance, hears the splash and returns home satisfied – for she is consumed by passion for Denzil herself and now sees the way clear to his embraces. Unfortunately, he finds her repellent, so she becomes a 'rampant' feminist instead.[24]

Another of Gissing's grudges against educated women is that their cultural pretensions have to be financed by their unfortunate supporting males. Flouncing round the continent in pursuit of culture, they have little thought for the husbands or fathers at home, who pay for it all.[25] The culture they acquire is, in any case, almost invariably superficial, and their vanity blinds them to any just estimate of their own gifts. An outstanding case is Alma Rolfe in *The Whirlpool*, who desperately wants to be a great violinist, though she has little talent and no love of music. In pursuit of her 'career' she obliges her husband to leave peaceful Carnarvon and move to the London suburbs. The 'whirlpool' of the novel's title is, in effect, Pinner and Gunnersbury – localities which, as Gissing conceives them, are awash with spendthrift, idle women working their husbands to death and having affairs under the guise of artistic activities. Alma becomes embroiled with a set of shady dilettantes, including Cyrus Redgrave, who keeps a love nest in Wimbledon, and the aptly named Mrs Strangeways, who is a procuress for him. 'What a grossly sensual life was masked by their airs and graces,' reflects Rolfe, at a musical evening given by his wife and her friends.[26] Seduced by the mirage of culture, Alma becomes deceitful, vain, hard, sexually lax and neglectful of her child. At least she has the decency, though, to take an overdose of sleeping pills at the novel's end.

Gissing's attitude towards the education of women, and towards the masses, was complicated by his personal history. The tragedy of his life, as is well known, was his dismissal from Owen's College, Manchester, when it was discovered that he had been stealing from fellow students. Up to then he had been an outstanding scholar and had won academic prizes. He later claimed that he had taken to stealing because he had fallen in love with a young woman whom he had picked up in the street, Marianne Helen Harrison ('Nell'), and wanted to save her from prostitution. According to another account, attributed to a college friend of Gissing's, he had been regularly frequenting prostitutes – and paying them with stolen money – when he met Nell in a brothel. What is certain is that after a month in prison and a year and a half in America he returned to England and married Nell. They lived in squalid lodging houses in the poorest London districts, amid vermin, dirt, drunkenness and violence. This was a deliberate choice on Gissing's part. He earned enough as a private tutor to raise him above the poverty level, and when he was twenty-one he inherited £500 from a trust fund. Also, he could have supplemented his income by journalism but refused to waste time on such 'trash' (so a pupil records). He preferred the role of social outcast, regarding himself, by reason of his art, as an 'aristocrat'.

His marriage reinforced this voluntary exile. Nell was ignorant, drunken and violent, and could not be cured of the habit of prostitution – or so Gissing told the few friends who knew of her existence. H. G. Wells, a close acquaintance in later years, came to doubt Gissing's word, however. According to Wells's son, Wells's inquiries led him to believe that Gissing treated Nell cruelly, and finally abandoned her. She died, alone and destitute, of starvation – or so Wells's informant maintained. Three years later Gissing married another lower-class woman, Edith Underwood, a Camden Town bootmaker's daughter. Again he gave disparaging accounts to friends of her drunkenness, ignorance and low habits. She bore him two sons, Walter and Alfred, but Gissing considered her unfit to be a mother and, against her will, he sent Walter to be reared by his relatives in Wakefield. He alleged that Edith was insane and wanted to murder the boy. Wells, again, doubted Gissing's account. He believed Gissing's sexual appetites required women who were his social and intellectual inferiors, and that he derived satisfaction from humiliating and punishing them once they were in his power. According to Wells's son, Gissing told Wells he had thrashed both his wives with stair rods, which he recommended to Wells as a handy implement for beating women.[27]

Whatever the truth of these reports, it seems clear that Gissing's sexual abnormalities were influential in formulating his view of the masses. The gulf between himself and the squalid paupers he lived among was a vital component of the ordeal he had chosen to undergo. So was his superiority to his coarse and ignorant wives. A sense of his estrangement from most other people seems to have been a necessary element in his self-esteem, and in his personal myth of early hardship valiantly borne, as outlined in *The Private Papers of Henry Ryecroft*. With women, as we have seen, his sense of estrangement frequently took the form of contempt, which led him to degrade them and strip them of their vaunted educational assets in his fiction.

It is true that, outside of fiction, he was capable of liberal views on women's education. He made himself responsible for the education of his own sisters.[28] 'I recognize no restraint whatever upon a woman's intellect,' he assured Gabrielle Fleury. 'Don't judge me in this respect from my wretched *books* – which deal, you know, with a contemptible social class.'[29] The examples cited above show that the animus against educated women in his books is not in fact restricted to the lower classes, but they are the main recipients of his scorn. It was the spectacle of their ignorance that prompted his railings against the 'crass imbecility of the typical woman', and his claim that the 'average woman' is intellectually on a par with 'the average male idiot'.[30] Observation of his second wife's speech defects and failures of logic afforded him many opportunities for reflecting on 'the stupidity of the vulgar at large' and 'the ignorance of the multitude'.[31] In his novel *The Odd Women*, which deals directly with the problem of the large numbers of unemployable and unmarriageable women in Gissing's England (where there were half a million more women than men), his heroine, Miss Barfoot, divides prospective trainees firmly along class lines. She runs a school where young women can learn typing, shorthand and book-keeping, and so become independent. However, she is adamant that social rank is 'anything but artificial'. The lower classes really are lower 'in every sense'. Consequently she wishes to be of use, she explains, only to the daughters of educated people. 'In the uneducated classes I have no interest whatsoever.'[32] For an educator, this might seem a restrictive proviso, but it corresponded closely to Gissing's own view.

His ideal woman, supposing he could have made up his mind on the point, would probably have been a clean, refined whore – nicely spoken, well behaved, but ignorant, and degraded by her vocation, and consequently irredeemably inferior to the educated male who becomes her lover, tutor and disciplinarian. This unlikely fantasy forms the basis of *The Unclassed*, in which the prostitute Ida Starr is beautiful, pure and always dressed 'in perfect taste'. Her eyes are the windows of a 'rich and beautiful soul', and she is so addicted to cleanliness that she gets a job in a laundry, where she revels in the 'dazzling white of linen'. She explains this enthusiasm to her lover, hearty, pipe-smoking schoolmaster and Gissing-surrogate Osmond Waymark, who is warm in his appreciation: ' "Yes, yes, I understand well enough," said Waymark earnestly. "The moving waters at their priest-like task of pure ablution round earth's human shores." ' Ida does not catch the allusion – which is gratifying too, since it gives Waymark an opportunity for more tuition. Perhaps Ida is what Gissing hoped Nell and Edith would be like, or would become under his management. If so, disappointment may contribute to his onslaughts on the brutish ignorance of the lower classes.

Actually it is hard to imagine him educating Ida, as Waymark does. For the primary function of culture in Gissing's scheme of things was to segregate him from other people. To qualify as culture, knowledge had to be abstruse. This evidently lent piquancy to his study of classical Greek metres. Morley Roberts remembers him saying with mock amazement: 'Why, my dear fellow, do you know that there are actually miserable men who do not know – who have never even heard of – the minute differences between dochmiacs and antispasts.'[34] It was important that culture, as Gissing understood it, should abolish the modern world as far as possible. He had 'a dread, almost a terror' of science.[35] Culture meant old books, preferably in dead languages. His love of classical literature was 'almost a mania'.[36] But it was curiously vague, dreamy and amateurish. Reardon, in *New Grub Street*, who wants to write about Diogenes Laertius, 'not learnedly, but in the strain of a modern man whose humour and sensibility find free play among the classic ghosts',[37] seems accurately to represent the level of Gissing's classical interests. His preferences were emotional and unargued – as a study of his classical scholarship confirms.[38] 'How the eyes grow dim with rare joy in the sounding of those nobly sweet hexameters!' is a fair sample of his critical acumen.[39]

Gissing's father had first encouraged his study of the classics, so his classicism was intimately bound up with happy recollections of family life before his father's death in 1870 – and his own disgrace. The classical age blended 'with those memories of youth which are as a glimmer of the world's primeval glory'.[40] Conceived in this way, classical literature represented a bolt-hole from reality.

Every man has his intellectual desire; mine is to escape life as I know it and dream myself into that old world which was the imaginative delight of my boyhood. The names of Greece and Italy draw me as no others.[41]

Culture, so constituted, can only be impaired by the intrusion of real people. When Gissing visited southern Italy, searching for vestiges of the antique, he was disappointed to find the Italians wearing modern clothes, 'the common, colourless garb of our destroying age'. Factory chimneys and other abominations had spread themselves over the classical landscape. Genuine peasants, such as abounded in classical times, were in short supply. Gissing did find one, though, ploughing near Taranto: 'His rude but gentle face, his gnarled hands, his rough and scanty vesture, moved me to deep respect.'[42] The man is, of course, no more to Gissing than a glorified garden gnome. Like other intellectuals, Gissing preferred peasants to almost any other variety of human being, since they were ecologically sound, and their traditional qualities of dour endurance, respect for their betters and illiteracy meant that the intellectual's superiority was in little danger from them.

Peasants were also favoured because they seemed pre-commercial. Their bond with the soil went deeper than mere economics. Commerce lay at the heart of Gissing's discontent with the modern. Intellectuals, he implies, should by rights be immune from the sordid pressures of the marketplace. This was, and is, a popular intellectual viewpoint, and Gissing's resentment of commercialism crystallizes around symbols, such as newspapers and advertisements, that many intellectuals found and find objectionable. The newspaper, *Thyrza's* Walter Egremont declares, 'is the very voice of all that is worst in our civilization'. It has supplanted the book. Thanks to its influence, 'every gross-minded scribbler who gets a square inch of space in the morning journal has a more respectful hearing than Shakespeare'.[43] John Pether, the revolutionary umbrella-maker in *Workers in the Dawn*, is an incurable newspaper addict, and burns to death when the piles of newsprint on his bed catch light. The dangers of inflammatory journalism could scarcely be more graphically illustrated.[44]

The menace of advertising is represented by *In the Year of Jubilee's* Luckworth Crewe, who aims to turn the unspoilt seaside village of Whitsand into a 'hideous brand-new resort of noisy hordes'. He shows an appalled resident his plans for Whitsand pier, glowing with placards and flanked by bathing machines pasted all over with adverts for soap and purgatives. (These, along with indigestion pills, were regularly selected by intellectuals as examples of advertised products, since they linked the classes to whom advertising appealed with dirt and unhealthy bodily functions.) Crewe is genuinely fired by what he regards as advertising's civilizing mission, and looks on his changes as real improvements. 'You remember the caves? I'm going to have them lighted with electricity and painted all round with advertisements of the most artistic kind.' This insensitivity only makes him more dangerous, of course. He is completely without breeding and a hooligan. Found as an infant on a doorstep in Leeds, he was reared by the wife of a millhand. His idea of fun is being in a crowd when it turns violent, smashes up property and stones the police.[45]

Gissing's horror of advertising, and his association of it with vulgarity and ill-breeding, were, of course, widely shared by the educated classes. A new periodical appeared in 1893 entitled *A Beautiful World: The Journal of the Society for Checking the Abuses of Public Advertising*. In the foreword to the first number Elizabeth Waterhouse, wife of the Society's president, distinguishes herself and fellow SCAPA members from the less sensitive majority: 'That most people do not mind these things, that many people – hideous thought – *prefer* them, is surely only another word on our side, for it shows the degradation they have wrought.'[46]

Even more sinister than advertising for Gissing was the behaviour of crowds, which confirmed his blackest fears of the mass. *In the Year of Jubilee* depicts the vast multitudes surging into London for the Jubilee procession. They are peaceful and make little noise – just numberless footfalls. But they suggest to Gissing 'some huge beast purring to itself in stupid contentment'. His heroine, Nancy, starts behaving in a vulgar and abandoned way the moment she joins the crowd. Her 'culture' vanishes instantly. She forgets her identity and ceases to operate as an individual.[47]

One of Gissing's most brilliant – though antagonistic – pieces of reporting is his description of a working-class Bank Holiday crowd at the Crystal Palace in *The Nether World*, published in 1889. Packed trains leave Holburn Viaduct station every few minutes. At the Palace there are swing boats, merry-go-rounds, coconot shies and trials of strength. Drunken brawls keep breaking out. Girls linked by the half-dozen, arm in arm, leap along, shrieking 'like grotesque maenads'. More crowds, sweltering under the glass canopy, listen to military bands, dust rising from the trampled boards. In the Shilling Tea Room sweating waiters dash about in a deafening uproar of voices. Afterwards there are fireworks, watched by a respectable, sober, 'deadly dull' horde. Every time a rocket goes up 'all the reeking multitude utters a huge "Oh!" of idiot admiration'. The young women are tawdry to look at, 'vulgarity and worse glares from all but every costume'; the older women are 'animal, repulsive, absolutely vicious in ugliness'. As for the men, 'four in every six have visages so deformed by ill-health that they excite disgust'. No one in the crowd knows what is meant by beauty or grandeur. They ignore the sunset and the casts of antique statues on show, caring 'as little for the glory of art as for that of nature'. Gissing surveys their degradation with gloomy satisfaction: 'Since man came into being, did the world ever exhibit a sadder spectacle?'[48] Drunk or sober, peaceful or violent, the crowd arouses his alarm and disgust. It is the mass taking bodily form.

The commercialization of literature suggested to him another version of the crowd – the unseen millions for whom journalists and popular writers cater. The spectre of this invisible multitude of readers, lurking just behind the columns of newsprint, drives Gissing's Will Warburton frantic as he scans the papers for situations vacant:

In spite of loathing and dread he began to read the thick-serried columns of newspaper advertisement. Wanted! Wanted! Wanted! Wants by the thousand; but many more those of the would-be employed than those of the would-be employers . . . To glance over these columns is like listening to the clamour of the hunger-driven multitude; the ears sing, the head turns giddy. After a quarter of an hour of such search, Will flung the paper aside, and stamped like a madman about his room. A horror of life seized him; he understood, with fearful sympathy, the impulse of those who, rather than be any longer hustled in this howling mob, dash themselves to destruction.[49]

The job columns catapult Will into the existential angst of an individual in a mass civilization. They are only silent newsprint, yet they seem to him a 'howling mob'.

The contrast between the coarse scribblers who entertain this mob and genuine writers is the theme of Gissing's greatest novel, *New Grub Street*. Here the struggling novelist Edwin Reardon, who believes in old-fashioned literary values, is modelled on Gissing. He has 'never written a line that was meant to attract the vulgar', and he dies destitute. His opposite number is the young journalist Jasper Milvain, ambitious, cold, shallow and prepared to do anything for money. 'Literature nowadays is a trade,' boasts Milvain. He aims to produce 'good, coarse marketable stuff for the world's vulgar'. He knows there is no value in what he writes. Given certain basic skills anyone with brains can succeed in 'out-trashing the trashiest that ever sold fifty thousand copies'. Encouraged by Milvain, his sisters start to write successfully for women's magazines. He warns them to avoid unusual ideas and confine themselves to 'vulgar thought and feeling', so that they will 'just hit the taste of the new generation of Board School children'.[50]

Milvain is unprincipled in love as well as art. He throws over his fiancée and weds Reardon's widow – a hard, ambitious woman who reads, of all things, social science. Milvain embodies myths still current among intellectuals. Gissing takes it for granted that in striving to reach a wide audience Milvain must write trash. The idea that popular writing might have 'literary value' is not entertained. It is assumed, too, that writing for a mass readership is easy. Anyone, or certainly any intellectual, could do it if he chose to debase himself.

The other character in *New Grub Street* intent upon catering for 'the new generation that is being turned out by the Board Schools' is Whelpdale, who founds a new paper called *Chit-Chat*. No article in it is to measure more than two column-inches. It is to contain 'bits of stories, bits of description, bits of scandal, bits of jokes, bits of statistics, bits of foolery', and it will appeal to the 'quarter-educated' – young men and women who can just read but are incapable of sustained attention.[51]

Gissing clearly intends this as a satirical reference to *Tit-Bits*, the immensely successful penny weekly started by George Newnes in October 1881. *Tit-Bits* was a regular butt of the intellectuals – Joyce, as we have seen, gives it to Leopold Bloom to read while he is seated on the outdoor privy – so it is perhaps worth digressing for a moment to put in a word for it. Each number of *Tit-Bits* offered about 40,000 words of solid print – there were no pictures – and by late twentieth-century standards the range of knowledge and interest assumed looks remarkably broad. Starting in May 1882, weekly numbers carried pages of excerpts from selected authors, among them Thackeray, George Eliot, Scott, Trollope, Charles Kingsley, Carlyle, Macaulay, Harriet Martineau, Oliver Wendell Holmes, Emerson, Edgar Allan Poe, Washington Irving, Jules Verne, Ruskin, Addison, Steele, Victor Hugo, Hawthorne, Lamb and Goldsmith. Other early issues carried a previously unpublished poem by Longfellow and an interview with an acquaintance of Dickens. Soon the paper was serializing novels. Conan Doyle's *The Sign of the Four* and *A Study in Scarlet* were run successively in 1893. Creativity in the readership was also encouraged. Every week a guinea was offered for a prize Tit-Bit, usually a short story. There was a weekly 'Answer to Correspondents' column and a '*Tit-Bits* Enquiry Column' began in February 1882 ('What is the best cement for making an aquarium watertight?'; 'What place has the lowest death rate?'), with a ten-guinea prize for the reader answering the most questions in a three-month period. The paper was astute at gauging the needs of its suburban readership. Its first Christmas issue in 1881 carried pages of round games, jokes, conundrums and ghost stories, and beginning in June 1882 weekly numbers carried rundowns of over fifty English and Welsh seaside resorts, giving details of rail fares, boarding-house charges, excursions in the nearby countryside, bicycling opportunities, piers, bands, shops and provision for children. The series concluded with a long article, extending over five issues, on the Lake District, providing routes for many walks.

As a means of awakening interest in books, arousing curiosity and introducing its readers to new ideas, *Tit-Bits* must compare very favourably with more acclaimed organs such as T. S. Eliot's *Criterion* and F. R. Leavis's *Scrutiny*, and its effects were infinitely more widespread. It encouraged new talent. H. G. Wells started in journalism by making up questions about science for *Tit-Bits*, and Arnold Bennett's first pen-money came when he won 20 guineas in a *Tit-Bits* competition. He followed this up with a guinea short story. Another enthusiastic contributor to *Tit-Bits* was Alfred Harmsworth, who took it as the model for his own *Answers*. Even James Joyce, as a schoolboy, wrote a story for *Tit-Bits* about Russian police and Nihilists, though he did not get round to submitting it.

Conrad and Virginia Woolf both submitted work and had it rejected.[52]

Gissing's opinion of the typical *Tit-Bits* reader can be gathered from his depiction of young Samuel Barmby (son of the reciter of *Paradise Lost*). Samuel enlivens his conversation with curious facts gleaned from his reading – as that the world's smallest tree is the Greenland birch, measuring only 3 inches when fully grown, and that if all the cabs in London were put end to end they would stretch 40 miles. When other young men go to the theatre or pub, Samuel and his friends gather to debate serious subjects, of which, Gissing assures us, they know 'somewhat less than nothing'. The result is 'a muddy flow of gabble and balderdash', and despite the revolutionary ideas they voice the debaters go quietly home to their mothers or landladies, sup on cheese and cocoa, and next day 'ply the cleric pen with exemplary zeal'. Samuel remains 'quite uneducated in any legitimate sense of the word'. The whole withering account brings sharply before us Gissing's jealous guardianship of education, and his refusal to believe that it could be acquired by uneducated young men with coarse accents and humble jobs.[53]

Like other intellectuals Gissing deplored the tainting effect of the suburban masses on the landscape as well as on culture. Streets of damp, jerry-built houses, flimsy and gimcrack, 'spreading like a disease', old estates being cut up into building sites, fields and woods transformed to foul heaps of builder's rubble and hoardings – these abominations figure repeatedly in his novels.[54] The destiny of every beautiful spot in Britain, Rolfe predicts in *The Whirlpool*, is to be built over.[55] But Gissing is singular in that he wrote a novel in which the process is, as if magically, reversed. This novel, *Demos: A Story of English Socialism*, is essentially a simple anti-socialist fable. We are shown that when working-class socialist Richard Mutimer comes into money, he is just as corrupt and despotic as any aristocrat. But also at issue in the novel is the fate of the beautiful Wanley Valley, with its fields and fruit orchards. Mutimer wants to develop it for industry. He is opposed by poor but gentlemanly Hubert Eldon, who grew up in the valley and cherishes it as his childhood paradise. Hugh is powerless against Mutimer's wealth, so streets of small houses spread over the orchards. The development is called New Wanley. Its industrial effluent blights the remaining apple and plum trees, and blackens the grass. Hubert, like Orwell's George Bowling, but half a century earlier, is aghast to see 'a malignant cancer spot spreading day by day' over the scenes of his boyhood bird's-nesting. He blames democracy. The masses have no appreciation of natural beauty, and they have grasped the sceptre. The twentieth century will not leave 'one green spot on the earth's surface'.[56]

But then a reversal occurs. A lost will comes to light, which shows that the fortune Mutimer inherited belongs by rights to Hubert. As soon as he takes possession, Hubert sets about the destruction of New Wanley. The mines are closed, the houses knocked down, the orchards replanted, the old fields marked out as before. Paradise returns.

This idyllic solution, dear to Gissing's heart, is, he obliges us – and himself – to see, vulnerable to certain objections. Earlier, when protesting against the imminent ruin of the valley, Hubert had pleaded with Mutimer on behalf of Nature. 'The Wanley Iron Works,' Mutimer had retorted, 'will soon mean bread to several hundred families; how many would your grass support?' This argument is later taken up by the novel's heroine, Adela, who, out of pity for the families who will lose their homes, tries to dissuade Hubert from destroying the town. Does he, she demands, 'think grass and trees of more importance than human lives'? Hubert replies that he sees no value in human lives from which grass and trees have vanished. Adela's intention, he admits, is to clothe and feed working people better, and give them more leisure, but in so doing she will: 'injure the class that has finer sensibilities, and give power to the class which not only postpones everything to material well-being, but more and more regards intellectual refinement as an obstacle in the way of progress.'

There is no doubt that Hubert's sentiments are those Gissing would instinctively echo. Yet his imaginative honesty impels him to subject them, by implication, to criticism. For Adela pursues her point, exposing the inhumanity inherent in Hubert's position. Is he content, she asks, that the majority should be 'kept to labour'? Hubert is forced to reply that he is, 'for I think it very unlikely that the majority will ever be fit for anything else'.[57]

Hubert, though fighting for what Gissing believed in, does not come unscathed out of the episode. On social questions he is shown, too, to be unthinkingly hypocritical. He sees everything through a filter of social snobbery. A proponent of sentimental, governing-class radicalism, he supports revolutionary movements abroad where they seem remote and romantic, but despises them at home. Russian Nihilism stirs his imagination. 'Fighting against a damnable tyranny – the best might sacrifice everything for that.' But English socialism is 'infused with the spirit of shop-keeping', and irredeemably vulgar, 'like everything originating with the English lower classes'.[58]

Hubert is not unique in being placed by his creator in an awkward position – even though he seems to stand for the right things. Gissing, the natural aristocrat, portrays in his fiction a series of natural aristocrats, spokesmen for Gissing's own prejudices, from whom he nevertheless distances himself. This may be due to the novel form's inherent tendency towards dialogue and dissent. Or it may be Gissing's social guilt emerging from behind his anti-democratic ramparts. Or perhaps both. At all events, the disowning of his own élitism is an unmistakable element of his creativity. In *Workers in the Dawn* it is the idle, selfish, cynical Gilbert Gresham who claims membership of the 'aristocracy of intellect', and believes that the masses are 'not to be classed with human beings but rather with the brutes'. 'I am by nature an aristocrat,' announces Osmond in *The Unclassed*,

because I am by nature an artist. The aristocratic and the artistic temperament have this in common, both are founded on egotism; conscious egotism. Of course, every man is an egotist, but the artist is so to a supremely conscious degree, and in consequence he becomes an aristocrat.

This shaky reasoning might lead us to suppose that Osmond would discover, by the end of the novel, that he had gone wrong somewhere. Sure enough, his faith in art fails him in his hour of need, and he recovers his zeal on behalf of the downtrodden masses.[59]

Godwin Peak in *Born in Exile* is another deluded superman. He believes himself 'an aristocrat of nature's own making – one of the few highly favoured beings who, in despite of circumstance, are pinnacled above mankind'. The uneducated revolt him: 'I hate them worse than the filthiest vermin. They ought to be swept off the face of the earth.' But Godwin is a pathetic case. His whole life is a fraud. A working-class scholarship boy, he worms his way into the confidence of a rich family, hoping to marry their daughter. Union with a 'perfectly refined' woman of high birth has always been his dream. There is a revealing scene when he stands in a crowd in Hyde Park, watching two aristocratic women drive by in their carriage. He feels, in himself, their fineness and their scorn for the herd.

They were his equals, those ladies; merely his equals. With such as they he should by right of nature associate . . . In his rebellion, he could not hate them. He hated the malodorous rabble who stared insolently at them and who envied their immeasurable remoteness.

These feelings – uncannily prefiguring D. H. Lawrence's attitude towards the high-born – were Gissing's as well as Peak's. 'Peak is myself – one phase of myself,' he admitted. The qualification is significant. It is as if Gissing stands both inside and outside Peak, feeding into him his own opinions, but exposing him to disgrace and failure. For the rich family find out about Godwin's deceit, and he dies shamed. His fate can perhaps be read as masochistic self-criticism on Gissing's part. But much of what Godwin believes in, Gissing himself never renounced or outgrew. Godwin's fulminations against the debasement of art and literature by popular taste, and against the kind of people whose spiritual guide is the Sunday newspaper – 'only a consuming fire could purify the places where they dwell' – are eminently Gissingite. So is Godwin's weakness for peasants and rural artisans – the only species of uneducated people he can tolerate. In creating the character of Godwin, Gissing performed some unsparing self-analysis, and the result is a base, deluded character. Yet Godwin never quite forfeits our sympathy, and Gissing seemingly felt ambivalent too. The photograph Godwin leaves with his friend Earwaker before going off to die shows a face 'which no two observers would interpret in the same way'. Even Gissing's usual confidence about physiognomy deserts him.[60]

There are striking resemblances to Gissing, too, in the discredited cheat Dyce Lashman, eponymous hero of *Our Friend the Charlatan*. Dyce masquerades as the inventor of a social theory called 'bio-sociology', which he has in fact discovered in Jean Izoulet's *La Cité Moderne*. The principle of bio-sociology is that the working classes are to be ruled for their own good by their biological superiors, and since Dyce regards himself as belonging to 'nature's aristocracy' he finds this plan attractive. Science, he explains, has made democracy obsolete. Darwinism proves the superiority of 'nature's elect'. He also admires Nietzsche's 'frank contempt of the average man'. By the end of the novel Dyce has been humiliated, and we are encouraged to enjoy his alarm at the prospect of having to earn his living ('Imagine *me* – *me* at the beck and call of paltry everyday people'). Yet his admiration for Izoulet is Gissing's, who wrote to his friend Eduard Bertz, recommending *La Cité Moderne*, and expressed the hope that 'the world will some day be reconstituted on a basis of intellectual aristocracy'.[61]

The last and most abject in this series of fraudulent supermen is the vain poseur Clifford Marsh in *The Emancipated* – a novel about English expatriates in Italy anticipating E. M. Forster's *A Room with a View*. Clifford is a talentless 'artist', living on money from his stepfather, who manufactures shoddy in Leeds. Though Gissing makes him despicable, he endows him with views remarkably close to his own. 'The multitude,' Clifford proclaims, 'will never be humanized.' Democracy is the enemy of art: 'From the standpoint of art, democracy is simply the triumph of ignorance and brutality.' Gissing sabotages his own beliefs in the same novel when Mrs Denyer complains about the 'miserable results of cheapened travel', and the low people one meets nowadays in hotels and railway stations. Soon, she fears, Genoa and Venice will resemble Margate.[62] Gissing takes considerable pains to show us that Mrs Denyer is vulgar, parasitical and pretentious, and that we should give no credence to her opinions. Yet while he was actually at work on the novel, he wrote to Bertz:

> How exasperating it is to see the kind of people who constitute the mass of foreign visitors to Rome. As sure as ever the English language fell on my ear, so surely did I hear words of ignorance or vulgarity! Impossible to describe the vulgarity of most of these people. Many of them are absolute shop-boys and work-girls. How in heaven's name do they get enough money to come here? . . . Every day I saw people whom I should like to have assaulted. What business have these gross animals in such places?[63]

Precisely Mrs Denyer's sentiments.

There is no point asking whether the 'real' Gissing is the one who snarled about the brutishness of the masses or the one who repudiated such views. It is clear he found both activities necessary for stabilizing his personality and sustaining his creative work. No careful reader of Gissing can fail to see why simple denunciation of the masses was insufficient in itself. For what distinguishes his writing is reporting of individual miseries that broad statements about the masses gloss over. No other English novelist can provide such accuracy, because no other novelist had lived for years in the squalid lodging houses of Tottenham Court Road and Camden Town. Other writers imagine, but Gissing knows. He knows how shop assistants' feet go dead as they toil through their long Saturday-night shift, and how they have to stamp them to get any feeling back. He knows how a cab-driver, coming off duty, has to struggle upstairs one step at a time, like a child, or someone carrying a heavy weight, because his legs are almost paralysed after sixteen hours sitting on the box. He knows how unemployed labourers, as they start to age, rub dye into their hair before joining job queues in the hope of passing themselves off as young. He knows that prostitutes, when they come to hospital for treatment and are asked their profession, use some euphemism such as, 'I'm unfortunate, sir.' He knows about the food of the very poor, how when they have money, they do not spend it wisely, as would the middle classes, on raw provisions to cook themselves, but squander it on cheap, satisfying fare – slabs of mincemeat cake, or dough puddings, which lie alluringly on zinc foil in the cookshop, with jets of steam to keep them hot, or treacle, bought 2 ounces at a time and eaten without bread. He has noticed how common vinegar-drinking is among working-class girls, how undernourishment and the dullness of their diet make them crave it as a toper does spirits, and how their lips are shrivelled up like dried orange peel from indulging the habit.[64]

As no other novelist, he can tell us exactly what it was like to visit a pawnbroker if you were a working-class girl with a dress to pawn. How the smartly attired youth behind the counter, with black greased hair, would superciliously offer you eighteen pence, and how this would actually mean you got seventeen and a half pence, because a halfpenny was deducted as commission, and how he would make out the ticket in duplicate, blotting it on a box of sand – a custom that survived in the conservative pawnbroking profession when blotting paper had replaced it elsewhere, and how the coins he handed you would be sandy and greasy and scratched.[65]

Gissing knows that when little slum girls are washed by middle-class ladies before being taken on charity treats, they are amazed at the whiteness of their own hands, and find it difficult to recognize themselves, and keep touching their faces and their newly combed hair. He knows, too, that there are typhus-stricken slum tenements where the rent collector will find the mother of the family in a coma, and young children playing with a dead kitten – their only toy – and a smell of rotten fish exuding from a corner where the body of another child lies on a piece of oilcloth.[66]

Knowledge of this kind cannot be mitigated or assuaged. It breeds, and bred in Gissing, both social guilt and its opposite – a black amalgam of disgust, despair and loathing that vented itself in denunciations of the masses and their degradation. About his social guilt, he was quite specific: 'I cannot look at the hands of a toiling man or woman without feeling deeply wretched. To compare my own with them, shames me.'[67] About his disgust and hatred of the masses he was voluble and specific, too. That was his problem, and is still a problem for intellectuals as a caste. In the end, he could not see what good he was – as a writer, a thinker or a creator of beauty. He tried to believe that what he called 'art' and 'culture' would somehow eventually 'leaven' the masses – by which he meant turn them into people with tastes and enjoyments resembling his own. He puts this hope into the mouth of one of his noble ladies, Helen in *Workers in the Dawn*. Men of artistic genius, Helen explains, are far more important than humble do-gooders like herself. Genius does not have to bother with philanthropy. It 'has always had, and always will have, laws to itself, laws not applicable to the rest of mankind'. The creations of genius – a beautiful picture, for example – may seem to please only rich dilettanti. But in reality 'its spirit permeates every layer of society' and 'leavens the whole mass'. So artists are the true social workers. 'Without the works of Raphael our civilization could not have been what it is now.'[68]

Gissing can hardly have failed to see the irony in Helen's words. By placing her in a novel which exposes the vileness and degradation of the masses, he prompts the reader to question whether, if this is what our civilization 'is now', Raphael's influence has been so beneficial after all.

6

H. G. Wells Getting Rid of People

H. G. Wells was born in Bromley, Kent, in 1866. It was just the wrong time to be born in Bromley. The railway had arrived in 1858, and a second station, Bromley North, was constructed when Wells was twelve. With the railway came 'development', which meant, in this case, new estates of speculative housing for London commuters. Between 1861 and 1881 the population of Bromley went up from 20,000 to almost 50,000 (a rate of increase four times the national average) and in the first ten years of this period the number of houses in Bromley rose by 86 per cent.[1] In his semi-autobiographical novel *The New Machiavelli*, Wells recounts how, as a child, he had to watch Bromley being ruined. 'All my childish memories are of digging and wheeling, of woods invaded by building . . . I realized building was the enemy.' Bromley's fields disappeared beneath rows of houses, its little river, the Ravensbourne, the haunt of trout and kingfishers, was filled with rubbish – 'old iron, rusty cans, abandoned boots'. It had, the narrator of *The New Machiavelli* recalls, been important in his imaginative life – the scene of early walks with his mother. By the time he was eleven, 'all the delight and beauty of it was destroyed'.[2]

As we have seen, what happened to Bromley was to happen to much of southern England. But suburban sprawl was only a particularly prominent and distressing feature of the much larger problem of population growth, which increasingly alarmed writers and intellectuals in the course of Wells's lifetime. When he published *The Shape of Things to Come* in 1933, he dedicated it to 'José

Ortega y Gasset, Explorador' – a tribute, presumably, to Ortega's role as the explorer of the new ethics that man's multitudinousness made necessary.

Anxiety about overpopulation, rooted in his childhood vision of woods and fields destroyed at Bromley, is the key to Wells's reading of modern history. 'The extravagant swarm of new births,' he declares in *Kipps*, 'was the essential disaster of the nineteenth century.'[3] No social improvement is possible, *A Modern Utopia* tells us, unless population is controlled. 'From the view of human comfort and happiness, the increase in population that occurs at each advance in human security is the greatest evil of life.'[4] The unprecedented improvements in the production and distribution of goods which the nineteenth century achieved have not made mankind richer, Wells's William Clissold observes, because population growth has kept pace with or outstripped them. Gains in productivity have been 'absorbed by blind breeding'.[5] Support for birth control becomes, for Wells as for Clissold, the vital test of a modern world view – the crucial factor distinguishing liberals from reactionaries. Wells's hostility to the Catholic Church arose from his perception that its opposition to birth control stood in the way of any improvement in the human condition.

He realized, of course, that the population problem was even more acute outside Europe. In *The Open Conspiracy*, the book which he offered as a plain statement of his essential ideas, the profligate fertility and 'inchoate barbarism' of the inhabitants of the Orient and Africa are seen as obstacles to any real human progress. In India, North Africa, China and the Far East, Wells regretfully reports, 'there goes on a rapid increase of low-grade population, undersized physically and mentally, and retarding the mechanical development of civilization'. In these 'decadent communities outside the Atlantic capitalist system', almost no intelligences would be found, he predicted, capable of grasping his plans for world improvement.[6]

The urgency of these plans arose in part from his remarkably clear perception of the ecological damage caused by mankind's irresponsible reproduction. He realized, much earlier than it was generally understood, how recklessly other species were being wiped out, and their habitats irretrievably destroyed. 'Man,' he concluded, 'is a biological catastrophe.'[7]

Despite, or perhaps because of, the vast scope of the problem, Wells, like other commentators, tended to focus his anxieties upon certain local and specific issues. His childhood experience of the rape of Bromley ensured that suburban sprawl would be one of these. 'England now for the half of its area,' he reported in 1926, 'is no better than a scattered suburb.'[8] The pain and anger this aroused permeate his fiction. London's suburbs in *Tono-Bungay* are a 'tumorous growth' – endless streets of undistinguished houses, shabby families and second-rate shops, with outcrops from the main cancer producing such horrors as 'ignoble' Croydon and 'tragic' West Ham.[9] In *Ann Veronica* the prosperous villas of Surbiton and Epsom shine out in their raw ugliness 'like a bright fungoid growth'.[10] The greyness of life in 'a Neo-Malthusian suburban hutch' – the sort of jerry-built receptacle that makes 'such places as Hendon a nightmare of monotony' – provides George Brumley with a fruitful topic in *The Wife of Sir Isaac Harman*.[11]

Wells notes, with a special pang, the galloping ruin of Britain's coastline. All but a small part of the south and east coasts, he laments has been cut up into building plots, with estate agents' boards everywhere, and ill-made, weedy tracks designated 'Trafalgar Avenue' or 'Sea-View Road'.[12] Mass tourism and its devastations are another nightmare. Writing in 1911, Wells depicts the future fate of Capri – the whole island converted into one enormous hotel, with miles of additional floating hotels offshore, and aeroplanes dropping out of the sky every afternoon bringing thousands of fresh pleasure-seekers.[13]

Equally dismaying was the new vigour that mass culture had given to the advertising industry. Public advocacy of anti-bilious pills, pickles and soap seemed to Wells degrading. It disfigured the countryside, and spread an atmosphere of pampered, lower-class consumerism that he found offensive. Failure to recognize the damage done by advertisements is a sure sign, in his fiction, of substandard intellegence – or worse. His sordid capitalist Sir Isaac

Harman, having desecrated various beauty spots with hoardings for Staminal Bread, seeks to erect one on Shakespeare Cliff at Dover. Harman's success, based on a chain of cafés, is inexorably linked to the whole depressing phenomenon of clerks, suburbs and commuterdom. It is Sir Isaac's enterprise that supplies 'the midday scone or poached egg' in all 'centres of clerkly employment in London or the Midlands'.[14]

Inextricably involved with advertising was the blight of popular newspapers. True, Wells's imagination was not immune to the feat of organization that ensured their daily appearance on the streets. A character in one of his futurist stories, looking back on the newspaper age, describes its effect as if it were something from science fiction: 'You must figure the whole country dotted white with rustling papers. It is just as if some vehement jet had sprayed the white foam of papers over the surface of the land.' But the same speaker, leafing through samples of early twentieth-century popular journalism, dismisses it as 'faded bawling', like 'screams and shouts heard faintly in a little gramophone'. Newspapers were dangerous, Wells believed, because the profit-motive forced them to appeal to the most crude and vulgar passions, such as patriotism and war-fever. This made them prime organs of mass hatred. A popular newspaper was, in a quite literal sense, 'a poison rag'.[15]

A more insidious evil than newspapers, and less resistible, was woman. Though Wells was highly susceptible to feminine allure, his considered view of woman's influence on civilization was not favourable. For one thing, it was undeniably woman's unchecked fertility that was to blame for the population problem. For another, women notoriously used their sex appeal to captivate young males and force them into marriage, thus tying them to the breadwinning treadmill and effectively ending their lives as thinkers. This fate overtakes Wells's Mr Lewisham, among others. The evidence suggests that Wells thought of women as by nature extravagant, and addicted to clothes, chatter and shopping. There is not a single woman, complains the consumptive Masterman in *Kipps*, 'who wouldn't lick the boots of a Jew or marry a nigger, rather than live decently on a hundred a year'.[16] These were not precisely Wells's sentiments, but he seems to have shared Masterman's exasperation. When Wells's women divulge to their menfolk the true nature of femininity, it is not a flattering picture. Women, Clementina tells William Clissold, are ungenerous, parasitic, fearful, vain, easily muddled, tired by brain-work and untruthful. They are also less highly individualized than men – though the romantic tradition pretends they are more so – and the vast industry of fashion, perfumery and cosmetics has come into existence solely to bestow on them the individuality they lack.[17] Marjorie, in *Marriage*, is similarly frank. 'What are we women?' she demands. 'Half savages, half pets, unemployed things of greed and desire.' Her husband, Trafford, though blinded by love at first, is brought to see that Marjorie is right after witnessing her wanton extravagance in the West End stores. 'I'm a deeper and bigger thing than you,' he discloses. 'I reach up to something you don't reach up to.' Marjorie entirely agrees. It is, she acknowledges, woman's craving for material things that has ruined mankind.[18]

Given that the need for children is minimal, on an overcrowded planet, woman's role as mother and homemaker is set to diminish, as Wells sees it, and it is not clear that she is really fitted for any other role. She may, of course, become a surrogate male, applying herself, not very outstandingly, to tasks traditionally carried out by men. But this seems unlikely to satisfy her natural desires. 'Our world is haunted by the superfluous dissatisfied woman,' sighs a male spokesman in *Apropos of Dolores*. 'She darkens the sky.'[19] The husband in this novel solves his immediate problem by murdering his wife. But the philosopher Karenin in *The World Set Free* suggests a more far-reaching remedy. The modern world, he cautions, has no room for 'sexual heroines', woman must stop flaunting her sexuality, and if she does not, men must remember that genetic engineering allows them to determine the sex of children. 'If woman is too much for us we'll reduce her to a minority.'[20]

Wells's less optimistic visions of the future, however, predict a world that is even more suffocatingly overcrowded than our own, and in which the illiterate masses have sunk to a condition of semi-human subjection and dependence. They are consumers of debased

mass media, and are incessantly bombarded with crude advertisements, beamed at them by televisual or radiophonic means. In his
novel of 1899, *When the Sleeper Wakes*, a character called Graham
comes out of a cataleptic trance to find himself 203 years in the
future. London has by this time become a huge glass-roofed
conglomeration of innumerable levels – 'a gigantic glass hive' – with
a population of 33 million. Down in the subterranean levels of the
city live the pale, toiling masses ('Masses – the word comes from
your days – you know, of course, that we still have masses,' a guide
explains to Graham). This submerged population talk in a crude
dialect and listen to 'Babble Machines' (the replacement for newspapers), which broadcast crude, false news items and shout slogans
– 'Blood! Blood!' or 'Yah!' – to attract attention. Even in the upper
city levels, Graham finds, there are no books any more, only videos
or porn-videos, labelled in simple phonetic English. He feels battered by the sheer size of the congested mass, and begs to be alone.
'Let me go into a little room,' he weeps.[21]

In his non-fiction works Wells committed himself to formulating
ways in which this dreadful future could be averted and the world
population controlled. As he saw it, the main problem was the mass
of low-grade humanity such as inhabits the underground in *When
the Sleeper Wakes*. All over the world, he observes in *Anticipations*,
published in 1901, 'vicious, helpless and pauper masses' have
appeared, spreading as the railway systems have spread, and
representing an integral part of the process of industrialization, like
the waste product of a healthy organism. For these 'great useless
masses of people' he adopts the term 'People of the Abyss', and he
predicts that the 'nation that most resolutely picks over, educates,
sterilizes, exports, or poisons its People of the Abyss' will be in the
ascendant.[22]

The word 'poisons' may sound extreme here, but getting rid of
these inferior types need not, Wells stipulates, worry the conscience
of the rulers of his New Republic. On the contrary, it may be looked
upon as an ethical duty. He derives his new ethics from two sources:
Malthus and Darwin. Malthus's *Essay on Population* has, he
argues, destroyed facile liberalisms once and for all, by showing that

unless the problem of reproduction is solved, all dreams of human betterment must be futile or insincere, or both. Meanwhile, Darwin's theory of natural selection has rendered untenable the belief in human equality implicit in every liberalizing movement.

It has become apparent that whole masses of human population are, as a whole, inferior in their claim upon the future, to other masses, that they cannot be given opportunities or trusted with power as the superior peoples are trusted, that their characteristic weaknesses are contagious and detrimental in the civilizing fabric, and that their range of incapacity tempts and demoralizes the strong. To give them equality is to sink to their level, to protect and cherish them is to be swamped in their fecundity.[23]

The ethical system that will obtain in Wells's New Republic will favour the procreation of what is fine and efficient, and check the procreation of 'base and servile types'. In the past, Nature killed these off, and in some cases killing will still be necessary. Nor, advises Wells, should this appal us. Death for such people will mean merely 'the end of the bitterness of failure, the merciful obliteration of weak and silly and pointless things'. Clearly the effecting of this will be morally justifiable.

The new ethics will hold life to be a privilege and a responsibility, not a sort of night refuge for base spirits out of the void; and the alternative in right conduct between living fully, beautifully and efficiently will be to die. For a multitude of contemptible and silly creatures, fear-driven and helpless and useless, unhappy or hatefully happy in the midst of squalid dishonour, feeble, ugly, inefficient, born of unrestrained lusts, and increasing and multiplying through sheer incontinence and stupidity, the men of the New Republic will have little pity and less benevolence.[24]

If 'the whole tenor of a man's actions' shows him to be unfit to live, the New Republicans will kill him. They will not be squeamish about inflicting death, because they will have a fuller sense of the possibilities of life. 'They will have an ideal that will make killing worth the while.' The killing, Wells explains, will not be needlessly brutal. 'All such killing will be done with an opiate.' Whether this will be administered forcibly, or whether the victim will be persuaded to swallow it, he does not reveal. Selected criminals will be destroyed by the same means. Those guilty of 'outrageous conduct' to women or children, or of 'cowardly and brutal assaults', together with the criminally insane, will be humanely put down, on the principle that 'people who cannot live happily and freely in the world without spoiling the lives of others are better out of it.' The death penalty will also be used to prevent the transmission of genetic disorders. People suffering from genetically transmissible diseases will be forbidden to propagate, and will be killed if they do.[25]

Even these wide-reaching reforms will, Wells realizes, still leave unsolved the problem of the black and brown races, whom he considers inferior to whites in intelligence and initiative, and who therefore seem to him to pose the general question to the Western world, 'What will you do with us, we hundreds of millions, who cannot keep pace with you?' Clearly administering opiates to the entire populations of China and Africa would raise some practical difficulties, and Wells does not present, in *Anticipations*, anything approaching a properly worked-out extermination policy. None the less, he appears convinced that genocide is the only answer. The 'swarms of black, and brown, and dirty-white, and yellow people', who do not meet the new needs of efficiency, will, he insists, 'have to go'. It is 'their portion to die out and disappear'.[26]

In later non-fiction works Wells applies his attention less to the extermination of inferior breeds and more to the application of birth-control within his New Republic itself. He concedes that the science of genetics is still imperfect, so selective breeding, such as eugenicists favour, is impractical. Not that he opposes, in principle, the idea that only certain couples should be allowed to have children, but the selection of those couples on genetic grounds surpasses, he warns, current human knowledge. Accordingly he proposes to restrict parenthood to those who have the money and intelligence to make responsible child-rearers. The authorities should set minimum standards of clothing, cleanliness, growth, nutrition and education, and if these standards are not met, the child will be taken away and reared by the state at the parents' expense. If the parents fail in their payments for the child's maintenance, they will be put into celibate labour establishments to work off their debt, and they will not be released until the debt is fully discharged.

These measures, Wells feels, will ensure a fall in the birthrate of 'improvident, vicious and feeble types'.[27]

He introduces these recommendations in *Mankind in the Making* in 1903, and they are refined and developed in *A Modern Utopia*, published in 1905. This is a story about two hikers in the Swiss Alps, the narrator and a botanist, who suddenly find themselves, as a result of a space–time warp, in another world which is 'out beyond Sirius, billions of light years away' but is identical in population and geography to our own world – everyone in our world, that is, has a double there. The difference between the two worlds is that the one the hikers find themselves in is conducted on rational lines. It has already become a world state, with English as its universal language.

Its rulers are representatives of Wells's proposed new governing class, which he designates at various times 'new Ironsides' or 'Cromwellians' or 'Samurai'. They are rational, advanced, scientifically trained people – technicians, engineers, doctors – and they are not democratically elected. Democracy, Wells believed, was fatal, since the only appeal democratically elected politicans could make to the electorate was patriotic, and patriotism inevitably led to war. Wells's Samurai constitute a voluntary, non-hereditary nobility, drawn from both men and women. To qualify, they must have passed an examination and have achieved something unusual, such as writing a book, painting a picture or obtaining an engineering degree. They must observe an austere rule of life, abjuring tobacco, drugs, alcohol and meat, and taking cold baths daily. Once a year they must also go on a journey, alone, to some wild, solitary region – ice fields, oceans and deserts are recommended – for at least a week.

Around this fiction Wells arranges discussions of other Utopian arrangements, including the treatment of failures.

It is our business to ask what Utopia will do with its congenital invalids, its idiots and madmen, its drunkards and men of vicious mind, its cruel and furtive souls, its stupid people, too stupid to be of use to the community, its lumpish, unteachable, and unimaginative people? And what will it do with the man who is 'poor' all round, the rather spiritless, rather incompetent low-grade man, who on earth sits in the den of the sweater, tramps the streets under the banner of the unemployed, or trembles – in another man's cast-off clothing, and with an infinity of hat-touching – on the verge of rural employment?²⁸

These people, Wells explains, must be 'in the descendent phase. The species must be engaged in eliminating them; there is no escape from that.' However, their elimination in *A Modern Utopia* is not to be effected by killing, as Wells had suggested in *Anticipations*. Killing would be Nature's remedy, and Wells lingers over it with some fondness: 'The way of Nature in this process is to kill the weaker and sillier, to crush them, to starve them, to overwhelm them.' But in *A Modern Utopia* only babies born deformed or diseased are killed. Adult degenerates of all kinds are merely prevented from breeding. The Utopian state insists that to have children you must be solvent, above a certain age (twenty-one for women, twenty-six for men), free of transmissible disease, physically developed to an approved level, not a criminal, and sufficiently intelligent and energetic to have reached a statutory level of education. If, defying these regulations, you do reproduce, the state will take away your offspring and make you pay for its upkeep. For a second offence, you will be sterilized. Meanwhile, all idiots, lunatics, drunkards, drug addicts, violent people, thieves and cheats – in fact, all those people who 'spoil the world for others' – are to be isolated on special islands, patrolled by guards, where the sexes are kept apart to stop procreation.²⁹

This kind of organization – applied to the whole population of the earth, which in *A Modern Utopia* is 1,500 million – presupposes a high degree of administrative control, and Wells imagines this being achieved by a massive bureaucratic effort. Each inhabitant of the world in *A Modern Utopia* has a number, and has his or her thumbprint taken and photographed. The central index is in a vast system of buildings in Paris, where an army of attendants labours day and night keeping the record of births, marriages, deaths and criminal convictions up to date. Because population is mobile, such a record, Wells points out, is inevitable in an organized world. Wells's science fiction sometimes accurately predicts modern technological advances. But here he predicts a need rather than an advance. The advance – computer technology – which could now provide the complete index to the world's population he required, was to come into being without his foreseeing it.

These, then, are the plans for population control that Wells outlines in his role as the prophet of modernity. As a writer of fiction he is able to go much further. The advantage of fiction is that it can cleanse the world of people more rapidly and spectacularly than birth control. In his early essay 'The Extinction of Man', Wells speculates about the different circumstances that might eliminate the human race. Giant crabs or octopuses might come from the sea and eat people. Alternatively the world's population might be devoured by ants. Both these ideas developed into Wellsian fictions. The ants appear in a story called 'The Empire of the Ants', set in the Amazon jungle, where two explorers, sent to investigate a plague of killer ants, find that the creatures have acquired intelligence. They have tools strapped to their bodies and their leaders wear uniform. They kill by poison, which they carry around in needle-like crystals. If they spread, the narrator predicts, they will wipe out the human race.[30]

As for crabs and octopuses, they are a recurrent nightmare in Wells. Usually they have long, flexible tentacles around their mouths, and horribly intelligent eyes. A swarm of these creatures appears off the Kentish coast in a story called 'The Sea Raiders', and starts to eat people.[31] The Martians in 'A Crystal Egg' have bunches of prehensile organs, like tentacles, immediately under their mouths,[32] and Wells's first men on the moon come across a breed of Selenites with whip-like tentacles and necks jointed like a crab's legs.[33] Similar crustacean man-eaters appear at the end of *The Time Machine*, when the time-traveller flicks his mechanism forward 30 million years and finds himself on a desolate shore. At this late point in world history, human life has become extinct. People have been got rid of entirely. The earth has ceased to revolve, and has come to rest with one face towards the sun, which never sets but glares out of the western sky. Approaching him the time-traveller sees a monstrous crab-like creature, its big claws swaying and its long antennae waving like whips. As he watches, he feels the tickling of a thread-like antenna on his cheek, and turning he finds another monster crab just behind him. 'Its evil eyes were wriggling on their stalks, its mouth was all alive with appetite, and its vast ungainly claws, smeared with an algal slime, were descending upon me.'[34] The psychological origins of this horror in Wells's writing are ultimately impossible to divine. But the hungry, slimy, fishy orifice, threatening to devour and surrounded by what seem like hairs, might, given his resentful feelings about women, prompt a sexual explanation.

As an alternative to man-eating ants or crabs, fiction could get rid of people by moving back to a period of time when human populations were still tiny. Wells's 'A Story of the Stone Age' takes this course, introducing us to the early inhabitants of the district beside the River Wey in Surrey now occupied by Guildford and Godalming. At the period the story describes, there are no buildings and the population is small enough to satisfy even Wells – just a scattering of savages wearing skins. The technological highpoint of the tale is the invention of the axe – achieved, needless to say, by a man, while his puzzled mate looks on uselessly.[35]

More sophisticated ways of getting rid of people exploit Wells's knowledge of science. In 'The Man Who Could Work Miracles' a clerk called Mr Fotheringay finds, to his surprise, that he has miraculous powers and, after successfully performing various conjuring tricks, he orders the earth to stop rotating – at the suggestion of a nonconformist minister who recalls Joshua's exploit in the Bible. There is instant, worldwide destruction. 'Every human being, every living creature' is killed. Mr Fotheringay had forgotten that the earth rotates at over 1,000 m.p.h. at the equator and at over 500 m.p.m. in our latitude, so that everything on earth 'had been jerked violently forward at about nine miles per second – that it is say, much more violently than if they had been fired out of a canon'.[36]

A similar technical oversight almost ends life on earth in *The First Men in the Moon*, where a scientist, Cavor, perfects a substance called Cavorite which is opaque to any form of radiant energy, including gravity. Since it cuts off gravitational attraction, all the air above it becomes weightless. The first piece of Cavorite manufactured is left to cool by his assistants. It acquires its gravitational opaqueness only at 60 degrees Farenheit, and when it reaches this temperature there is a huge explosion and tornado-like winds spread havoc for 20 miles around. These are caused by the air rushing into the space above the Cavorite, which has become free of gravity. Luckily, the sheet of Cavorite is itself sucked upwards and disappears. Otherwise the whole atmosphere of the earth would have gone howling up through this gap in gravity, and every living thing would have suffocated. The Cavorite 'would have whipped the air off the world as one peels a banana, and flung it thousands of miles. It would have dropped back again, of course – but on an asphyxiated world.'[37]

Vivid as these ways of getting rid of people are, they have the disadvantage of being relatively unlikely. Also, they leave no ruins, or none the stories permit us to inspect. We are not allowed to savour the shattered remains of the towns and suburbs with which mankind has defaced the earth. Nor can we watch the hated masses of humanity reduced to terrified fugitives, and eventually to corpses. The first Wells story to provide these satisfactions was *The War of the Worlds*, published in 1898. This tale of a Martian invasion of the earth is sited precisely in the areas of London's suburbs that had caused most heartache to sensitive, thinking people in the later nineteenth century. The first Martian spacecraft lands at Weybridge. Armed with heat rays and poisonous black clouds, the Martians rapidly wipe out most of inner and outer London. Weybridge and Shepperton are early victims; Woking becomes a heap of fiery ruins; Richmond is destroyed by gas attack.

Much of the excitement comes from place-names. The destruction is less a matter of human casualties than of postal districts being cleared. Towards the end, the narrator walks through suburban London – Mortlake, Putney, Roehampton, Fulham, Ealing, Kilburn, South Kensington – and finds it quite empty of people. Vegetation is returning. A red weed, introduced from Mars, spreads everywhere, burying the remnants of houses in its rampant growth.

The preface to this disaster had been panic. Law and government had broken down. London's population had turned into terrified refugee columns, heading out of the city.

If one could have hung that June morning in a balloon in the blazing blue above London, every northward and eastward road running out of the infinite tangle of streets would have seemed stippled black with the streaming fugitives, each dot a human agony of terror and physical distress . . . Never before in the history of the world had such a mass of human beings moved and suffered together . . . without order and with a goal, six million people, unarmed and unprovisioned, driving headlong. It was the beginning of the rout of civilization, of the massacre of mankind.[38]

The element of relish in this account is indicated by the position Wells allocates to himself – safe above the fugitives, composedly putting the phenomenon into historical perspective. In the novel the narrator does not confess to any joy in destruction, but Wells introduces another character who does. On Putney Hill the narrator meets an artilleryman who plans to collect a band of brave, ruthless men and women like himself, and perpetuate the breed. He is exhilarated by the megadeath around him. 'The useless and cumbersome and mischievous have to die,' he urges. 'They ought to die.' This is just what Wells recommends three years later in *Anticipations*, and the tame, inert types the artilleryman condemns resemble the suburban lower-middle classes, lacking in ideas and initiative, who are excluded from Wells's Utopias. 'All those damn little clerks,' the artilleryman labels them – cautious, law-abiding, with 'no proud dreams and no proud lusts', just railway season tickets, life-insurance policies and small, safe investments. They will all, he rejoices, be wiped out. 'Life is real again.'[39]

The exultation in death that sweeps through *The War of the Worlds* is unmistakable, but it is counterbalanced by the loathsomeness of the victors – the Martians – who are another version of Wells's nightmare crabs. They have big, staring eyes, tentacles and horrible mouths that quiver, pant and drop saliva. Their steeds, the Handling Machines, are explicitly 'crab-like'. The Martians eat human beings – or, rather, suck the blood out of them – and the narrator gets a close look at one prospective meal, a well-dressed middle-aged man with shining studs and watch-chain, as he is lifted, shrieking, to his killer's mouth.[40]

In the end the Martians are defeated, succumbing to germs and bacteria which their systems, unlike ours, cannot cope with. Just ten years later, in 1908, Wells published a fantasy of world destruction, *The War in the Air*, which offers no such get-out for the world's millions. The destroyers this time are men in aircraft. Written soon after the advent of manned flight, the novel predicts the effects of air war, and foresees its major drawback – that it can effect only the destruction, not the occupation, of its target.

The novel makes it clear that the world deserves to be destroyed, because it has become so ugly, and the eyesores are those that dismayed the young Wells in suburban Bromley. The story opens in a London suburb called Bun Hill, where a gardener and greengrocer, Tom Smallways, tends the last patch of country in an area invaded by urban growth. Tom's garden is overshadowed by building site hoardings. The cables of the suburban monorail darken the sky above. The roof of Tom's mushroom shed carries advertisements, facing upwards to catch the eye of monorail travellers. Tom's father can remember Bun Hill when it was a Kentish village. But the old estates were cut up for building, the Crystal Palace was built, 6 miles away, then the railway came, and the gasworks, and an ugly sea of workmen's houses, and the pretty River Otterbourne became a putrid ditch. It is the story of Bromley from *The New Machiavelli*.

The penalty the novel metes out for this sacrilege is the destruction of virtually the whole civilized world. We watch it through the eyes of Bert Smallways, Tom's brother, who by a series of mischances gets aboard an airship in the German fleet just as it is taking off to bomb New York. As the fleet sails over northern England, we get a last glimpse of the ignoble landscape which is to be erased. Manchester and Liverpool lie below, a 'sprawl of undistinguished population', like London slums run to seed, with a few last bits of agricultural land caught in its net. Once over New York, the Germans wipe out the city with its 'black and sinister polyglot population', then global war develops, destroying all the world's major cities. Economic systems collapse; millions die of starvation.

When Bert returns to England he finds most of the population has died in a plague called the Purple Death. London is a ghost city, full of skeletons, dogs and rats. The few survivors of the English people live in rural peasant communities, subsisting by primitive agriculture. They have returned, Wells observes, from 'suburban parasitism' to what had been the life of the European peasant since the dawn of history. There are few children, because most of those born die within a few days. Adverts for canned peaches survive grotesquely in a medieval landscape of waste land and starving vagabonds.

Wells implies that this is all for the best. The old suburban life was not rooted in history or the earth. The life of the survivors is. Bert and his wife, Edna, rear pigs and hens 'among the clay and oak thickets of the Weald' – a stalwart English address, if rather vague. 'They loved and suffered and were happy.'[41]

With time, the obliteration of human life in Wells's fiction becomes more violent and thorough. *The World Set Free*, published in 1914, foresees nuclear fission and the outbreak of atomic war. Wells's atom bombs trigger chain reactions, so that they go on exploding indefinitely, turning their targets into man-made volcanoes. Leo Szilard, one of the scientists who worked on the Hiroshima bomb, said the idea of chain reaction first came to him after reading this book.[42] In the story atom bombs destroy most of the world's capitals in the late 1950s, killing millions. Economy and industry are paralysed. Government breaks down. Plague, cholera and famine follow the holocaust, greatly reducing the populations of India and China, and so easing the problem of those 'swarms of black, and brown, and dirty-white, and yellow people' whose presence on earth worried Wells in *Anticipations*.

Nuclear war, though it has a healthy effect on population figures, also destroys property. Twenty years later, in 1933, in *The Shape of Things to Come*, Wells hit on a way of eliminating people that would leave buildings intact. His futurist fantasy tells how germ warfare developed around 1940, and how an accidental release of yellow fever in India left much more open space on that subcontinent. The 1930s also saw the refinement of poisonous gases, culminating in Permanent Death Gas, which was used in a world war in the 1950s. Between May 1955 and November 1956 half the world's population perished, either from warfare or subsequent plagues and epidemics. 'In India the tigers and in Africa the lions came into the desolate streets, and in Brazil the dead population of whole districts was eaten chiefly by wild hog, which multiplied excessively.' The European scene is marginally less bleak. One Titus Cobbett, making a cycling tour from Rome along the Riviera to Bordeaux in 1958, describes deserted châteaux and overgrown gardens, 'blind tangles of roses, oleanders, pomegranates, oranges', and derelict railways overgrown with wild flowers. London's suburbs, however, are not even beautiful in their overthrow. Cobbett finds them a 'ruinous desolation'.[43]

Wells is often thought of as a rationalist, bringing science to the succour of mankind and planning technological Utopias. This view is not false, but it is incomplete. Many aspects of modern mass-mankind repelled him – newspapers, advertising, consumerist women, cities. A return to peasant life was preferable. The development of his fiction suggests that destruction lured him even more powerfully than progress. Reducing the world's population became an obsession. In fantasy he took – again and again, and with mounting savagery – a terrible revenge on the suburban sprawl that had blighted Bromley.

7

H. G. Wells Against H. G. Wells

Wells's greatness as a writer depends not only on the intensity with which he hates but on the imaginative duplicity that qualifies his hatred. He is nearly always in two minds, and this saves him from mere prescription. The utopias he invents seem to waver and change into dystopias as we watch, robbing us of certainty. Significantly the two astronauts in *The First Men in the Moon* react in opposite ways to the Selenites. Bedford, appalled, hits out and smashes them like toadstools. Cavor is fascinated by their intelligence, and remains behind when Bedford returns to earth. There is no saying who is 'right'. The Selenites, adapting all individuals to specific functions (like Huxley's Brave New Worlders, who derive from them), have eliminated discontent, war and all destructive instincts. They deserve Cavor's admiration. But a hand protruding from a jar in which a young Selenite is being processed into a machine-minder seems to express 'a sort of limp appeal for lost possibilities'.[1]

Such indecisions go back to a primary indecision in Wells about the validity of hope. For all his campaigning, his science taught him that the human race was doomed. The cold, empty world at the end of *The Time Machine* was the coming reality, and this made dreams of progress futile. Sometimes he feels there must be a way out. Perhaps men will survive, like Selenites, in underground galleries beneath the snow and ice.[2] Or perhaps they will fly to other planets and perpetuate the race. Man will 'stand upon the earth as upon a footstool, and reach out his hand among the stars'. This is what Trafford proclaims in *Marriage*, and the young giant Cossar's son in

The Food of the Gods, and Rufus in *The World Set Free*, and Wells in a speech to the Royal Institution in 1902[3] But for all that, he knew that space travel could not outsoar the second law of thermodynamics. Entropy, not evolution, would prevail – and as for reaching out among the stars, the Martians in *The War of the Worlds* had done just that, and their example was not propitious. A subsidiary desolation, but important to a writer, was that writing would perish too. Ruined libraries and rotting books are a feature of Wells's futurist waste lands. So his attitude to failure was divided. Failure was ignoble and should be eradicated; failure was universal and inevitable. This basic split spreads through his consciousness, disturbing all certainties.[4]

Even areas where he had seemed most dogmatic become dubious. Suburbs, it seems, are not necessarily evil. The spread of houses over beauty spots is positively welcomed in *Anticipations* – for should not people live among beauty, Wells demands? In his rational future 'every open space of mountain or heather' will be dotted with houses.[5] The futurist hikers in *A Modern Utopia* find suburbs all over the Alpine foothills, and defend this against a simple-lifer of the nut-eating breed, who likens houses to 'bacteria' on the face of the earth. 'All life is that,' retorts the Wellsian narrator scientifically, and inquires whether the simple-lifer does not himself live in a house.[6]

True, the world Wells anticipates in these instances is happily less congested than our own, much of its population having been wiped out. So suburbs are correspondingly less offensive. But Wells can also sigh for perfectly ordinary London suburbs, with their 'foolish little gardens of shrub and geranium', when he contemplates the bleak fields of swedes and carrots, sprayed with deodorized sewage, that will replace them in his rational utopia.[7] The poetry of the suburbs is in his blood. *The New Machiavelli* grows rapt about suburban Penge.

With Penge I associate my first realizations of the wonder and beauty of twilight and night, the effect of dark walls reflecting lamplight, and the mystery of blue haze-veiled hillsides of houses, the glare of shops by night, the glowing steam and streaming sparks of railways trains.[8]

Chesterton could not have said more for suburbs – would not, indeed, have said as much. For Wells goes on to describe the mating rites of lower-middle-class youngsters – the twilight promenades which are 'one of the odd social developments of the great suburban growths'. 'Stirred by mysterious intimations', these shop apprentices, work girls and young clerks spend their first-earned money on cheap finery, and venture forth into the vague, transfiguring gaslight to walk up and down and eye one another meaningly.

It is a queer instinctive revolt from the narrow, limited, friendless homes in which so many find themselves, a going out towards something, romance if you will, beauty, that has suddenly become a need – a need that hitherto has lain dormant and unsuspected. They promenade. Vulgar! – it is as vulgar as the spirit that calls the moth abroad in the evening and lights the body of the glow-worm in the night.[9]

Wells's transformation of the masses to moths is, it is true, a kind of evasion – a surreptitious shift into pastoral, like Orwell's rose-hip prole woman or Yeats's confusion of the breeding young with birds and mackerel. But it allows Wells to see what others (himself included) often miss – that the suburbs are not outside nature but part of it.

Advertising is another Wellsian bugbear that yields up its romance once he turns from contempt to imagination. The marvel-medicine Tono-Bungay, marketed at seven pence a bottle and possessing no scientific properties beyond being mildly harmful to the kidneys, sweeps Edward Ponderevo to wealth solely because he discovers in himself a genius for advertising. He understands the kind of lies you must tell, and the pictorial stimulus that will make people want to believe them. The advertiser and the novelist, Wells perceives, are alike. Both market illusions. Both fill otherwise empty lives with colour and interest.[10]

Further, advertising had shown itself to be the most successful form of mass-persuasion ever conceived, so it cannot be ignored in the building of the Wellsian New Republic. The second volume of *The World of William Clissold* is devoted to this idea. Dickon Clissold promises that advertising will control the world's food supply, and pour population 'from district to district like water'. This had been Wells's aim in *A Modern Utopia*. Dickon's scorn for old-style education also has a Wellsian ring. In effect, advertising *is* modern education, he explains. It teaches ten times as much as schools or universities. 'The only use I've got for schools now is to fit people to read advertisements.'[11] When Wells's own great enterprise in popular education, *The Outline of History*, appeared, it betrayed no aversion to advertising. Its twenty-four monthly parts carry advertisements for Gibbs Dentifrice, Kkhova Health Salts, Fry's Cocoa and many other benefits. Its illustrated section on 'Tribal Gods' (Britannia, Germania, etc.) prompts the reader to contrast these national symbols, for which millions have died, with the benign icons of advertising.[12]

Even Wells's allegiance to the idea of the superior individual, which is the linchpin of his programme for world reform, wears thin when his duplicitous imagination gets to work. True, some of his fables accept it in a fairly unquestioning fashion. The likeable young giants in *The Food of the Gods*, who have grown 40 feet tall through exposure to a revolutionary chemical and find themselves ostracized, clearly represent the fate of exceptional people in a world of mediocrities. Their spokesman declaims with Nietzschean vigour against Christianity's defence of the weak and puny, which allows them to 'multiply and multiply until at last they crawl over one another'.[13]

But in other stories – *The Invisible Man, The Island of Dr Moreau, The Country of the Blind* – the superiority of the singular individual is by no means apparent. The murderous, invisible Griffin and the crazed vivisectionist Moreau are prodigies that seem to endorse the ordinary man's suspicion of ruthless scientific genius, and Nunez, the sighted man who hopes to exploit the blind, is in the event horribly caught out. Wells will not let the issue become clear-cut. Moreau is certainly evil, but the masses do not come well out of the story either. When the narrator, Prendrick, gets back to civilization, he cannot rid himself of the idea that the crowds in London are composed of mutant beasts such as roamed the horror-island.

I would go out into the streets to fight with my delusion and prowling women would mew after me, furtive craving men glance jealously at me, weary pale workers go coughing by me, with tired eyes and eager paces, like wounded deer dripping blood . . . Particularly nauseous were the blank expressionless faces of people in trains and omnibuses; they seemed no more my fellow creatures than dead bodies would be, so that I did not dare to travel unless I was assured of being alone.[14]

The fable is as much about the repellent masses as about the wicked scientist, and Prendrick himself chooses the life of a hermit-astronomer, finding solace in the 'vast and eternal laws of matter'.

Wells makes it harder to guess his standpoint by putting what seem to be his views about the individual and the mass in the mouths of decidedly sinister characters. Ostrog, the bullying dictator in *When the Sleeper Wakes* lectures Graham about the merits of aristocracy and the necessary extinction of the unfit millions: 'The world is no place for the bad, the stupid, the enervated. Their duty – it's a fine duty too! – is to die.'[15] This, after all, is what Wells advocated in *Anticipations*, yet Ostrog is evil. And where are our sympathies meant to lie when the otherwise exemplary Professor Keppel in *Star Begotten* delivers his opinion of mankind?

I hate common humanity. This oafish crowd which tramples the ground whence my cloud-capped pinnacles might rise. I am tired of humanity – beyond measure. Take it away. This gaping, stinking, bombing, shooting, throat-slitting, cringing brawl of gawky, under-nourished riff-raff. Clear the earth of them![16]

Blaming humanity for bombing and shooting sounds reasonable enough. But for being under-nourished? And are we meant to notice how strangely disapproval of bombing and shooting combines with a wish to wipe humanity off the face of the earth? Did Wells himself ever decide how he felt on these issues? Or was fiction a means of keeping decision at bay? *The Research Magnificent* seems to be a satire on the whole notion of the intellectual aristocrat, as propounded in Wells's non-fiction. Rich young William Benham decides to devote his life to pursuing an ideal of aristocracy which will include the conquest of fear and pain, and adventures in the wild places of the earth, far from men who 'stew in cities'. Intellectuals, he proclaims, must become 'lords of the world', and advance civilization in the face of 'the inertia, the indifference, the insubordination, the instinctive hostility of the mass of mankind'. It sounds just like a Wellsian Samurai. Yet Benham emerges as priggish, ineffective and cruel: ' "Accursed things," he would say, as he flung some importunate cripple at a church door a ten centime piece, "why were they born?" '[17]

Benham's opposite number is his Cambridge friend William Prothero – scholarship boy, socialist, son of a Brixton dressmaker ('We're suburban people,' he chirps). In a straightforward novel he would capture the sympathies Benham forfeits. But actually he turns out to be a weak, sex-starved don. Neither democrat nor aristocrat appeals. Wells, as in much of his later fiction, seems anxious to put forward ideas but not to be held accountable for them. Some part of ⌐him – his imagination? his story-telling gift? – does not trust the creeds his brain formulated. His heroes and heroines can sound Nietzschean, and they share Nietzsche's enthusiasm for alpine glaciers and mountaineering as denoting superiority to the 'grubby little beasts down there'.[18] Yet the avowed Nietzscheans in Wells's fiction – Edward Ponderevo or young Walsingham in *Kipps* – are always preposterous.[19]

Though the idea of the superior individual was vital to Wells's whole programme, then, his doubts about it persistently enrich his fiction. Despite his contempt for failures, failures are his only successes. Failures alone, among his characters, have warmth and life. His servant-class origins, his life as a draper's assistant, his love for his drop-out father, his wretched clerkly physique (which he used to compare dejectedly, as a young man, with the statues of Apollo in the British Museum) – all these fed his art much more dependably than aspirations to *Übermensch* status. It is with a housemaid that his angel in *The Wonderful Visit* falls in love. Depth comes to his writing only in lower-middle-class contexts, or in contexts of loss and breakdown, as when poor crazed Mr Britling sits under a hedge, carefully drawing boundaries in red ink on the maps in his atlas. Wells never wrote anything more moving that the passage where Britling hears that his son Hugh has been killed on the Western

Front, and remembers how lovely the boy was alive, how his hair looked when he was born, how he liked long words as a child. Britling's red-inked plans for a world republic that will prevent such slaughter in future are a sad parody of all Wells's New Republican dreams, an elegy for his own hopelessness and failure. Cavor's glimpse of the young Selenite's hand protruding from a jar, expressing 'a sort of limp appeal for lost possibilities', is a truly Wellsian glimpse because lost possibilities were his one tragic subject. His sympathy for the young who see themselves as inferior comes unexpectedly from a vilifier of the inferior, yet it provokes one of the noblest insights in his writing.

Going to work is a misery and a tragedy for the great multitude of boys and girls who have to face it. Suddenly they see their lives plainly defined as limited and inferior. It is a humiliation so great that they cannot even express the hidden bitterness of their souls. But it is there. It betrays itself in derision. I do not believe that it would be possible for contemporary economic life to go on if it were not for the consolations of derision.[20]

Perhaps it was because Wells felt this so tenderly that he could shut out the feeling only by cold violence towards the weak and inferior, such as we find in *Anticipations*. Certainly it was only because he could write that passage that he could create his jaunty, woebegone clerks and pupil-teachers and shopkeepers – Mr Lewisham, Kipps, Mr Polly, and Hoopdriver in *The Wheels of Chance*.

All these characters are victims of lost educational opportunities. Mr Polly went to a National School at six and a dingy private school to 'finish off', and learned nothing. Kipps was sent to a rotten lower-middle-class 'academy'. Hoopdriver did algebra and some Latin and French, and 'wasn't backward', but he had to leave at fifteen and start as a draper's assistant. Together they represent the wastage of the English educational system at the start of the twentieth century. They justify Wells's rage at the national expenditure on armaments, which, he proclaimed, had stunted the lives of millions of children and robbed them of the chance of fine living.[21]

They all try to educate themselves after leaving school. Mr Polly reads Shakespeare, Boccaccio ('Bocashieu') and Rabelais ('Rabooloose') in a cheerfully uninstructed way with other draper's assistants. Like Mr Britling's son, he loves words, especially odd or made-up ones ('Sesquippledan verboojuice'). Hoopdriver, a Sherlock Holmes fan, goes to extension lectures to study Elizabethan drama and woodcarving. Kipps struggles with Shakespeare and Bacon's *Advancement of Learning* and Herrick's poems, which he buys from a chap who is hard up.[22] Wells, of course, thought such studies a stupid waste of time – but it is not Kipps's fault. He is misled by the 'cultured' middle class, and wants to be like them.

Lewisham, the brightest of the bunch, wins scholarships and gets as far as the Normal School of Science, South Kensington. But then he drops out, worn down by poverty and an unwise marriage. His fate illustrates 'the shameful and embittering' choice between education and sex, which, in Wells's world, was forced upon gifted young men with no money.[23] Wells, the model for Mr Lewisham, knew all about this, and sets out Lewisham's finances, down to the last penny, in double columns: 'These details are tiresome and disagreeable, no doubt, to the refined reader, but just imagine how much more disagreeable they were to Mr Lewisham.'[24]

What Wells depicts in each of these figures is not just deprivation but the pain of exclusion. They are sensitive enough to know that they are shut out, and to know, with horrible shame, that they deserve to be. What they are shut out from is an ideal of culture that is repeatedly projected as female. Whereas woman, in Wells's meliorist diatribes, is a clog to the aspiring male, in his human-interest stories she is an enticing, unattainable prize. Cycling through the Surrey countryside Mr Polly, a failed shopkeeper, comes upon a ravishingly pretty, brown-stockinged schoolgirl in a short blue skirt, sitting astride the wall which goes round the grounds of her school. She does not see him at first and he, delicately, pretends not to have seen her. But then they talk. She is called Christabel and is upper-class. Her 'people' are in India. She uses schoolgirl slang like 'beastly rot'. Mr Polly cannot hide his adoration, and she gives him, moved by his pleading, 'a freckled, tennis-blistered little paw to kiss'.[25]

The scene recapitulates one in *Tono-Bungay* in which young George Ponderevo, the housekeeper's son at Bladesover (i.e. Up

Park, Sussex, where Wells's mother was housekeeper), is in love with the aristocratic Beatrice, and she lets him kiss her on the lips as she sits, in black stockings, astride the park wall, her governess shrieking 'Beeee-e-e-a-trice!' from the house.[26] The symbolism of exclusion dominates both scenes: the wall, the girl tantalizingly astride it, her posture 'opening' her sexually, and indicating that the boundary can be crossed – by her. Can there be something in this symbolism of the rigid wall, and the girl's open, soft sex pressed against it, and her waving black, or brown, legs – something that becomes, through reversal, or resentment, those threatening Wellsian crabs with their rigid carapace and soft, moist, hair-circled mouths, and waving tentacles? Not that such a thought would ever occur to chivalric Mr Polly. What he feels is the shame of exclusion, as, having grazed his face slipping down from the wall, he staggers, bleeding, away, muttering, 'You blithering fool!' to himself.

Hoopdriver, a draper's assistant on a cycling holiday, finds his icon of refinement astride not a wall but a bicycle. She is impulsive, eighteen-year-old Jessie (an early sketch for Ann Veronica), who has eloped with a middle-aged art critic, Bechamel, only to find that he is not content with beautiful friendship but wants to seduce her. Hoopdriver arrives in the nick of time and escorts her to safety. To impress her, he makes up wild stories about lion-hunting in South Africa, but then, ashamed, confesses he is just a 'counter jumper'. Jessie encourages him to educate himself, and promises to send books. He returns to drapery, resolved to 'catch up' with the cultured in six years.

That lower-class Hoopdriver ever could come back and claim Jessie is, however, inconceivable. He belongs to a different kind of fiction. Significantly, when Jessie first asks Hoopdriver his name he makes up a series of false ones (Carrington, Benson, etc.). He is forced to do this by the fictional mode he finds himself in. His actual name belongs to a Punch-style caricature cockney cyclist, not a character in a realist novel. To admit he was called Hoopdriver would be like saying he was called John Bull. Exclusion so possesses him that it is stitched into his name – a name that does not qualify him to appear in the same book as Jessie.

Kipps is Hoopdriver plus an inherited fortune, and he chooses deliberately to exclude himself from the feminine ideal of 'high' culture Hoopdriver and Mr Polly are debarred from. When, out of the blue, he finds himself rich, he almost marries nicely spoken Miss Walsingham, who taught him art at evening classes, and is prepared to overlook his vulgar tastes. But he marries his childhood sweetheart, Ann, instead. Though in comfortable circumstances, he remains at heart what he has always been – a jaunty, irreverent draper's assistant, who likes a good read but hates everything 'stuck up'.[27] Nothing could be less like a Wellsian Samurai. The integrity and interest of all these lower-middle-class types – Polly, Hoopdriver, Kipps – depend on their not possessing those qualities which, Wells believed, should rule the world.

Wells's attitude to them – as we should expect by now – is divided. He feels for them, but does not quite treat them as men. They do not even have men's bodies. In front of a mirror, Hoopdriver ruefully inspects his narrow shoulders, hollow chest and weedy neck (those clerkly field-marks), and Wells interjects that, had you seen him in bed, you would realize he was 'only a little child asleep', despite his 'treasured, thin and straggling moustache'.[28] Mr Polly is a child, too. He and Mr Rusper the ironmonger, engaging in absurd fisticuffs on the pavement outside their shops, are smilingly characterized by Wells as 'these inexpert children of a pacific age'.[29] With Kipps the child theme becomes strident. Kipps exchanges kisses 'as frank and tender as a child's' with Ann, who has 'the face of a wise little child'.[30] Wells visualizes a lumpish monster – Stupidity – 'the ruling power of this land', which shuts Kipps and Ann out from 'the sunshine of literature' and the true apprehension of beauty which 'we favoured ones' enjoy.

I see through the darkness the souls of my Kippses as they are, as little pink strips of quivering, living stuff, as things like the bodies of little, ill-nourished, ailing, ignorant children – children who feel pain, who are naughty and muddled and suffer, and do not understand why. And the claw of this Beast rests upon them![31]

This is not the way we talk about equals. It reduces Kipps and Ann to pets. Mr Polly is a pet, too, and Hoopdriver. Only Mr Lewisham escapes Wells's condescension. Tearing up his plans for self-education, and resigning himself to dismal suburban marriage, he is treated like an adult – perhaps because his fate was so nearly Wells's.

But if Wells's kindliness to lower-middle-class characters betrays some of the disparagement it is supposed to be renouncing, it is still kindliness. And if we ask what sort of readership Wells wrote his science fiction for, the answer is that it was for the Mr Pollys and Hoopdrivers and Kippses, rather than for the intellectual heroes of later novels like Professor Trafford or William Clissold. Wells's science fiction is popular and sensational. It has nothing to do with 'the vast and eternal laws of matter' to which Prendrick in *The Island of Dr Moreau* allegedly devotes himself,[32] nor with that 'remotest of mistresses', scientific truth, that George Ponderevo pursues.[33] Science, for Wells, does not mean anything abstract at all. It means nights flapping by like a black wing, and trees growing and changing like puffs of vapour, as the time-traveller speeds through the centuries. It means water boiling and bubbling with the friction as a steel bathyscope plummets towards the ocean bed, and water shooting into the same bathyscope like a jet of iron, spreading the sea-explorer over his own smashed cushions like butter over bread.[34] It means the Invisible Man finding, when he shuts his eyes, that he can see through his eyelids, because they have become invisible too. It means the seeds on the surface of the moon cracking open, putting out shoots, starting to grow, becoming trees and plants, covering the moon with foliage, fruit and flowers, then dwindling, dying, disappearing – all in the course of a single lunar day.[34] These sensational effects were designed to attract not intellectuals but the Mr Pollys of the new reading public, who could not claim to be educated or scientific or interested in 'ideas', but who had a craving for a good read and liked to be astonished and entertained.

Freedom is what links Wells's science-fiction fantasies with his Mr Pollys, Kippses and Hoopdrivers. Science fiction is free because it transgresses the constraints of technology, turning natural laws to lawless ends. Mr Polly and Hoopdriver are free because Wells releases them, by romance, from their cramped lives. What he releases them into is a dream of the English countryside. 'There were miles of this, scores of miles of this before him,' thinks Hoopdriver on the first day of his cycling holiday, 'pinewood and oak forest, purple heathery moorland and grassy down, lush meadows where shining rivers wound their lazy way, villages with square-towered flint churches, and rambling, cheap and hearty inns.'[36]

Other writers, too, encouraged this cult of the open road – Chesterton and Jerome K. Jerome and Richard Jefferies, who, like Wells, vengefully imagined the London of the future as a desolate swamp.[37] The cult was an anti-urban idyll, pursued in defiance of encroaching suburbia and of clerkly cares. But it had its realistic side, too. The bicycle and the electric tram really had put the countryside, or what was left of it, within reach of the clerks.

> We have discovered Richard Jefferies' *Open Air* philosophy and read his books. There is now a series of small handbooks indicating the possibilities of woodland paths and downland tracks, with avoidance of road walking. We seize these and begin happily to explore the countryside . . . Electric trams will carry us to Purley or Wimbledon; Purley is the jumping-off spot for a day on the Downs . . . We shake the dust of the city from our feet, and turn southward to walk miles of turf and track, to laze in a hay-meadow, to eat sandwiches sitting on the low, rounded wall of an old churchyard . . . David knows the flora of the lanes better than I, and our talk is often mixed with incidental study of botany.[38]

The writer here is post-office-clerk-cum-pupil-teacher Helen Corke, and 'David' is her fellow pupil-teacher in Croydon, D. H. Lawrence. Hiking and tramping were discussed by pale young men in city offices. Forster's Leonard Bast tells the Schlegel sisters how, one Saturday after work, he took the underground to Wimbledon and walked all night. Getting clear of the suburbs took a long time – 'It was gas lamps for hours' – but then he tramped over the North Downs, through woodland and gorse bushes till dawn. 'There's been a lot of talk at the office lately about these things,' he tells them. 'The fellows there said one steers by the Pole Star.'[39]

This common factor of freedom helps to explain why Wells stopped writing lower-middle-class adventures like *Mr Polly* and science-fiction fantasies like *The Time Machine* – and why he stopped writing both at roughly the same time. The reason is that system replaced freedom as his ruling principle. He had always been torn between system and freedom, and continued to be. But from about 1910 system began to prevail. Worry about population was one cause of this. Freedom was all very well, but it choked the earth with bodies. Only by system could humanity's rampant growth be checked, so Wells began to work out programmes of world reform. He was aware of the losses involved. System meant the end of individuality. Mr Polly, Kipps and Mr Lewisham are individuals. But the people who occupy Wells's utopias and dystopias are representatives, like the people in adverts. They illustrate a design.

Once system is accepted, categorization follows, and abstractions like 'the masses' swallow up individual Mr Pollys and Mr Lewishams. Wells can be found mocking this tendency. 'I don't call the people we get here a Poor – they're certainly not a proper Poor. They're Masses. I always tell Mr Bugshoot they're Masses, and ought to be treated as such,' quacks Mrs Hogberry of Beckenham in *Tono-Bungay*.[40] But Wells himself, in the grip of system, uses terms like 'the masses' without misgiving. Moreover, it is only too clear that 'the great useless masses of people'[41] who are to be swept away by Wells's New Republicans will include confused, ignorant, common, unambitious little types like Mr Polly and Kipps.

As time went on Wells began to doubt not only whether individuality could be allowed but whether it existed at all. We can trace his struggles with this idea in his writing. At the end of *Kipps*, Art and Ann go for a row on the canal one summer evening, leaving the baby with a minder, and Art remarks what a Rum Go life is. 'Queer old Artie!' teases Ann – and Kipps agrees: ' "Ain't I? I don't suppose there ever was a chap quite like me before." He reflected for just another minute. "Oo! – I dunno," he said at last, and roused himself to pull.'[42]

Wells did not know either. Towards the end of his life he wrote a thesis for his D.Sc. which argues that the individual's belief that he is an independent entity is an illusion. The only reality is the collective existence of the species.[43] Forty years earlier he had maintained just the opposite. In a paper read to the Oxford Philosophical Society in

1903, he questioned the validity of logic, pointing out that its components, such as the syllogism, depend on an acceptance of the objective reality of classification, which Wells rejects. Logical categories are really, he observes, a device for allowing the mind to ignore individual differences, and thus to comprehend an otherwise unmanageable number of unique realities. It follows that we must regard as false all reasoning that arises from 'the fallacy of classification, in what is quite conceivably a universe of uniques'.[44]

This position, if adhered to, would render science invalid also – since science, like logic, depends on classification – and it would destroy at one blow the whole basis of Wells's later thinking. For his thought, as we have seen, became increasingly dominated by classification – into those who are fit to survive and those who are not; into the black and yellow races and the Europeans; into the natural aristocrats and the masses. His paper of 1903 renders all this illusory.

Wells keeps trying to articulate compromises between the two positions. *A Modern Utopia* divides people up into the imaginative, the administrative, the dull, the base and so on, yet protests that 'every being is regarded as finally unique'.[45] William Clissold (who says that he has discussed the matter with Jung) looks forward to the evolution of a 'collective human person', a 'common mental being of our race', that will nevertheless not replace individuals – they will be 'different' but 'enlarged'.[46] Wells himself, in *The Shape of Things to Come*, prophesies that the whole human race, in history's modern phase, will become 'confluent' – 'as much a colonial organism as any branching coral or polyp' – a real 'mass', in fact. Yet this will apparently not impair individuality, but merely turn it to 'higher aims'.[47]

The tragedy of the individual engulfed by the mass prompts some of his most poignant images. In *Tono-Bungay* Marion's absurd little wedding procession, with its three white-ribboned carriages, passes through London's traffic 'like a lost china image in the coal-chute of an ironclad'.[48] But system demanded individuality's extinction, and in Wells's later fiction the irreverent, irresponsible individuality of a Kipps or a Mr Polly is nowhere to be found. To Remington in *The*

New Machiavelli the individual is not a struggling, vulnerable self but just a source of muddle. Individualism means 'a crowd of separate and undisciplined little people'.[49]

Not that even Remington can make up his mind about it for long. His memory of Bromstead, overrun by suburbia, has set him against individual freedom, but when he meets the Baileys (modelled on Beatrice and Sidney Webb) he realizes that system is a mirage. The Baileys believe social classes are '*real* and independent of their individuals'. They see people only as samples and types. 'If they had the universe in hand, I know they would take down all the trees and put up stamped green tin shades and sunlight accumulators.'[50] Remington revolts against the sameness inherent in system. Threading the grimy chaos of London's streets, he finds himself losing faith in system altogether, and 'swaying back' to the belief that the huge, formless spirit of the world will not fit into categories.

This does not stop him – or Wells – trying to make it fit. Remington's New Tory party takes as its slogan 'The World Exists for Exceptional People'. By extending educational opportunity, it aims to select and develop the exceptional. No longer will they be lost in the crowd, marrying 'commonplace wives' and becoming 'commonplace workmen and second-rate professional men'. No longer will they be waste, 'as the driftage of superfluous pollen in the pine forest is waste'. One of Remington's audience protests at this point: 'Decent honest lives! *Waste!*'[51] That voice, and Remington's, are both Wells's. If the salvation of the world is what matters, then these scattered, unfulfilled lives – like Mr Lewisham's – really are waste. But to the individual they are not waste but life.

Wells shuttled inconclusively between these two perceptions, and they came to dominate his creative thought. Ellen, in *The Wife of Sir Isaac Harman*, earns praise for the gift – rare, says Wells, among philanthropists – of 'not being able to classify the people with whom she was dealing'. To her they are 'individualized souls', as distinct and considerable as herself.[52] But Trafford, in *Marriage*, wants to end the multiplicity and diversity of human existence, because he sees that if people do not grow more alike, and do not adopt the same ideals of world reform, then the world cannot be saved. The sight of the shopping crowds in Oxford Street exasperates him.

This rich and abundant and ultimately aimless life, this tremendous spawning and proliferation of uneventful humanity! These individual lives signified no doubt enormously to the individuals, but did all the shining, reflecting, changing existence that went by like bubbles in a stream, signify collectively anything more than the leaping, glittering confusion of shoaling mackerel on a sunlit afternoon?[53]

Trafford's mackerel, like Yeats's, are a version of the mass. But they do not reflect the intellectual's benign acceptance of brainless humanity. Trafford wants men to stop being mackerel. He takes a special interest in his cockney technical assistant, Dowd, a rabid socialist, spotty and dyspeptic from eating tinned food, whom he gradually comes to see as representative of the mass.

It seemed to him that in meeting Dowd he was meeting all that vast new England outside the range of ruling-class dreams, that multitudinous greater England, cheaply treated, rather out of health, angry, energetic, and now becoming intelligent and critical; that England which organized industrialism has created.[54]

'It *seemed* to him': Trafford's thinking epitomizes Wells's problem. As Dowd develops into a representative, so his individuality fades. He turns into an example – and, inevitably, an inadequate one. For Trafford is wrong to think he meets the 'vast new England' in meeting Dowd. Such an illusion negates the individualities of the millions for whom Dowd has come to stand but who are not Dowd.

Wells does not 'solve' the problem of the individual versus the system, but neither does he allow us to imagine it can go unsolved if we are to survive as a species. His value as a writer is that he faces us with facts beyond the normal scope of fiction. He teaches that unless population is controlled, all dreams of human betterment are futile. He knows that adequate control must involve a degree of interference, extending to every living person, which would outrage old-world concepts of individual freedom. He sees that in an overpopulated world human beings are a plague. It was not easy for him to reach these conclusions. As the pioneer of scientific fantasy and the apostle of free love, he was temperamentally averse to compulsion. He had, as he told a friend in a letter of 1907, no 'organizing capacity', but was a 'thoroughly immoral person', 'discursive, experimental and flunctuating'.[55] Yet increasingly he devoted his life to imagining a 'common social order' for the entire population of the planet, with a single language, a single monetary system and a rigorous central control that would arrest the spontaneous, disorderly breeding that had characterized earlier eras.[56]

He did not pretend that improvements could come about without widespread death and suffering. Some types of people, and some races, must be exterminated. He acknowledged that a transitional period of 'grim systematization', dictatorially imposed by the ruling élite and lasting perhaps many years, would be necessary before mankind was ready for happiness. But after that would come the green world. Mankind would live rationally in a pollution-free global garden, with the population kept below the safety limit of 2,000 million. Education would eliminate religion. Poverty, war and disease would be obsolete. The world's forests would grow again. Biological research would multiply plant varieties. Animal species would be preserved in vast wild-life parks, closed to humans.[57] This was Wells's dream. But it carried with it the shadow of poor crazy Mr Britling scribbling red lines on his map of the world.

8

Narrowing the Abyss: Arnold Bennett

Arnold Bennett is the hero of this book. His writings represent a systematic dismemberment of the intellectuals' case against the masses. He has never been popular with intellectuals as a result. Despite Margaret Drabble's forceful advocacy, his novels are still undervalued by literary academics, syllabus-devisers and other official censors. Many students of English literature know of him, if at all, only through Virginia Woolf's scornful estimate in 'Mr Bennett and Mrs Brown', and they naturally, though mistakenly, assume that Bennett, not Woolf, is diminished by that sally.

Bennett's origins and upbringing provided easy targets for the intellectuals' disdain. He came from the provincial shopkeeping class. His grandparents kept a tailor's shop in Burslem, and he was born in 1867 in his father's drapery-cum-pawnbroking shop in the same town. He left school at sixteen and worked for his matric at night school. The Bennett home, though beneath contempt from the viewpoint of metropolitan culture, seems to have been lively and artistic. The family enjoyed papers like *Tit-Bits* and *Pearson's Weekly*. Bennett later recalled that his 'principal instrument of culture' was *The Girl's Own Paper*, which advised on aesthetic matters. He also devoured best-sellers, his early favourite being Ouida, whom he read long before he sampled any of the classics.

At the age of twenty-one he went to London and joined the despised breed of clerks, working in a solicitor's office for 25 shillings a week. A fellow clerk called John Eland was a bit of a bibliophile and the two young men would talk books together and converse in French. Eland (later Aked in *The Man from the North*) introduced him to the British Museum reading room and second-hand bookshops. It was at this stage that Bennett developed his taste for the modern French and Russian writers Zola, Maupassant, the Goncourt brothers, Turgenev – ' my gods', as he called them. He won a guinea *Tit-Bits* prize for a story about an artist's model, and began sending short stories to evening papers. Within four years of arriving in the capital he had become assistant editor of *Woman*, writing 'Gwendolen's Column' and learning about frocks, household management, central heating, and other topics invaluable for the kind of writer he wanted to be.[1]

Later, when he had made his mark as a novelist, these humble antecedents were not forgotten by the intellectuals. He was 'an insignificant little man and ridiculous to boot,' declared Virginia Woolf's brother-in-law, the art critic Clive Bell. 'He was the boy from Staffordshire who was making good, and in his bowler hat and reach-me-downs he looked the part.' According to Somerset Maugham, Bennett looked like 'a managing clerk in a city office', and was 'rather common'. Wyndham Lewis sneered at his 'grocer origins'; Virginia Woolf at his 'shopkeeper's view of literature'. Bertrand Russell found him so 'vulgar' that he could not bear to be in the same room. T. S. Eliot told his cousin in a letter of 1917 how annoyed he had been when he was discussing psychic research with W. B. Yeats and a red-faced man 'with an air of impertinent prosperity and the aspect of a successful wholesale grocer' came up and interrupted them, in 'a most disagreeable cockney accent'. This, he discovered, was Arnold Bennett. It particularly aroused the intellectuals' venom that Bennett should have presumed to make money from literature, as they could not. D. H. Lawrence described him to Aldous Huxley as a 'sort of pig in clover', and Ezra Pound satirized him as the corrupt, venal and philistine Mr Nixon, pontificating in the 'cream and gilded cabin of his steam yacht'.[2]

Bennett did indeed make enough money from his writing to buy a yacht – in fact, two. His second, the *Marie Marguerite*, which he bought in 1920, had a crew of eight. 'She's not a yacht, she's a ship,' he announced jubilantly. His determination to make literature a livelihood first showed itself in 1898, when he took the decision to write sensational serial novels that he could sell to syndicates for publication in popular magazines. At his second attempt he scored a phenomenal success with *The Grand Babylon Hotel*, which sold 50,000 copies in hardback and was translated into French, German, Italian and Swedish. This venture represented precisely that commercialization of literature bemoaned by intellectuals like Gissing, and Bennett defends himself in his deliberately provocative – and very funny – autobiographical sketch *The Truth About an Author*, published in 1903. Here he explains that he had meant to keep himself 'unsullied for the pure exercise of the artist in me', and his first novel, *The Man from the North*, had been written 'in the vein of the *écriture artiste*'. But it had made no money, and his exclusive dedication to art and penury melted away 'the instant I saw the chance of earning the money of shame'.[3]

Bennett did not renounce art, of course, but he did not expect others to keep him while he produced it. In *The Truth About an Author* he goads the apostles of art by insisting that what an author labours for is ultimately 'food, shelter, tailors, a woman, European travel, horses, stalls at the opera, good cigars, ambrosial evenings in restaurants'. His recognition of this has allowed him to approach the business of self-promotion systematically: 'I wanted money in heaps, and I wanted advertisement for my books.' His reviewing has also been strictly businesslike. On average, he reckons, he reviews a book and a fraction of a book every day of his life, Sundays included. He fits reviewing into unoccupied corners of time, and can polish off five novels inside three hours, earning three guineas. He does not, he admits, read every word, but, being an expert, he does not need to.[4]

The Truth About an Author was an exercise in intellectual-baiting and should not be taken too seriously. Bennett's reference to 'the money of shame', for example, was a joke, for he by no means thought it shameful to write for money. His aim was to mediate between highbrow and lowbrow culture. Intellectuals, he believed, should write so as to appeal to a wider audience, and he did not see why what the masses liked should automatically be accounted trash. In *Fame and Fiction* he analyses a number of best-sellers – by Marie

Corelli, J. M. Barrie, etc. – to show that their popularity rests on genuine qualities which demand respect, and which only those besotted with the 'dandyism of technique' could ignore. This is what he would have expected to find, for between the popular and the highbrow reader there was, he argued, no essential difference.

Not only is art a factor in life; it is a factor in all lives. The division of the world into two classes, one of which has a monopoly of what is called 'artistic feeling', is arbitrary and false. Everyone is an artist, more or less; that is to say, there is no person quite without that faculty of poetising, which by seeing beauty creates beauty, and which, when it is sufficiently powerful and articulate, constitutes the musical composer, the architect, the imaginative writer, the sculptor and painter. To the persistent ignoring of this obvious truth is due much misunderstanding and some bitterness. The fault lies originally with the minority, the more artistic, which has imposed an artificial distinction upon the majority, the less artistic.[5]

The exclusiveness of the intellectual minority has, Bennett concludes, divided the world into two hostile camps, and it will remain divided until the minority makes an effort to understand the majority, inaugurating a 'democratization of art'. He welcomes H. G. Wells as an intellectual who has taken this step and written for the 'intelligent masses'.[6] But if other intellectuals do not follow suit, Bennett predicts, the movement of mass culture will sweep them aside. The 'trash' on bookstalls that literary reactionaries groan about signals a social revolution. Praisers of the past overlook the Education Act of 1870, and the new, eager reading public it has created, with 'no tradition of self-culture by means of books'. *Tit-Bits* and its imitators have been welcomed by the masses, Bennett notes, because they are hungry for a culture they can understand. This is 'the germ of a tremendous movement'.[7]

The lower middle classes, especially in the industrial Midlands and the north, are what Bennett identifies as the great potential reading public. He instances the Manchester suburbs, where Boot's Circulating Libraries offer their borrowers (mainly women) contact with living literature. Nelson's Cheap Modern Classics (seven pence for fiction, one shilling for belles-lettres) are creating book-buyers where there were none before. Even though they sell 20,000 volumes a week, they only scratch the surface. The lower-middle-class reading public, 'if it is cultivated and manufactured with skill', will surpass 'immeasurably in quantity, and quite appreciably in quality' the middle-class readership for which Bennett felt he and his contemporaries were catering.[8]

In politics, he displayed a matching optimism: the spread of education will heal the rift in English culture. 'The abyss between the mentality of the true leaders and the mentality of the people narrows and must narrow every year.'[9] His own contribution to narrowing the abyss was book reviewing, which educated the taste of the English public. Without being either patronizing or élitist, he introduced his readers to what he believed was truly valuable in modern literature. Writing for the *New Age*, he addressed a cross-section of the public that included 'board-school teachers, shop assistants, servants, artisans, and members of the poor generally'. Later, in Beaverbrook's *Evening Standard* his weekly book articles commanded a still wider audience. A list of the writers he praised quickly dispels any charge of philistinism. He selected Turgenev's *On the Eve* as 'the most perfect example of the novel yet produced in any country', and placed *The Brothers Karamazov*, *The Charter-house of Parma* and *Crime and Punishment* among the 'supreme marvels of the world'. His enthusiasm for Dostoevsky encouraged Constance Garnett to undertake her translations, and his admiration for Chekhov led to publication of Chekhov's short stories in the *New Age*. When the audience at the first London performance of *The Cherry Orchard* walked out in disgust, Bennett defended the play's 'daring naturalism'. Among French writers he championed Mallarmé, Valéry and Gide. He recognized Conrad's genius as early as 1908 – long before Leavis enrolled Conrad in the Great Tradition – and acknowledged D. H. Lawrence as 'far and away the best of the younger school'. In 1915 Bennett was one of only two writers to protest publicly about the banning of *The Rainbow*. He admired, supported or defended T. S. Eliot, Proust, James Joyce, E. M. Forster and Aldous Huxley, and boosted the unknown William Faulkner. Robert Graves recalled Bennett as 'the first critic who spoke out strongly for my poems in the daily press'.[10]

On painting, Bennett's views were likewise modern, unaffected and unafraid. The Post-Impressionist Exhibition of November 1910, which gave London its first sight of Cézanne, Van Gogh, Gauguin, Vuillard and Matisse, reduced critics and public alike to splutters and guffaws. But Bennett came out firmly on the side of the artists, acknowledging that if a writer were to do in words what they had done in paint, he might have to begin his own work all over again and renounce the 'infantile realisms' and photographic fidelities in which he had dealt. Among young painters, he helped Paul Nash and Ben Nicholson, and wrote an introduction to the catalogue for a 1919 exhibition which included Dufy, Vlaminck, Utrillo, Matisse, Picasso and Modigliani. The show provided, he wrote, 'an education to the islanders; and of course it is equally a joy'.[11]

As might be expected of an educator with an in interest in the Board School readership, Bennett alludes to the Board Schools in his fiction with consistent approval. Maidie, whom Ralph Furber in 'The Limits of Dominion' prefers to the exotic women his wealth has made available, is a Board School mistress. So is the clever, ambitious heroine of *Helen with the High Hand*, who 'for something less than thirty shillings a week' teaches sewing, mathematics, cookery and piano, and is representative, Bennett stresses, of thousands of efficient women teachers all over England.[12]

Bennett's reactions to crowds, seaside trippers, journalism and advertising also distinguish him from run-of-the-mill intellectuals. Brighton, which gave Gissing the shudders, was a spectacle of 'exciting humanity and radiant colour' to Bennett.[13] Organizing trips for the seaside crowds at Llandudno provides one of Denry Machin's most joyous coups in *The Card*.[14] The pampered intellectual Matthew Park in 'The Paper Cap', who shrinks from mass vulgarity and gramophones, comes to his senses in the end and marries a boisterous concert singer, deciding to 'adapt himself to the planet instead of sulking because the planet would not adapt itself to him'.[15]

Not that Bennett was immune to the spectre of the crowd. The 'dark torrent of human beings' cramming themselves into commuter trains at Hornsey Station, 'all frowning in study over white newspapers', strike Hilda Lessways as something alien.[16] But they do not disgust her. Crowds evoke pity in Edwin Clayhanger. As he watches workers streaming home at night past 'enamelled advertisements of magic soaps', he feels keenly that he is one of the exploiters.[17] Bennett sees subjects like journalism and advertising from the inside, not as plagues but as products of hope and pride. By selecting printing as the Clayhanger family business, he is able to plan his great novel and its sequels around typography's advance into the era of mass culture. The building of Edwin's new printing works coincides with the rise of lithography. His huge new litho machine, printing, four at a time and in two colours, advertisements for the Knype Mineral Water Company, would appal any self-respecting aesthete, but Bennett shows how it is interwoven with Edwin's private sanctities. In *The Old Wives' Tale*, when Constance and Sam disrupt the even tenor of the Baines' shop by designing eye-catching new labels – 'Exquisite 1/11' – Bennett recognizes them as 'the forces of the future'. Innocent and resourceful, they have added their small weight to advertising's advance.[18]

As a working journalist Bennett strongly contested, too, the intellectuals' disparagement of newspapers. In *Journalism for Women: A Practical Guide*, published in 1898, he insists that journalism is an art, and he welcomes the 'gradual Americanizing of the English press', which was the highbrows' bugbear. The born journalist knows 'that nothing under the sun is uninteresting'. Whatever he does – catching a cold, cutting a finger – he is impressed anew by 'the interestingness of mundane phenomena'. Most people find life dull. It is the journalist's job to make them see it is not, and for this the journalist must be gifted with 'the inexhaustible appreciative wonder of a child'.[19]

Conceived in this way journalism does not differ much from literature as Bennett describes it in *Literary Taste: How to Form It* of 1909 – another of his educational ventures, providing suggestions for reading and a guide to cheap editions. The makers of literature, Bennett tells his students, feel 'the miraculous interestingness of the universe'. Their lives are 'one long ecstasy of denying that the world is a dull place'.[20]

In Bennett's fiction, art and journalism are challengingly equated. Edwin Clayhanger thrills with 'a passion for great news' as he reads a newspaper transcript of a political speech, and Bennett breaks in defensively: 'I say his pleasure had the voluptuousness of an artistic sensation.'[21] Hilda Lessways, as a sub-editor on the *Five Towns Chronicle*, is caught up in the adventure of news-gathering, and this gives her a special feeling when she buys a paper and reads about the military disaster of Majuba Hill – 'horror-stricken desolation', but also 'an extraordinary sense of fervid pleasure'.[22]

The rights and wrongs of popular journalism are the subject of Bennett's play *What the Public Wants*, in which millionaire newspaper proprietor Sir Charles Worgan clashes with indignant intellectuals, including his brothers Francis and John and theatre-manager St John Holt. Sir Charles hates being despised by intellectuals, and donates £100,000 to Oxford University to get himself an Hon. DCL, though he does not know what the letters stand for. He is shown to be ruthless and unprincipled. But the highbrows are not much better. John is a prig and an intellectual snob; Francis, a dilettante; and Holt, champion of 'art' and scorner of public taste, has talent for little beyond losing money. Sir Charles takes over his ailing theatre and revamps it, introducing new costumes for the programme girls and a rule that they must be under twenty-five and pretty. Things immediately look up, and Sir Charles's popular productions of Shakespeare are a great hit.[23]

The contrast between the lowbrow who can make art pay and the incompetent intellectuals who hate him for doing it was also Bennett's theme in *A Great Man*, 1904. The hero, Henry Knight, is a young solicitor's clerk of impeccable conventionality who earns 3 guineas a week and lives quietly with his widowed mother and aunt in Dawes Road, Fulham. While recovering from measles he decide to write a novel, and the result, *Love in Babylon*, is a runaway best-seller. Though he takes a naïve delight in the high life to which wealth gives him access, Henry does not let it go to his head and remains cautious, sensible and modest. He and the reader learn a good deal in the course of the novel about the financial realities of authorship – agents, contracts, US serial rights – and this rampant commercialism is viewed not glumly but with infectious brio. Like *The Card*, the novel brims with the happiness of success. Set against Henry is his cousin Tom, who becomes an impecunious sculptor in Paris, styling himself Dolbiac, and is esteemed a genius by the highbrows and himself. He derides his cousin's books, and so do the highbrow reviewers, who suggest Henry should have been a grocer not a novelist. However, Tom is a liar and thief, and does not pay his debts, whereas Henry's success, Bennett lays it down, is due to 'the genuine enthusiasm of the average, sensible, healthy-minded man and woman'.[24] By the end of the novel, with two more best-sellers to his credit, Henry owns a London mansion in Cumberland Place and a country house in Hindhead, and is earning £10,000 a year.

A more sexually charged but equally decisive defeat of the intellectuals by a lowbrow comes in Bennett's 'The Perfect Creature', in which the snobbish, cultured Revestres endure a visit from a distant relative, Henry Clixham, a young chemical engineer with brilliantined hair who rides a motorbike. He cares nothing for philosophy, history, pictures, sculpture or literature, and seems to Mrs Revestre a 'barbaric, uncouth, maladroit specimen of the outer hordes of humanity plunging into her delicate and perfect home'. But her daughter Elvira thrills to his coarse masculinity, and falls wildly in love with him. Watching him mend the Revestres' electricity generator she gets oil on her fingers and rubs 'her jewelled hand on her short skirt, deliberately' – combining in a single gesture sexual invitation, self-abasement and rejection of her own effete, impractical culture.[25]

Bennett's whole quarrel with intellectual contempt for the masses is that it is a kind of deadness, a mark of inferior not superior faculties – a dull, unsharpened impercipience shut off from the intricacy and fecundity of each human life. Hence for Bennett the heightened sensibility of the artist is not antagonistic to the masses but looks to the masses – or, rather, to the hidden lives which that crude metaphor deletes – for its natural succour.

This is the point of his first novel, *The Man from the North*, which, as we have seen, he valued in retrospect for its pure artistry. It was written under the influence of Flaubert and Maupassant, and when he had finished it he could not think of it except as pure art: 'All I knew was that certain sentences, in the vein of the *écriture artiste*, persisted beautifully in my mind, like fine lines from a favourite poet.'[26] Yet the subject of this refined artwork was not some facet of high culture but the suburbs and the clerks.

The novel announces its main theme when the old clerk Aked, soon to die, holds forth to his niece Adeline about the literary potential of the suburbs. Suburbs, even Walham Green and Fulham, are full of interest, he advises, for those who can see it.

'Walk along this very street on such a Sunday afternoon as today. The roofs form two horrible, converging straight lines, I know, but beneath there is character, individuality, enough to make the greatest book ever written. Note the varying indications supplied by bad furniture seen through curtained windows, like ours' (he grinned, opened his eyes, and sat up); 'listen to the melodies issuing lamely from ill-tuned pianos; examine the enervated figures of women reclining amidst flower pots on narrow balconies. Even in the thin smoke ascending unwillingly from invisible chimney-pots, the flutter of a blind, the bang of a door, the winking of a fox terrier perched on a window sill, the colour of paint, the lettering of a name, – in all these things there is character and matter of interest, – truth waiting to be expounded. How many houses are there in Carteret Street? Say eighty. Eighty theatres of love, hate, greed, tyranny, endeavour; eighty separate dramas always unfolding, intertwining, ending, beginning, – and every drama a tragedy.'[27]

Aked suggests to the young clerk Richard Larch, the novel's hero, that they should write a book together called *The Psychology of the Suburbs*, which will disabuse revilers of suburbia, and show that 'the suburbs *are* London'. Aked dies before the project can start. But Larch is captivated by his vision. 'It seemed to him that the latent poetry of the suburbs arose like a beautiful vapour and filled these monotonous and squalid vistas with the scent and colour of violets, leaving nothing common, nothing ignoble.' In the upturned eyes of a shop girl on the arm of her lover 'he divined a passion as pure as that of Eugénie Grandet'.[28]

Larch's enlightened perspective on the suburbs is, of course,

Bennett's, for Larch is the young Bennett, though he might equally be Forster's Leonard Bast seen with sympathy and insight. He comes to London from the Potteries and gets a job as a shorthand clerk at 25 shillings, rising to £3, a week. He does the usual clerkly things – eats in ABC tearooms, goes on Saturday trips to Littlehampton – but he is mad about books and poetry, reads Zola and Maupassant, and tries to educate himself at evenings and weekends, getting a piano on hire purchase, taking music lessons, haunting concerts and picture galleries. But he fails. Like Wells's *Love and Mr Lewisham*, this is a portrait of the artist as he might have been without that extra bit of luck or determination. Larch tries to write a novel, modelled on Stevenson, but gives up after 14,000 words because it is so awful. He marries a cash-desk girl, Laura Roberts, because he must have a woman and cannot meet any others. He knows he is laying up years of regret. Laura will soon be like her sister Milly – plump, with eyes of 'cow-like vacancy'. He knows he will never be a writer. He will become 'simply the suburban husband, pottering in the garden, dutiful to employers'. But he thinks that perhaps a child of his may turn out to have literary ability. 'If so – and surely these instincts descended, were not lost – how he would foster and encourage it!'[29]

So the suburbs emerge from this novel as the site of lost illusions, not peripheral but central to life's tragedy. Bennett was capable of other attitudes to the suburbs, but he never fell for the simple intellectual sneer – partly because he was sensitive to intellectual disparagement of the Potteries, and recognized anti-suburbans as tarred with the same brush. So he sympathized with those who longed to escape from the suburbs and with those who longed to escape into them. The heroine of his typist-novel *Lilian* loathes the 'prison' of suburban Putney, and flees to the yachts and luxury hotels of the Riviera, whereas Priam Farll, the famous painter in *Buried Alive*, breaks free of the smart set by giving it out that he has died and settles comfortably in Putney, where he is at leisure to paint 'one of the most wonderful scenes in London: Putney High Street at night'.[30]

What Bennett seeks, wherever his stories are set, are the depths that lie within ordinary, not-particularly-intelligent people. 'If I cannot take a Pentonville omnibus and show it to be fine,' he pledged, 'then I am not a fully equipped artist.'[31] *Clayhanger* and *The Old Wives' Tale*, his masterpieces, are Pentonville omnibus novels. We know by the end that their characters are not remotely ordinary, but unforgettably singular. Yet they are also commonplace. Edwin, on the day he leaves school at the start of *Clayhanger*, is a clumsy, ignorant youth. He knows nothing of art; he has never seen a great picture or statue or heard great music. He has been taught nothing about literature. But his fineness does not depend on his acquiring these masteries. It is there already in the unshaped boy. A flame burns with 'serene and terrible pureness' in his head. No one notices it, except Bennett and us. 'It was surprising that no one saw it passing along the mean, black smoke-palled streets.' In *The Old Wives' Tale* the same benign irony is brought into play when Sophia falls in love with Gerald Scales. 'No one else in Wedgwood Street saw the god walking along by her side. No one else saw anything but a simple commercial traveller.'[32]

In this way Bennett gives us access to the realities that blaze and coruscate inside dowdy or commonplace bodies. Delicacy is, he shows us, a quality of Edwin's flame. His 'sense of delicacy' later makes him unwilling to intrude on the strike-meeting, despite Hilda's eagerness; and after shaking hands with her he carries away 'a delicate photograph of the palm of her hand printed in minute sensations on the palm of his'.[33] This delicacy, though it makes Edwin special, is not special to him. Bennett discloses it repeatedly behind his characters' mundane façades. Constance and Sophia, two unremarkable adolescent daughters of a draper, are 'like racehorses, quivering with delicate, sensitive, luxuriant life'.[34] Edwin's delicacy, which eludes common eyes, is apparent to Darius, his father.

Darius was aware of a faint thrill. Pride? Perhaps; but he would never have admitted it. An agreeable perplexity rather – a state of being puzzled how he, so common, had begotten a creature so subtly aristocratic . . . aristocratic was the word.[35]

This is a very different matter from the natural aristocrat of the intellectuals' vaunting fantasies. What Darius perceives has nothing to do with overlordship, rather the contrary. It springs from vulnerability – innocent, fragile, defenceless. It is gentle and seeks gentleness. This, too, is echoed in *The Old Wives' Tale*, in Sophia's love for Gerald. Her 'aristocratic instinct' makes her seize on his gentlemanly manners 'like a famished animal seizing food'. In another mood entirely, Sophia believes that she forms an 'aristocracy of intellect' with her schoolmistress Miss Chetwynd, and Bennett smiles at that.[36] But he does not smile at the aristocracy that Darius perceives in Edwin, or that makes Sophia flee brutality, for that is not intellectual arrogance but the delicacy of the young, fiery and vulnerable.

Nor does Bennett unearth these refinements only in the relatively precious soil of young middle-class Burslemites. One of his greatest stories, 'Elsie and the Child', is about a London housemaid, Elsie Sprickett, who first made her appearance as the Earlforwards' servant in *Riceyman Steps*, and who by the time this new story begins is working for cultivated, artistic Dr and Mrs Raste in Myddleton Square, Clerkenwell. Elsie is fat, stupid and ignorant, 'a dull, slow, heavy ex-charwoman'. Nothing resembling culture has ever glimmered in the 'almost primeval night of her brain'.[37] But she is also sensitive, wise and frightened – more sensitive, wiser and more frightened than anyone else in either story. She might almost be Bennett's answer to T. S. Eliot's sneer about the 'damp souls of housemaids' in 'Morning at the Window'. We watch Elsie lying on her side in bed, blinking at the electric light, 'like an animal', but, Bennett advises us, 'an animal with a soul highly developed'. It is her soul that suffers when she waits at table for the Rastes. To her they are 'the feared, worshipped and incalculable rulers of the universe', and she is terrified of making mistakes. As she lifts the covers from the food she trembles with stage fright, like a Shakespearean heroine on a first night. Standing unoccupied by the sideboard is an agony, for she has to struggle to control 'those unruly vassals – her hands, terrorized by a sickening self-consciousness'. The ceremonial code which forbids her employers to talk to her during dinner, or she to them, alarms her, and she cannot adapt herself to its inhumanity. When she makes a slip she offers Mrs Raste 'a miserable and touching little smile of excuse, a smile entirely unauthorized by the code'.[38]

The Raste dinner party, seen entirely from their servant's viewpoint, is one of Bennett's most humane disclosures. It ends in a domestic row, because the Rastes' twelve-year-old daughter, Miss Eva, breaks down and sobs at the prospect of being sent away to boarding school. Elsie weeps in sympathy. 'There Miss Eva sat, far more elegant and stylish than either of her parents, fresh, exquisite in contours, sensitive, proud, defenceless, set apart, so young in her twelve years, childlike, childlike, childlike – broken!'[39] Bennett's narrative method does not allow us to say whom these thoughts occur to. But the triple 'childlike', with its note of helpless sympathy, suggests Elsie, though they are ideas she would not have been able to articulate. She sees in Eva what Darius sees in Edwin, and loves it. Her own life has little tenderness. Her first husband was killed in the war. Her second, Joe, fought in it and is shellshocked and sometimes violent. She has no children. Eva supplies that want, and Elsie's strength and gentleness draw Eva. Their love is physical, though disguised as the attentions of a servant to a young mistress.

'I'll come up with ye,' said Elsie. She ought not to have said it. To see the child into bed on such a night was wicked self-indulgence, bad for her and bad for the child too, very bad for the child. The temptation, however, was too strong, too sweet . . .
[Miss Eva] yielded her long, snake-like, aristocratic body to be undressed, and Elsie's hard muscles, moving over her, grew as soft as Elsie's affection. Self-indulgence, but exquisite! Miss Eva dropped on the bed, lying stretched on the top of the eiderdown, and sighed.
'Oh, Elsie, couldn't you carry me into the bathroom?'
Elsie did so. Wickedness: that was what it was![40]

There are two Elsies here. The inner voice – 'wicked self-indulgence', 'Wickedness' – speaks for a simple Elsie whose notions of respectability, so quickly overcome by sexual desire, we can afford to smile at. But the Elsie whose hard muscles grow soft as she undresses Eva is not an Elsie of voices, inner or outer, but of sensations that outrun words. The word 'aristocratic', which Darius fumbled for and found when thinking of Edwin, is supplied by Bennett on Elsie's behalf. She would not have known this was the word for the delicacy that excited her in Eva's body.

Bennett's alertness to the body's intense, wordless life prefigures D. H. Lawrence, who read him attentively. Sophia, for example, walking along Wedgwood Street beside Gerald, converses in mundane phrases, 'and meanwhile a miracle of ecstasy had opened – opened like a flower'.[41] This could be Lawrence's Yvette, entranced by the stranger's maleness in The Virgin and the Gipsy – 'Like a mysterious early flower, she was full out.'[42] Elsie's physical passion for Eva, like Sophia's for Gerald, admits her to a level of seriousness where she can no longer be regarded, either by Bennett or us, with a patronizing twinkle. She escapes from intellectual belittlement into a region where the intellect has no place. Bennett recurrently makes this shift, to register the extraordinary in ordinary people. It happens, for instance, in These Twain when Minnie, Aunt Hamps's fat, dim servant girl, gets pregnant. Edwin thinks how grotesque she is as she kneels blubbering before his sister Maggie.

And then some glance of her spectacled eyes, or some gesture of her great red hand, showed him his own blindness, and mysteriously made him realize the immensity of the illusion and the disillusion through which she had passed in her foolish and incontinent simplicity . . . 'Compared to her,' he thought, 'I don't know what life is. No man does.' And he not only suffered for her sorrow, he gave her a sacred quality. It seemed to him that heaven itself ought to endow her with beauty.[43]

The despised whom Bennett rescues are often – like Elsie and Minnie – women, largely because he saw they were more despised than men, especially by intellectuals. The idea for The Old Wives' Tale occurred to him when he was sitting in a Parisian restaurant in the autumn of 1903 and an old woman came in to dine. She was fat, shapeless and ugly, and loaded with small parcels that she kept dropping. Her voice and gestures were ridiculous, and she attracted attention to herself by choosing one seat and then, not liking it, choosing another, and then another. In a few minutes the whole restaurant was laughing at her. But to Bennett she seemed tragic. He deduced from her mannerisms that she lived alone. She had once, perhaps, been slim and beautiful, he thought, and she was probably unaware of her oddity. It should be possible 'to write a heart-rending novel out of the history of a woman such as that'. So *The Old Wives' Tale* was conceived.[44]

Not that women alone, among the downtrodden, win Bennett's reappraisal. He frequently draws attention to the slave class, male as well as female. Samuel Povey, up late one night, catches a glimpse, as he passes a bakehouse, of bakery workers, stripped and labouring through the hours of darkness. He never again eats 'a mouthful of common bread without recalling that midnight apparition'.[45] Hilda Lessways, noticing George Cannon's cuffs, imagines the women who have sighed and grumbled amid wreaths of steam and suds and sloppiness, 'so that the grand creature might have a rim of pure white to his coat-sleeves for a day'.[46] The one moment of dreadful and sinister power in the otherwise thinnish novel *The Pretty Lady* comes when wealthy Gilbert Hoape visits a high-class West End bootmaker. The fawning attendant shouts 'Polisher' down a speaking tube, and through a trapdoor in the floor 'a horrible, pallid, weak, cringing man' comes up out of the earth of St James's, kneels before Gilbert, makes his shoes like mirrors and then vanishes, 'silently, and dutifully bent' through the trapdoor. It does not shut properly, so the manager 'stamped on it, and stamped the pale man definitely into the darkness underneath'.[47]

But it would be wrong to claim Bennett as predominantly the kind of social-problem novelist that these instances suggest. Aiming, as he did, to narrow the abyss between highbrow and lowbrow, he had to find a theme that was wider and more permanent than social problems – a universal theme that would have meaning for human beings at every level of intelligence and culture. The theme he chose was youth and age. This subject, inexhaustible in its implications and relevant to every mortal, is the keystone of his writing. What most pained him when he saw the old woman in the Paris restaurant who inspired *The Old Wives' Tale* was not so much her helplessness and disarray as the fact that those who laughed at her included a beautiful young waitress, whom he had especially admired. This set him thinking about the process that transforms a girl into a stout, ageing woman, and about how 'it is made up of an infinite number of infinitesimal changes, each unperceived by her'. *The Old Wives' Tale* is about these changes, and about 'the profound, instinctive cruelty of youth'. Sophia and Constance, Bennett assures us, are nice, kind girls, but they are ruthlessly intent, as all young creatures are, on displacing, conquering and eventually eliminating their elders. Their elders, in the shape of Mrs Baines and Aunt Harriet, are equally intent on fighting tooth and nail against the terrifyingly strong young minds and bodies which they have reared and nurtured, but which are now crushing them to the earth. The battles in this universal conflict are waged over seemingly trival matters, but they are life-and-death encounters. When Sophia, for the first time in her life, refuses to take castor oil at her mother's command, it is a fatal defeat for Mrs Baines, and she knows it: 'She held herself in dignity while the apocalypse roared in her ears.' This is not a joke – or, rather, like all jokes, it is an attempt momentarily to lighten the pitiless advance of death. For Mrs Baines's failure shifts her one more notch down the scale towards uselessness, senility and oblivion. In the novel's last pages Sophia and Constance have themselves almost reached the end of that scale – two tired, aching old women, bullied by their young servant, 'an impudent girl of about twenty-three', with a 'cruel, radiant and conquering' gaze, who waggles her hips as she carelessly lays the table, 'as though for the benefit of a soldier in handsome uniform'.[48]

The battle of youth against age also means, sometimes, victories for age – temporary, like all victories, but horrible and crippling none the less; envious counterattacks launched by stiffening bodies and hardening brains. *Clayhanger* is planned around just such a fight. Edwin, fiery and delicate but helpless, is reduced to 'blubbering' obedience by his father, Darius, and compelled to renounce his hopes of beauty and art and an architectural career. It is perfectly commonplace, like all Bennett's most dreadful scenes. Countless adolescents are talked out of their dreams in this way by reasonable, brutal, well-meaning parents. Edwin, furious and impotent, silently vows revenge: ' "When you're old, and I've *got* you" – he clenched his fists and teeth – "when I've *got* you and you can't help yourself, by God it'll be my turn." ' But because in the wars of youth against age the victors are constantly becoming the vanquished, and acquiring all the pitiable trappings of defeat, revenge when it arrives is never as satisfying as we had expected. The tyrants we wished to avenge ourselves upon are no longer there, but have turned into victims. When Darius, stricken with softening of the brain, has grown senile, Edwin learns the limits of vengefulness. 'As he looked at the poor figure fumbling towards the door, he knew the humiliating paltriness of revenge.'[49]

Throughout Bennett's work the shattering, momentous, utterly everyday subject of youth and age is pursued, reformulated, analysed. It is present in Mr Ipple's alarming encounter with a cool young actress who seems to have no respect for senior drama critics,[50] and it is present in the feud over money between Anna Tellwright and her father in *Anna of the Five Towns*. It is never simplified or packaged into moral conclusions. Hilda Lessways, like all Bennett's young people, has a 'deep unconscious conviction of the superiority of youth to age',[51] and she is both right and wrong. Age can mean envy and venom, as it does when the boarding-house servant Louisa refuses to change the sheets on the bed of a housemaid who has eloped with one of the guests.

'I ain't going to touch her sheets, not for nobody!' Louisa proclaimed savagely. And by that single phrase, with its implications she laid unconsciously bare the sordid baseness of her ageing heart; she exposed by her mere intonation of the word 'sheets' all the foulness of jealousy and thwarted salacity that was usually concealed beneath her tight dress and neat apron.[52]

But age can also mean old Shushions in *Clayhanger*, the former Sunday School teacher who long ago rescued Darius and his parents and siblings from the workhouse. Though feeble and tedious, Shushions sheds 'epic' tears, [53] and he earns this epic status because his fine and generous past is encompassed within, yet also absent from, his crack-brained present. He both is and is not the man he was. He is Time's 'obscene victim', and Edwin is revolted by the spectacle of young louts baiting him in the street. 'He was astonished that they were so shortsighted as not to be able to see the image of themselves in the old man, so imprudent as not to think of their own future, so utterly brutalized.'[54]

It is, though, because the louts will become feeble like old Shushions – or die first – that it is needless to read them a moral lesson about youth and age. Time has pre-empted the moralist's role, and no one is excused from watching the retributive process. Typically Bennett uses common or garden objects to symbolize the tragic contrast between youth and age – like the secondhand satin shoe which Elsie in *Riceyman Steps* ties for good luck to the Earlforwards' bed on their bridal night – a shoe 'which some unknown girl had once worn in flashing pride'. Later, when both Earlforwards are dying, Elsie cannot bear to look at the shoe. With its curved high heel and pink ribbon, it seems to represent 'all the enigma of the universe'.[55] That phrase suggests why youth's defeat by age, and age's by youth, were such valuable subjects for Bennett. They are enigmatic, in that understanding is of no use against them. They cannot be solved by intelligence. Faced with their inevitability, the intellectuals' advantages evaporate.

The theme of youth and age naturally draws Bennett's attention to children and the hopes parents invest in them. This is an interest that distinguishes him sharply from early twentieth-century intellectuals. The intellectual code regards fondness for children as suburban or middle class. According to this view, parenthood is a distraction from the serious pursuit of culture. 'There is no more sombre enemy of good art,' warns Cyril Connolly, 'than the pram in the hall.'[56] Literary intellectuals in the first half of the twentieth century tended to opt for childlessness or child neglect. Wyndham Lewis, for example, refused to have children by his wife, and took no responsibility for the illegitimate children his mistresses gave birth to. His son and daughter were both given away. 'I have no children, though some, I believe, are attributed to me,' he told a friend. 'I have work to do.'[47] The novelist Jean Rhys left her first child, a son, near an open window in midwinter, so that it caught pneumonia. It was sent to a hospice for the poor and died there aged three weeks while Rhys and her husband, the Dutch writer Jean Lenglet, were drinking champagne in their Paris flat. Rhys's second child, a daughter, spent much of her early life in institutions.[58] When Olga Rudge bore Ezra

Pound a daughter in 1925, the baby was handed over to a peasant couple to be reared in a remote village in the Austrian Tyrol.[59]

Bennett, by contrast, appreciated that for normal people parenthood is the most important thing that ever happens. When Constance in *The Old Wives' Tale* gives birth to Cyril, her life and that of her husband, Samuel, are utterly transformed. They cease to be 'self-justifying beings', and never think of themselves afterwards except as their son's parents. Constance, having known the pains of childbirth – 'the shattering army, endless, increasing in terror as they thundered across her' – is a different woman ever after. She offers her breast to the child 'with the unconscious primitive savagery of a young mother'. Fatherhood gives Samuel – though he is only, from an intellectual viewpoint, a rather common little draper – a universal dimension.

He walked home, as he had decided, over the wavy moorland of the country dreaming in the heart of England. Night fell on him in mid-career, and he was tired. But the earth, as it whirled through naked space, whirled up the moon for him, and he pressed on at a good speed. A wind from Arabia wandering cooled his face. And at last, over the brow of Toft End, he saw suddenly the Five Towns a-twinkle on their little hills down in the vast amphitheatre. And one of those lamps was Constance's lamp – one, somewhere. He lived, then. He entered into the shadow of nature.[60]

Parenthood is not only mysteriously elevating for Bennett's people; it is also joyfully physical. The smell of children – rank, sweet, vital – is a potent and secret delight. At the Bainses' children's tea-party:

Although the window was slightly open, the air was heavy with the natural human odour which young children transpire. More than one mother, pressing her nose into a lacy mass to whisper, inhaled that pleasant perfume with a voluptuous thrill.[61]

As Cyril grows to boyhood, Constance loves to feel him and gaze at him 'and to smell that faint, uncleanly odour of sweat that hung in his clothes'.[62] Only a parent could understand that (or so we might say – but when Bennett wrote it fatherhood was still many years in the future for him). It is because he knows about parents and children that he can describe the drama of a baby being bathed, and the sexual rivalry it arouses in the parents, without being sentimental,[63] and can appreciate, too, the ache of childlessness. The charming little social comedies he weaves around Stephen and Vera Cheswardine have Vera's barrenness ('bitterly regretted') as the shadow to their sunlight.[64] Though he shows how children are treasured, he never gushes over them. He acknowledges their greed and selfishness, taking it as natural behaviour in young animals. When Cyril, after his father's death, wins a National Scholarship and decides to go to London to study art, Constance is aghast. But she realizes it would be fruitless to plead, much as she dreads the gap he will leave behind. 'She knew that she might as usefully have besought mercy from a tiger as from her good, industrious, dreamy son.'[65]

Bennett's concern with parenthood is an aspect of his tendency to see people not as brains but as organisms. This is another of his perspectives that rescues the world from intellectuals. Biology is no respecter of thinkers. The thoughtless, as Bennett keeps reminding us, are just as apt for its purposes as the clever, and it links ordinary people with the timeless. Constance and Sophia, having their first adolescent quarrel about a man, sense their beauty changing into something sinister and cruel, because 'the eternal had leapt up in them from its sleep';[66] Mrs Baines feels her powers wane, because 'the everlasting purpose' had made use of her and 'cast her off';[67] Sophia, striving to attract Gerald Scales, becomes simply the 'expression of a deep instinct to attract and charm';[68] Mr Baines, paralysed, is 'a mere mass of living and dead nerves on the rich Victorian bedspread'.[69] Intellectuals, used to regarding themselves as more than just cellular syntheses, are likelier than most people, Bennett suggests, to be hoodwinked about their motives and significance. In *The Pretty Lady* Gilbert Hoape tries to fathom what it is that binds him to the disreputable Christine – 'imagining himself to be on the edge of a divine mystery, and never expecting that he and Christine were the huge contrivances of certain active spermatozoa for producing other active spermatozoa'.[70]

What are real, from this angle, are not the pastimes intellectuals value – literature, art, philosophy – but the offices of deathbed and sickroom, where man is reduced to matter. Edwin Clayhanger appreciates this as his dying father struggles in the throes of what Edwin learns is called Cheyne-Stokes breathing: 'Nothing was real except imprisonment on a bed night and day, day and night for weeks . . . Let them see a human animal in a crisis of Cheyne-Stokes breathing, and they would know something about reality!'[71] Watching old Aked die in *The Man from the North*, Richard Larch comes to see that life is more terrible than he had thought, and feels new respect for the professional nurse: 'He abased himself before all doctors, nurses and soldiers in battle; they alone tasted the true savour of life. Art was a very little thing.'[72] Bennett, we have seen, planned the book as a Flaubertian artwork – 'in the vein of the *écriture artiste*'. So in Larch's testimony art renounces art. Intellectuals are denied any real knowledge of life, compared to quite humble functionaries.

Bennett's biological perspective allowed him to take a tougher view than intellectuals about suburban sprawl and industrial squalor. They became marks of man's justifiable hostility to nature. For he saw that if nature means grass and trees, it also means cancer, bacteria and the torments of natural death, and in this guise it is obviously hateful. Besides, the desecration of landscape by houses and factories can itself be seen as a natural process, expressing man's industrializing and urbanizing instincts. Bennett offers both these justifications. Of the smoke and pollution in *Anna of the Five Towns* he submits:

this disfigurement is merely an episode in the unending warfare of man and nature, and calls for no contrition. Here indeed is nature repaid for some of her notorious cruelties. She imperiously bids man sustain and reproduce himself, and this is one of the places where in the very act of obedience he wounds and maltreats her.[73]

Whom God Hath Joined defends the ravaged urban landscape of the Five Towns as 'the natural, beautiful, inevitable manifestation of the indestructible force' within man. If this prospect is not beautiful, Bennett insists, 'then flowers are not beautiful, nor the ways of animals'.[74] According to Bennett's universal time-scale, the mark made by man on the planet is, in any case, temporary, so the question of whether it is ugly or beautiful is ultimately of little moment. Like Wells, he foresees a world without people. Expounding the vital role of pottery (and so of his beloved Potteries) in human life, he predicts: 'The last lone man will want an earthen vessel after he has abandoned his ruined house for a cave, and his woven rags for an animal's skin.'[75]

Logically Bennett's projection of humankind as a temporary biological event might seem to devalue individuality. Character traits cannot matter much if we are all just organisms programmed to reproduce and die. However, Bennett is not logical, and he keeps both ideas in play. Further, they serve the same purpose. He invokes his biological perspective for anti-élitist ends – to assure us of the basic sameness of people, despite social and educational differences. He also insists on the absolute singularity of each person, especially of seemingly unimportant people, and this underwrites anti-élitism too.

He holds to this second idea so strongly that it resembles religious faith. Like religious faith, it depends on ignorance (no one can *know* that everyone else in the world is unique). In effect it was Bennett's religion. To everything else that usually comes under the heading of religion, he was unremittingly hostile. 'Pietistic humbug,' and the narrow-mindedness it breeds, came high on his list of hates. As we have seen, he employs phrases like 'the eternal' and 'the everlasting purpose' to denote the force that drives the universe, but they have for him no theological content. He believed people were singular and important in themselves, not because they were prized by some notional divine proprietor.

His fiction is committed to illustrating this belief. Edwin Clayhanger, watching Hilda's child, little George, shriek with ecstasy as he soars and plunges on a garden swing, is awestruck by the 'miraculous' advent of a new human being, 'with character and volition of its own; unlike any other individuality in the universe'.[76] This doctrine of individual distinction, on which Bennett pins his most serious thoughts about people, crosses the barriers intellectuals erect between themselves and the masses, for it is combatively unexclusive. Samuel Povey, though outwardly a funny little man, has in him, Bennett divines, 'the vein of greatness which runs through every soul without exception'.[77] Nor, Bennett stipulates, can even the most 'ordinary' people be completely known. Their distinctiveness extends beyond thought. At the end of *The Old Wives' Tale*, after Constance's death, Bennett imagines her friends trying to fathom what her life had been like, and failing: 'No one but Constance could realize all that Constance had been through, and all that life had meant to her.'[78]

This emphasis on everyone's unusualness is not what we should expect from (to return to our starting point) Virginia Woolf's 'Mr Bennett and Mrs Brown'.[79] Woolf there contends that Bennett's characters are conventional, and that in constructing them he concentrates merely on external details. Meeting Woolf's hypothetical old lady Mrs Brown in a railway carriage, he would, she predicts, observe with immense care the pictures of Swanage and Portsmouth displayed in the compartment, the way the cushions bulge between their buttons, and 'how Mrs Brown wore a brooch which had cost three-and-ten-three at Whitworth's Bazaar'.[80] While accumulating these trivia, Bennett would, Woolf alleges, miss the real Mrs Brown, because his eye would not penetrate to what was unpredictable, incalculable, surprising and complex in her thoughts and feelings. The younger novelists, on the other hand, such as E. M. Forster, D. H. Lawrence and, she implies, herself, would omit the external and conventional and transcribe 'their own direct sense of the oddity and significance' of the character.

To support this travesty of Bennett's methods Woolf quotes from the opening paragraphs of *Hilda Lessways*, in which Bennett describes, with great precision, the house Hilda and her mother live in, defining its social ranking in the locality with reference to rateable value and the occupations of neighbours. That Woolf does not see the relevance of these lowly considerations to Hilda's inner self illustrates her upper-middle-class obtuseness – or affectation. But the really breathtaking aspect of her attack is her appropriation to herself and fellow moderns of precisely those unexpected shifts of thought and feeling that give Bennett's characters their depth. He persistently sees past the ordinary to the odd and unpredictable, as

Woolf claims the moderns do, and Hilda Lessways herself could have supplied Woolf with abundant testimony of this.

When Cannon first kisses Hilda, for example, Bennett shows how her senses go on busily registering the incidentals of the scene, despite her emotion: 'She could see in a mist the separate hairs of his tremendous moustache and the colours swimming in his eyes.'[81] 'Tremendous', with its half-comic suggestion of grandeur, indicates the moustache's distorting proximity to Hilda's face, and the 'swimming' colours signal his body going about its organic processes, unmarked by him. Hilda's dispassionate, distracted notation of these oddities seems precisely to meet Woolf's criteria for 'modern' writing, though her essay gives no inkling of such a dimension in Bennett. When, later, Hilda learns that Cannon has married her bigamously, she feels none of the indignation or vengefulness convention would require. On the contrary, she is curiously proud of him, and finds herself remembering, in the flash of her shock, his triumphs in the hotel-management line. 'With an extraordinary inconsequence she dwelt upon the fact that, always grand – even as a caterer, he had caused to be printed at the foot of the menu-forms which he had instituted, the words: "A second helping of all or any of the above dishes will willingly be served if so desired." '[82]

There is a connection between bigamy and second helpings, of course, which makes Hilda's reaction believable as well as bizarre. But it is worlds away from the humdrum externals Woolf maintains Bennett's characters are composed of. Sophia in *The Old Wives' Tale* is another of the band of characters that could be called in Bennett's defence. What she hears when, having eloped with Gerald, she tries to get to sleep in an uncomfortable French hotel is entirely unexpected, yet as ordinary as breathing: 'She pressed her face into the pillow and listened to the irregular, prodigious noise of her eyelashes as they scraped the rough linen.'[83] Had any character in fiction listened to that noise before? The comparisons that occur to Sophia as she surveys her new world are just as startling and commonplace. Comforting the ageing whore Madame Foucault, she notes that the woman's tears have turned her face into a kind of smudged palette, 'like the coloured design of a pavement artist after a heavy shower'.[84]

Through Sophia, Bennett also shows the importance of the ordinary in defining people's lives, and shows – what is more surprising – that as the ordinary becomes more ordinary, so it becomes not ordinary at all but precious. After living for years in the Rue Lord Byron, Sophia finds that the turning down of the gas burners in the street lamps at a particular time each night has grown so accustomed it is 'a portion of her life', and dear to her. 'If it is possible to love such a phenomenon, she loved that phenomenon.'[85] This perception of how love gathers round habit, and builds the world out of it, tallies with the feelings Sophia and Constance have, as children, about their shared bed: 'If Constance had one night lain down on the half near the window instead of on the half near the door, the secret nature of the universe would have been altered.'[86]

The apotheosis of the ordinary in Bennett carries an anti-intellectual charge. It reminds us that what is most valued in most people's lives has nothing to do with art, literature or ideas, and it admonishes us that such lives are no less sensitively lived for that absence. The character Dr Stirling in *The Old Wives' Tale* makes the mistake of supposing the contrary when, back in England, he meets Sophia and asks her whether she has read Zola's *La Débâcle*. It emerges she has read almost nothing since 1870, and has only the vaguest impression of Zola, whom she thinks of as 'not at all nice'. Dr Stirling 'had too hastily assumed that the opinions of the bourgeois upon art differ in different countries'.[87] Yet this exchange does not diminish Sophia and the bourgeoisie, as it would in an intellectual novel. For we know that Sophia was actually in Paris throughout the siege and commune, which are the subject of Zola's novel. She does not have to depend, like Stirling, on Zolaesque realism. She knows reality.

For Sophia the siege and commune were, Bennett shows, far removed from Zola's crowd scenes and bloodshed and novelistic coincidences. She was occupied with more sensible affairs, such as hiring a boy for two sous an hour to wait in bread queues, and selling the food she had hoarded at a marked-up price to neighbouring housewives. What the siege meant most vividly to her was a notice across the shuttered windows of her local creamery: 'Closed for want of milk'.[88] The commune which followed was an inconvenience, since the streets were not always safe and she had to give orders to the butcher over the courtyard wall.[89] But she never witnessed any violence, being too busy keeping alive and feeding her lodgers amid the havoc caused by men and politics.

It is a feminist view of a historical event that Sophia validates, and also a populist one. Bennett got the details for his account from an old railway employee and his wife called the Leberts whom he was lodging with in a village near Fontainebleau. He knew they had lived in Paris during the 1870 war, so he asked the old man whether he was right in thinking they had been through the siege of Paris. 'He turned to his old wife and said, uncertainly, "The Siege of Paris? Yes, we did, didn't we?" ' This halting answer brought it home to Bennett that the siege had been only one incident among many in their lives, and it gave him the perception 'startling at first, that ordinary people went on living very ordinary lives in Paris during the siege, and that to the vast mass of the population the siege was not the dramatic, spectacular, thrilling, ecstatic affair that is described in history'.[90]

Of course, what the 'vast mass' felt or thought was not of much concern to Virginia Woolf. Snobbery is the most prominent of the various energies running through 'Mr Bennett and Mrs Brown'. The essay was originally delivered as a paper to a Cambridge undergraduate society, and it reverberates with the mirth of upper-class young people contemplating the sordid lives of their social inferiors. One can almost hear the well-bred laughter as Woolf impersonates Arnold Bennett planning a fictional character: 'Begin by saying that her father kept a shop in Harrogate. Ascertain the rent. Ascertain the wages of shop assistants in the year 1878. Discover what her mother died of. Describe cancer. Describe calico . . . '[91] Woolf, at the start of her essay, distinguishes the modern from the Victorian age by reference to the changes observable in the character of 'one's cook'. The modern cook, she reports, is much more open and friendly with the 'woman of genius' she serves than her formidable Victorian counterpart. This allusion to the servant problem is quite in keeping with the social tone of her piece, and of Bloomsbury and modernism as a whole.

But Bennett would have been more likely to see the matter from the cook's angle. A feature of his work mocked by intellectuals like Woolf was his emphasis on domestic convenience and labour-saving home design. The house Denry builds for his mother in *The Card* has a self-washing doorstep, black china wipe-clean door knobs, rounded corners at the junctions of all interior walls, floors and ceilings to speed dusting, enamel wall surfaces, steam central heating, electric light, a bathroom and a vacuum cleaner.[92] The chapter in which these wonders are listed is the most serious in the novel. Likewise in *Clayhanger*, when Edwin moves with his family into their new house, its hot and cold water system inspires him 'like a poem'. 'You of the younger generation,' Bennett interjects, 'cannot understand that.'[93]

Nor could anyone of the older generation, for whom the production of hot water was the servants' concern. Shown over Denry's masterpiece, his mother exclaims significantly, 'I could run this house without a servant.' The elimination of domestic servants was a major impulse behind the movement towards rational home design, and partly for that reason it was not England but the more egalitarian America that led the way. In *The Card*, first published in 1911, Bennett was clearly influenced by American ideas, and was, for an English writer, unusually progressive. He was also unusual in being male, for the pioneers in the movement were all women. The emphasis in American works of mass education, such as Catherine E. Beecher's *The American Woman's Home*, was, as in Bennett, on labour-saving. The male concept of the home had been primarily visual; the new women writers concentrated on efficiency within the small, servantless, suburban family house. A notable American feature in Denry's house is the bathroom. In Europe portable baths lasted until well into the twentieth century. The 'American' bathroom, once adopted, meant that water did not have to be carried about. 'No porterage of water anywhere' is prominent in Bennett's commendation of the Denry plan.[94] It was in America, too, that electricity first revolutionized household appliances. Denry's vacuum cleaner must have been an early model as, even in the States, vacuum cleaners did not become widely available until 1915.[95]

No modernist writer took the least cognizance of this revolution in home economy, though it enriched the lives of millions of women and was much more important for most people than any revolution in art or literature – including modernism itself. Bennett realized his singularity in bothering about such vulgarities, but he was not ashamed – nor above taunting intellectuals about their misplaced priorities. In *These Twain* Edwin installs a new radiator, and takes as much pride in it as in the photogravure of Bellini's 'Agony in the Garden' which hangs nearby. To highbrows that could only seem the height of bourgeois philistinism. But it does not count against Edwin in Bennett's book.[96]

Yet Bennett, after all, was an intellectual, and he was torn. He devoted himself as a writer to showing how profound, intricate and delicate, how momentous and elemental, how unknowable, are the lives of unliterary, commonplace people like Constance and Sophia. Yet he also maintained that a knowledge of literature was vital to complete living. Thousands of people who know nothing of literature go around under the delusion that they are alive, but 'without literature you can't see, hear or feel in any full sense'. What – we may protest – about the young Baines girls, 'quivering with delicate, sensitive, luxuriant life'? What about Elsie Sprickett and her 'highly developed' soul? Not alive? Does Bennett subscribe, after all, to the intellectual myth that the masses are dead? There is no reconciling this opposition. Bennett's is the dilemma of every intellectual who resents and renounces the exclusiveness of intellectuals, yet values literature too much to pretend that its lack does not maim. Nor did he believe that literary values were just subjective, and that what the majority liked might be as good as the minority's choice. The classic texts are classic, he teaches, because they appeal to the 'passionate few' who know what is right. What the majority prefers is always second-rate.[97] The Bennett who propounds these intellectual orthodoxies seems ruled by different priorities from those that direct the writer of his fictions. That is because his fictions were designed to narrow the abyss between himself and those from whom his intellectual orthodoxies estranged him.

9

Wyndham Lewis and Hitler

Wyndham Lewis is the intellectuals' intellectual. 'There is no one,' Rebecca West attested, 'who can more deeply thrill one.' T. S. Eliot called him 'the most fascinating personality of our time' and 'the greatest prose master of style of my generation'. He encouraged Lewis to contribute to every issue of the *Criterion*. For Osbert Sitwell, Lewis shed 'a new and illuminating light' on every subject he touched upon. Edgell Rickword applauded him for trying to arrest 'the degradation of values on which our civilization seems to depend', and for 'reasserting the terms on which the life of the intellect may regain its proper ascendancy'. It is symptomatic of the priorities of the Lewis lobby that Arnold Bennett should appear in Jeffrey Meyers's biography of Lewis as a 'complacent and philistine *parvenu*', a 'middlebrow novelist', who 'adopted the obtuse attitude of the common reader'.[1]

Comparison of Wyndham Lewis with Hitler is, of course, prompted by Lewis's eager championship of the Führer in *Hitler*, published in 1931, *Left Wings Over Europe*, 1936, and *Count Your Dead*, 1937. There are a number of obvious similarities between the two figures. Both were obsessive, and expounded their relatively small collection of ideas with unflagging repetitiveness. Both regarded themselves as unjustly neglected artists, and took this neglect as the central fact around which to construct their distorted and vindictive models of the societies in which they lived. Both were powered to a considerable degree by hatred and resentment. In the second part of this chapter I shall investigate these and other correspondences between the Lewis of the inter-war years and the mind that is revealed in Hitler's *Mein Kampf* and *Table Talk*, and I shall also suggest more general parallels between Hitler's social views and what I have been characterizing in this book as the intellectuals' attitude to the masses.

WYNDHAM LEWIS AND THE FEMINIZATION OF THE WEST

Contempt for woman, or for a sexual stereotype that he identified as woman, was a key component in Lewis's thought about art and society. It seems probable that this derived from personal problems. When he was eleven his father had run off with a housemaid, leaving Lewis and his mother to struggle along in shabby-genteel poverty. This betrayal may lie behind the resentment and insecurity evident in his adult treatment of women. He needed a constant stream of mistresses to reinforce his virile self-image, and often boasted about having VD, which he thought a sign of potency. (He did, in fact, contract gonorrhoea, and underwent several operations in the 1930s.)² To show disregard for women and children was, he believed, the proper 'masculine' intellectual stance.

His consequent neglect of his offspring was, as I pointed out in the previous chapter, only an extreme case of an attitude common among early twentieth-century intellectuals. He abandoned his first child and its mother in France in 1908, later giving it out, probably untruthfully, that he had dropped and killed the baby. Between 1911 and 1920 Olive Johnson and Iris Barry each bore him two illegitimate children, all of whom were quickly disposed of. When Iris returned from hospital with the second child, a daughter, Lewis was having sex with the shipping heiress and cultural groupie Nancy Cunard in his studio, and Iris had to wait on the steps until they had finished.³

Lewis's wife, Anne Hoskyns, was a working-class girl from Teddington, eighteen years his junior, who served him in the capacity of cook, secretary and artist's model, and seems to have been completely subservient ('a masochistic doll', as one acquaintance put it). She connived at his infidelities, and did not dispute his decision that their union should be childless. Since he wished to appear to the world as a free and dashing artist, not a husband, he also insisted that their marriage should be kept secret. Even close friends did not know of Anne's existence, though they would hear her scuttling into hiding when they came to call, or catch a glimpse of her hands through the serving hatch at mealtimes. Geoffrey Grigson recalls Lewis saying in the middle of a conversation, 'Stay to dinner. I've a wife downstairs. A simple woman, but a good cook.'[4]

This high-handed, 'manly' treatment of weaker beings was modelled to some degree on the teaching of Nietzsche, whom the young Lewis greatly admired. His early essay 'The Code of a Herdsman', first published in the *Little Review* in July 1917, adopts the familiar Nietzschean symbolic landscape, with artists and intellectuals dwelling on the mountain tops and the 'Yahooesque and rotten herds' seething and stinking in the valleys below. The intellectual is particularly warned to beware of the insidious appeal of women and children, since they will only submerge him in the vulgarities of the mass.[5] As Nietzsche became more popular among those who aspired to be considered intellectual, so Lewis's admiration for him underwent some strain. In the preface to *Tarr*, published in 1918, Nietzsche's books are said to have 'made an Over-man of every vulgarly energetic grocer in Europe',[6] and *The Art of Being Ruled* denounces Nietzsche as an archetype of the vulgarizer, appealing to the half-educated and encouraging attorney's sons and farmer's daughters to feel like barons and baronesses.[7] Despite these reservations, Nietzsche continued to be a potent influence on Lewis. Kriesler in *Tarr* reads and quotes Nietzsche (including the notorious, 'When you go to a woman, you should be careful not to forget your whip'), and *The Art of Being Ruled* acknowledges him as 'a very great writer'.[8]

However, it was Lewis's own peculiar psychology that drew him to Nietzschean ideals. Fierce 'masculine' spiritual freedom attracted him because he found it difficult to reconcile his intellect with his bodily functions. This type of inhibition, common in adolescent boys, was unusually prolonged in Lewis's case. Activities such as swallowing and evacuating revolted him, and he felt degraded by the physical aspects of sex. His hostility to children seems to have stemmed, likewise, from physical repulsion.[9] Detestation of the human body is evident throughout his writing. In his satirical novel *The Apes of God*, published in 1932, for example, the men are mostly homosexual, impotent or predatory, and the women are lesbians or aged vamps. Much play is made with dentures, farts, belches, 'drink-puffed lips' and skin 'anchovy-tinted with traces of eczema'. The ordeals of Dan Boleyn (alias Stephen Spender), who is dressed in a frock and woman's underclothes by the raucously dominant Mrs Bosun, and physically humiliated by various other ladies, suggest that fear of women may have been an element in Lewis's contempt for them.

He persistently characterizes the female in terms of repellently soft or fluid textures and consistencies. His own cold, hard, masculine intellect is contrasted with the 'intestinal billowing' and 'gushings' of a world 'literally inundated with sexual viscera' that he finds in the work of D. H. Lawrence. He envisages himself, in his own writing, constructing a causeway, in 'Roman fashion', across 'an inconvenient and insanitary bog' of feminine sensibilities. 'Softness' and 'flabbiness' and the 'effluvia of feminine scent' are regarded as antithetical to the artistic impulse, which is essentially classical, rational, aristocratic and male.[10]

This nexus of gender-tagged physical apprehensions seems to have been decisive in the generation of Lewis's ideas. His 'thought', indeed, seems to consist of little more than the translation into propositional form of these sensory prejudices. The only factor of comparable influence on his thinking was his lifelong and much-resented poverty, which ensued upon the failure of his books to find a market. To readers of Lewis, this unpopularity will be readily understandable. But he himself regarded it as a persecution. He blamed democracy, which fostered, he believed, an inbuilt hostility to genius and imposed its 'box-office and library-subscription standards' upon the products of the intellect.[11] 'No artist,' he stipulated, 'can ever love democracy.' The democratic system, on Lewis's reckoning, hates and victimizes intellectuals, because 'mind' has, by its very nature, an 'aristocratic colour' which offends the masses.[12]

Lewis managed to draw together these two strands in his psyche – his anti-woman prejudice and his anti-democratic prejudice – by arguing that democracy, in its modern form, is deeply imbued with feminine characteristics. The twentieth century was, he maintained, undergoing a new kind of cultural decay, attributable to the erosion of traditional male values by the female. He and his contemporaries were faced with 'an increasingly feminine world', in which 'the natural feminine hostility to the intellect' was running amock. He took it for granted that abstract thought had always been offensive to the female, and that women were naturally dimmer and duller than men. 'A stupid, or slow-witted, not very ambitious, conventional, slothful person,' he explained, 'has necessarily a great many feminine characteristics.' However, these well-established womanly defects had not become troublesome or assertive until the modern period, when the advent of mass democracy had inaugurated a wholesale feminization of Western cultural values, with disastrous results for all true intellectuals.[13]

The signs of this change were, in Lewis's account, various and widespread. They included the high frequency of homosexuals among modern males – for the sexual invert adopts, Lewis argued, the characteristic feminine antagonism to the intellect, out of a wish to belittle genuinely masculine types of success.[14] Another portent was the frenzied conduct of women shoppers in department stores which Lewis identified as a contemporary manifestation of the blind, purposeless Will that, in Schopenhauer's theory, drives the world: 'It causes, daily, millions of women to drift in front of, and swarm inside, gigantic clothes-shops in every great capital, buying silk underclothing, cloche-hats, perfumes, vanishing creams, vanity bags and furs.'[15] Also to blame for the destruction of Western values was a miscellany of writers, past and present, who were either actually women or, in Lewis's view, just as bad as women. Among these were Virginia Woolf, and the other 'tittering old maids' of Bloomsbury, the 'girlish' Oscar Wilde, and the 'essentially feminine'

Pater, whose influence was ultimately responsible, Lewis held, for the 'droopings and wiltings' of Eliot's Prufrock.[16]

However, all these instances of mind-rotting femininity took second place to what Lewis referred to as the 'time-cult' or 'time-mind', the evils of which he expounded at length in *Time and Western Man*, published in 1928. This book exhibits with peculiar clarity the dependence of Lewis's thought upon sensory preferences, since the assumption behind all its muddled vehemence is that flux or fluidity (which he characterizes as 'feminine') is inferior to hard, static, changeless and 'masculine' states of matter. Lewis detects feminine flux in the whole drift of modern civilization, but the chief individual culprits he selects are Einstein, Proust, Joyce and the French philosopher Henri Bergson, whose lectures he had attended in Paris. All of these had sinned, as Lewis saw it, against the hard-edged 'classical' model of reality he favoured. Bergson had privileged *durée*, or fluid psychological time, over the strict limitations of clock time, and his account of the mind as a string of temporal happenings undermined stable old-world concepts of personality. It had influenced stream-of-consciousness fiction, and this linked Bergson with Joyce, whose *Ulysses*, Lewis objected, 'imposes a softness, flabbiness and vagueness everywhere in its Bergsonian fluidity'. Einstein's space–time looked, from Lewis's mathematically uninformed angle, 'identical' to Bergson's *durée*, and the 'welter' of relativity theory seemed yet another erosion of solid, traditional manly truths. As for Proust, he was obviously another Bergsonian 'time-worshipper', and a sexual invert to boot. Against these apostles of time, which, Lewis decided, was 'the feminine principle', he advocated space, the masculine. Whereas time sucked one into a soft, obnoxious intimacy where things were for ever 'penetrating' and 'merging', space offered a healthy outdoor scene, with things standing apart, 'the wind blowing between them, and the air circulating freely'.[17]

This Boy Scoutish metaphysic might seem an odd choice for Lewis, given his sexual morals, but it is a further illustration of the difficulty he encountered in reconciling his 'high' intellectual aspirations with his 'low' bodily functions. It reflects, too, the influence of the solitary male mountaineer so important in the Nietzschean ethic. Art and the artistic impulse were, Lewis stressed, essentially chaste. He regarded with manly distaste such contemporary effeminacies as Diaghilev's Ballets Russes ('an epicene circus').[18] His whole stance on the time question was, indeed, strongly Victorian. Despite his ultra-modern mannerisms, his beliefs cannot be taken seriously as a contribution to twentieth-century debate. They mark him out, rather, as a curious historical throwback. He resembles Matthew Arnold both in his sexual prudery and in his adherence to 'classical' standards which he conceived of as antagonistic to 'such enormous, sprawling, proletarianized societies as ours'.[19] Like Arnold, he believed that cultural and artistic values had been established once and for all. Art was 'timeless', its values 'static'. The great figures of history and the great works of art could not be reinterpreted or altered by succeeding generations, but existed in a metaphysical vacuum, beyond human contamination.[20] The modern idea that value judgements are relative, and culturally determined, Lewis dismissed as a feminine invention.

In common with other intellectuals both before and since, Lewis justified his belief in timeless artistic values by declaring that God's tastes coincided with his own. This meant that his cultural preferences were not mere preferences but tantamount to cosmic laws. Furthermore, it was God's artistic taste that, in Lewis's view, constituted His best claim to Godhead. Other attributes, such as divine love, do not even qualify for mention. God's highest conceivable activity is enjoying or inspiring artworks.

We can assert that a God who swam in such an atmosphere as is produced by the music of a Bach fugue, or the stormy grandeur of the genii in the Sistine Chapel, or the scene of the Judgement of Signorelli at Orvieto, who moved with the grace of Mozart – anyone may for himself accumulate such comparisons from the greatest forms of art – such a God would be the highest we could imagine.[21]

We should, Lewis advises, dismiss the claims of those who pretend that they can imagine a greater God than this, to whom all human achievement would be imperfect. Such people merely show themselves congenitally incapable of appreciating the great works of art to which he refers. Lewis's God, in other words, not only agrees with Lewis's taste in art; He is powerless to do anything more Godlike. Any other 'material of deity for the construction of God is meaningless to us'. No God need feel ashamed to 'put His name to the *Oedipus* or *King Lear*'. The Sistine Chapel ceiling is 'worthy of the hand of any God which we can infer, dream of, or postulate. We may certainly say that God's hand is visible in it.'[22]

Like other intellectuals, Lewis had his own personal selection of hates which for him characterized democratic society. Photography – an irritant we have come across before – was among these. Taking photographs betrayed, for Lewis, subservience to the time cult since it showed attachment to past moments. It was therefore vulgar and feminine. With (for him) unusually accurate prescience, he foresaw the advent of the home video.

A quite credible domestic scene of the future is this. Mr Citizen and his wife are at the fireside; they release a spring and their selves of long ago fly on to a screen supplied . . . to all suburban villas. It is a phono-film; it fills the room at once with the cheery laughter of any epoch required. 'Lets have that picnic at Hampton Court in such and such a year!' Mrs Citizen may have exclaimed. 'Yes, do lets!' hubby has responded. And they live again the sandwiches, the tea in the Thermos, the ginger beer and mosquitoes, of a dozen years before.[23]

Lewis's phrasing makes it apparent that disdain for lower-middle-class speech and manners reinforces his philosophical objections to photography. He argued that 'mechanical photographic reality' was opposed to art: 'The intelligence to which this method is natural is the opposite of the creative, clearly.' He called James Joyce's stream-of-consciousness technique 'snapshotting', and declared it inevitably inferior to the 'masculine' formalism of Egyptian or Chinese art. In his critique of Rodin, Lewis's dislike of photography amalgamates with other phobias – commercial success, soft, fluid textures, and feminine sexuality. Rodin poured out on the world 'a stream of vulgar ornaments . . . flowing, structureless, lissom, wave-lined pieces of commercial marble'; the whole philosophy of flux is 'palpitating and streaming' in Rodin's 'cleverly dreamified stone-photographs of naked nature'.[24]

Not surprisingly, newspapers and advertisements also qualified for Lewis's denunciation. He blamed them, along with cinema and wireless, for destroying individuality in the masses. Despite the modern belief in expressing personality, he asserts, most people have none to express, only a group consciousness imposed by the mass media. Moreover, 'the values and tastes of the cinema mob' have begun to infiltrate even the educated classes. Everyone is being reduced to a Lyons-tea-shop level by 'a systematic forcing down of civilized standards'. Advertisements, being a 'glorification of the life of the moment' with 'no absolute or universal value', are a pure expression of the Bergsonian time cult. Their 'mesmeric methods' hypnotize the 'so-called democratic masses' into 'a sort of hysterical imbecility'.[25] One advantage of Fascism, to Lewis's way of thinking, was that it would put an end to 'the sickly rage of advertisement'. In a totalitarian economy there would be only one state brand of soap, so giant hoardings telling the public how to keep their schoolgirl complexions would be unnecessary.[26]

Given these views, Lewis might be expected to favour popular education, since it would provide an antidote to the deceptions of the mass media. However, while proclaiming that the mass of people are 'in mental equipment and outlook, savages', he strongly opposed any spread of knowledge. Should the masses have access to the discoveries of the 'learned and splendid few', he argued, they would turn them to evil. A book such as Tolstoy's *War and Peace*, for example, written to raise the consciousness of the oppressed, should be kept from the 'ignorantly inflammable' masses, lest it provoke them to lawless actions. Only the rulers should be allowed to read such books.[27] Lewis can elsewhere be found arguing that popular education does not, in fact, make people think independently, but merely programmes them, turning them into gullible robots.[28] Clearly this objection does not tally with his view of education as a spur to revolt. But his feelings on such topics went deeper than reason or consistency, as we have seen.

Lewis was also disturbed by the mobility which the masses were displaying, abetted by increasing leisure and access to travel. He saw that global tourism would become an increasingly urgent problem as world populations increased. People moved 'in great herds' to the seaside, only to find that a sea of people rather than of water awaited them. It was exhausting, and they did not enjoy it. If a travel permit were required before tickets could be bought, much congestion and wear and tear on the roads would be avoided. Most people are 'born molluscs' and would be much happier staying at home. Mass tourism is, in any case, an 'absurdity', since only scholars are really interested in cathedrals and artworks. The tourists who gawp at them are filled with boredom and self-reproach, and would never, Lewis contends, have dreamed of such a pastime had not holiday advertisements contrived to turn them into sham students and fake cosmopolitan aristocrats.[29]

Other modern cultural movements Lewis deplored were the 'vulgarization' of literature by writers catering for the new reading public, the (as he saw it) subversive tendencies of Freudian psychoanalysis, and the rise of science. He accused authors such as Wells, Shaw and Aldous Huxley of 'complicity with the dreariest of suburban library readers'.[30] Shaw's *Back to Methuselah* made Adam and Eve speak in 'the jargon of the city tea-shop', like 'a London bank clerk and his girl'.[31]

Freudian psychoanalysis displeased Lewis because he took the distinction between ego and id, and between conscious and unconscious, to be a reflection of the social division between the ruler and the masses. The unconscious is 'really what Plato meant by "the mob of the senses".' The advent of psychoanalysis internalized politics, so that 'inside us also the crowds were pitted against the individual . . . the Many against the One'. The ego, 'a sort of primitive king of the psychological world', cannot hope to survive in the democratic environment. Freudianism can be seen, from this angle, as an effect of democracy. Man, hating power and authority, turns his 'bloodshot eyes inward' and sees his own mind lording it over his animal being. So he dethrones it, with 'a grin of diabolical malice'.[32]

As we saw in Chapter 2, Lewis's belief that the ego–id distinction could be interpreted politically concurred with Freud's view. But the idea that Freudianism favoured the id and aimed to elevate it over the ego was, of course, mere fantasy. Like other intellectuals, Freud thought that the élite, who were prepared to pay the price of instinctual renunciation, had a right to rule the masses, and he used the ego–id model to illustrate this: 'Our mind is to be compared with a modern state in which a mob, eager for destruction, has to be held down by a prudent and superior class.'³³

On science, Lewis's pronouncements were hampered by his lack of scientific education, but this did not prevent him from speaking out strongly against it, as anti-individual, anti-intellectual and culpably implicated in the mass media. The so-called benefits of science amounted to little more than that 'a million sheep's heads in London' could listen simultaneously to 'the bellowing of Dame Clara Butt'. Science had turned the white populations into 'a horde of particularly helpless children' by releasing upon them 'a gigantic plague of numberless mechanical toys'. The uniformity which this process entailed meant that science, in the modern age, was 'the expression of the aggregate or crowd'.³⁴

Lewis's contempt for the masses was at its most vehement in *The Art of Being Ruled*, a work which gained enthusiastic tributes from fellow intellectuals. It is noticeable that his image of mass man in it wavers between the extremes of robot and wild beast (not, of course, that he was alone among intellectuals in embracing these contradictory stereotypes). On the one hand, he asserts that most men, scientists included, are 'mad and brutalized', and it is criminal to pretend, from some motive of egalitarian vanity, that they are otherwise. However, he also dismisses most men as automata, 'obedient, hard-working machines, as near dead as possible'. Freedom does not appeal to these mechanical anthropoids, whatever illusions they may harbour to the contrary. All they desire is a well-disciplined, well-policed herd life. Educating them makes no difference, for education will merely provide them with a system of habits that concur with their neighbours', 'and from this coma they never wake'.³⁵

To try to wake them would, in any case, be a mistake, Lewis believed. Though he attacks those who control the press, cinema and radio for assuming that the public is infinitely stupid, and despising it, they are, he admits, right. Totalitarian regimes are to be admired for perceiving that human beings are naturally subservient, like a horse or a dog or 'a very helpless child', and treating them accordingly.[36] On this, as on other subjects, Lewis's vehemence issues in self-contradiction. He deplores the collectivism of the industrial world, 'herding people into enormous mechanized masses',[37] and laments the standardization imposed by mass production. 'The mass mind' is debased because it 'is required to gravitate to a standard size to receive the standard idea'. Yet he urges that this stultifying process should be stepped up, because as the mass becomes more and more comatose, the few 'free intelligences' will be isolated and thrown into prominence, and this will create an intellectual caste system. Interbreeding within the intellectual caste may result, Lewis suggests, in beneficial biological mutation. For though mankind as a whole will never be ready for civilization, the isolated intelligent few may generate a new species of superior being.[38]

Ideally the intelligent few will govern. Lewis proposes that in his Fascist state admission to the 'inbred and highly organized body of rulers' will be by competitive examination, rather than by the 'brutal and unsatisfactory' methods of the commercial world. The consequent caste system will not, he predicts, cause resentment, because most people not only must be but enjoy being underlings. Besides, the rulers will lead a severe life, rather like Wells's Samurai, 'full of the shock of the forces of outer vastness, from which the masses are sheltered'. There will be no bourgeois relaxation or laughter for them; by nature they will be disillusioned and ascetic – clones, in fact, of Nietzsche's mountain-pacing, rabble-scorning solitary.[39] Vindicating their right to rule, Lewis appeals to nature and to God. Natural law, as opposed to sentimental morality, 'recognizes what is due to character, to creative genius, to personal power'. It is neglect of that law in modern democratic times that has sanctioned personal attacks upon the great men of literature, and other forms of cultural 'sansculottism'. Such disrespect for the truly gifted is, in the last resort, an offence against divinity. For the deference due from one creature to another superior one is 'in reality due to God'. This,

Lewis stresses, is not a mere ethical standpoint but an intellectual compulsion.[40]

However, the world has tragically lost sight of the natural ascendancy of Lewis and his kind, and his report on the current situation is pained.

We, by birth the natural leaders of the White European, are people of no political or public consequence any more . . . We, the natural leaders of the World we live in, are now *private citizens* in the fullest sense, and that World is, as far as the administration of its traditional law of life is concerned, leaderless. Under these circumstances, its soul in a generation or so will be extinct.[41]

Part of the appeal of Fascism for Lewis was that it promised a strong leader to halt this drift into chaos. Several aspects of Hitler's public persona attracted him, not least his racism. For Lewis's diagnosis of Europe's ills maintained not only that the mass culture ushered in by industrialism had led to a 'pulverization of our intellectual life', nor only that through science 'all our standards of existence have been discredited', but also that the world was becoming a 'melting pot', where different races and nationalities were no longer distinguishable.

This degeneration provided him with his subject in *Paleface: The Philosophy of the Melting-Pot*, published in 1929. Ostensibly he directs this work not against blacks but against the cult of the Negro and the primitive among educated whites. However, this distinction soon fades. Whiteness, Lewis suggests, is 'in a pigmentary sense aristocratic', and the proper colour for a 'gentleman'. Blackness is 'irretrievably proletarian'. This law may, he thinks, be 'an absolute, established in our senses'.[42] The Negro's gift to the white world is jazz, which Lewis interprets as 'the aesthetic medium of a sort of frantic proletarian subconscious'. He does not deny that, given equal opportunities, the blacks might have produced poets and philosophers. But in fact their sole contribution to culture is 'a barbarous, melancholy, epileptic folk-music, worthy of a patagonian cannibal'.[43] Jazz, as developed in the West, is for Lewis unmistakably degraded and degrading, expressing the mindless energy of the mass. It is the 'slum peasant' and the 'city serf' that rejoice in its 'gross proletarian nigger bumps'. Its 'idiot mass sound' is ultimately 'marxistic'.[44]

Despite his laments over the ills of industrialism, he denounces Western admirers of pre-industrial cultures on the grounds that they venerate mere mindlessness. Lawrence's description of the Indians in *Mornings in Mexico* values, Lewis notes, their 'visceral' consciousness above European intellect. However, though he ridicules this preference, he does not question Lawrence's assessment of the Indian mind. The 'average Hopi or Negro' is, he agrees, a man who squats and drums, not a man who thinks. As he warms to his subject, the pretence that he is attacking only romantic configurations of the Negro wanes. He refers to the 'jigging, laughing and crying, yapping and baaing, average Negro', and to the 'ignoble, slothful, shambling, jazzing, laughing-and-crying, sort of big black baby, with silly, rolling eyes, and big characterless lips, as the average "Nigger" is apt too much to be'.[45] The white and black races, he suggests, should stay apart, for they are essentially different, and there is no practical reason for their physical or spiritual merging. We should see 'less and less' of these 'other kinds of men'.[46] Lewis may have been influenced in all this by Nietzsche, who suggested that black skin could be viewed, from an evolutionary angle, as the effect of frequent attacks of rage, which denoted animality, whereas white skin had arisen from the frequent onset of fear – a mark of intelligence. For the intelligent white races to interbreed with blacks was inadvisable, Nietzsche cautioned, for racial purity always generates strength and beauty.[47] Lewis's resentment of Jews was even more forceful than his contempt for Negroes, since it was easier for him to see them as representatives of the underbred, commerce-crazed masses that were destroying Western civilization. As Meyers notes, his anti-Semitism was not abated by the spectacle of Jewish persecution. He continued to express strongly anti-Semitic views even after Hitler came to power and implemented the Nuremberg Laws, which dispossessed the Jews, in September 1935.[48] Lewis argues that Jews provoke their own persecution. In the USA, for example, 'the anti-Semitism that does exist is sustained solely by the extremely bad manners and barbaric aggressiveness of the eastern slum-Jew immigrant'. *Left Wings Over Europe*, published in 1936, mocks the concern of English churchmen about the fate of German Jews.[49] A year later, in *Count Your Dead*, Lewis seeks to arouse anti-Jewish feeling in England by pointing to the social and financial advantages enjoyed by 'gilded immigrants' who are in truth 'of no better birth . . . than their domestics'. He professes to feel sorry for Jews – for it must be 'bitterly unpleasant' to be treated by everybody as an inferior. But he feels even sorrier, he declares, for true-born Englishmen who find themselves in competition with Jews. He presents it as a scandal that 'a man of the same blood as Chaucer and Shakespeare' should, because his parents have not had the 'low cunning' to accumulate money, be obliged to abase himself before 'some offspring of an asiatic bazaar tout'. If we take such wrongs into account, Lewis suggests, we will understand that there is no need to hate Hitler just because he is 'impolite to Jews'.[50]

It is difficult to decide how far Lewis's account of Hitler proceeds from a wish to falsify, and how far it was the result of mere carelessness and self-delusion. However, it seems inconceivable that anyone who had read *Mein Kampf* even cursorily could conclude, as Lewis does, that Hitler was essentially a 'man of peace' who, if he obtained power, would show 'increasing moderation and tolerance'.[51] Certainly Lewis's dismissal of Hitler's anti-Semitism as a 'mere bagatelle' which should not stand in the way of our blood kinship with the Nazis has the appearance of deliberate misrepresentation, especially as Lewis goes on to plead that we in England cannot understand the depth of Nazi animus against Jews, since English Jews are integrated into the population, whereas in Germany 'the traditional jewish figure of melodrama or of comedy' is a familiar sight.[52] Such a defence tacitly concedes that German anti-Semitism is by no means inconsiderable.

The best that can be said for Lewis is that in depicting Hitler and the Nazis, his anxiety to overcome English resistance to Fascism led him to prefer fantasy to truth. The attraction of Fascist regimes for him seems to have been not so much political as aesthetic – inextricable from ideas of strong, healthy masculinity, strenuous effort, and the kind of rigid control and hard, exact outline that he favoured in his writing on literature and art. He praises the 'disciplined' Fascist party in Italy for combining a 'new, healthy type of freedom' with a 'rigidly organized' bureaucratic state.[53] Mussolini has saved Italy from the 'humbug' of democratic suffrage. He represents, for Lewis, individual will overcoming the confusions of the mass. His example shows how a 'tyrant or dictator, with virtual powers of life and death', who is astute enough to employ a loyal band of assassins, and who clamps down on newspapers, placing them under the direct control of central government, can restore social health. Mussolini, Lewis believes, has banished politics and economics. These 'boring and wasteful sham sciences', which have sprung up in support of 'the great pretences of democracy', will simply die out in the Fascist state.[54]

Behind all this we can detect Lewis's artistic preference for classical authority and marble rigidity as opposed to the 'softness' and 'flabbiness' of female flux. His depiction of Hitler similarly stresses the Führer's rigorous, clean-living masculinity. The 'celibate inhabitant of a modest alpine chalet – vegetarian, non-smoking, non-drinking', Hitler 'has remained the most unassuming and simple of men'. His myrmidons, the Nazi storm-troopers, have, Lewis assures his readers, been much misunderstood in England. Far from being armed roughs and hoodlums, they resemble a 'picked police force'. Legality is their watchword. The mere sight of them is enough to allay civilized fears.

These hefty young street-fighting warriors have not the blood-shot eyes and furtive manners of the political gutter-gunmen, but the personal neatness, the clear blue eyes, of the police. The Anglo-Saxon would feel reassured at once in the presence of these straightforward young pillars of the law.[55]

Lewis's championship of changeless, absolute 'law' in art and culture which resists female flux is here carried over into politics. His allegiance to manly, marmoreal classicism ('pillars') and his racial prejudice conspire to produce a travesty of historical fact which is nevertheless entirely faithful to his aesthetic tastes.

ADOLF HITLER'S INTELLECTUAL PROGRAMME

In the introduction to his edition of Hitler's *Table Talk*, Hugh Trevor-Roper maintains that Hitler's ideas on culture were 'trivial, half-baked and disgusting'.[56] This seems questionable. At least, there are marked similarities between the cultural ideals promulgated in the Führer's writings and conversation and those of the intellectuals we have been looking at. Further, Hitler believed just as strongly as the intellectuals in the eternal value of what intellectuals consider great art.

His account of his adolescence in *Mein Kampf* subscribes as eagerly as, for example, Gissing's *Private Papers of Henry Ryecroft* to the Western intellectual stereotype of the poor student, high-minded and half-starved, spending his last few coins on erudite tomes and scorning the fat burghers whom he glimpses through the plate-glass of restaurants or from his miserable perch in the gallery of a theatre or opera house. As a student in Vienna, Hitler tells us, he would go hungry to buy books, and would register righteous disgust at the low level of culture he saw around him. He felt pain at the multitude's regrettable weakness for 'smutty literature, artistic tripe and theatrical banalities'. Like many English intellectuals, he blamed this degeneracy on the mass media, deploring the poison spread among the masses by 'gutter journalism' and 'cinema bilge'.[57]

His own inclinations were undeviatingly highbrow. He would bring home books by the kilo from the lending library on art history, architecture, religion and philosophy. Nietzsche was often on his lips, and he could quote Schopenhauer by the page. He admired the works of Cervantes, Defoe, Swift, Goethe and Carlyle. Among musicians his heroes were Mozart, Bruckner, Haydn and Bach, and he idolized Wagner. In painting it was the achievement of the old masters, particularly Rembrandt and Rubens, that he applauded.[58]

He strongly advocated state subsidies for the arts. The great galleries like those at Dresden, Munich and Vienna should, he urged, have at least 2 million marks a year to buy new pictures. Germany should have more theatres. Though Berlin already had three opera houses, it should have four or five for its 4 million inhabitants. On the other hand, even the present state of affairs was enough to prove Germany's superiority to the materialistic society of the United States. The Americans, Hitler conceded, possessed cars, clothes and refrigerators, but the German Reich could boast 270 opera houses and a standard of culture of which America could have no conception. This contempt for the vulgar materialism of America was, of course, shared by many European intellectuals, from Gissing to the Leavises and beyond.[59]

Hitler also believed just as firmly as, say, T. S. Eliot or Wyndham Lewis in the permanence of aesthetic values. In *Mein Kampf* he contrasts the all-time greats, such as Shakespeare, Schiller and Goethe, with the degeneracy of modern culture. The creative spirit of the Periclean age, as manifested in the Parthenon, is one of his touchstones. He venerates the 'divine spark' as it flashes forth from the 'shining brow' of genius. Art is higher and more valuable, he insists, than science or philosophy, and more permanent than politics. 'Wars pass by. The only things that exist are the works of human genius. This is the explanation of my love of art.' Music and architecture record the path of humanity's ascent. Nothing can take the place of the great painter or poet. The highest realm is that of artistic creativity. The inner force of a nation comes from its worship of men of genius.[60]

It is hard to see what could be accounted trivial, half-baked or disgusting about these propositions from the standpoint of early twentieth-century intellectuals, or, for that matter, from the standpoint of a late twentieth-century intellectual such as George Steiner. It is true that Hitler goes on to suggest that the feat of producing the great achievements of Western art effectively establishes the supremacy of the Aryan race: 'It is evident that a people which is endowed with high creative powers in the cultural sphere is of more worth than a tribe of negroes.'[61] However, even this would meet with no demur from twentieth-century intellectuals such as H. G. Wells and Wyndham Lewis.

Like Lewis, Steiner and many other intellectuals, Hitler believes that it is the presence of a divine spark that makes great art great.

God underwrites the music of Mozart, the plays of Shakespeare and other intellectual preferences, and it is precisely this underwriting that establishes them as more than just intellectual preferences. The power of great artists and writers is, *Mein Kampf* affirms, 'an innate product of divine grace'. Since only the Aryan race has, in Hitler's view, produced great artists and writers, the cultural achievements of the West serve neatly to endorse the status of Aryans as 'the highest image of God among his creatures'.[62] This is, of course, only a modification of the tactic by which intellectuals invoke God's artistic preferences in order to endorse their superiority as intellectuals.

The opposition between the natural aristocrat and the mass is another large element of Hitler's thought that finds a counterpart in twentieth-century intellectual orthodoxy. The principle underlying all nature's operations, he stresses, is 'the aristocratic principle'. This conforms with 'the eternal Will that governs the universe'. For Hitler, as for other intellectuals, it follows that there is or should be some connection between cultural eminence and political power. The supreme natural aristocrat, Hitler argues, is the genius, and it is the shining example of genius that makes clear the baseness of the mass and the folly of parliamentary democracy. The creative act of genius is 'always a protest against the inertia of the mass'. Democracy, by vesting power in 'the dunderheaded multitude' flies in the face of 'the aristocratic principle of nature'. In common with other disciples of Nietzsche, Hitler conceives of a moral universe in which the 'dead weight' of the mass is pitted against 'the eternal privilege of force and energy' in the gifted individual. He also shares the customary intellectual scorn for the *nouveaux riches*, whom he regards as false aspirers to nobility, unacceptable 'from the standpoint of good breeding'. As we have seen, this curiously old-style appeal to 'breeding', together with a hatred of plutocracy, are relatively frequent components in schemes of natural aristocracy devised by intellectuals, D. H. Lawrence among others.[63]

Like other intellectuals, Hitler becomes rather muddled over his advocacy of individualism. Intellectuals naturally regard themselves as individuals, and strongly support individual freedoms in that context. On the other hand, the mass, in opposition to which intellectuals construct their individuality, is by definition not composed of individuals, so cannot expect to be treated with the consideration individuals merit. An uneasy situation emerges, in which some human beings are individuals, but most are not. This is the situation that obtains in Hitler's writing, as in Wyndham Lewis's. Hitler hymns the individual genius, and attacks Marxism on the grounds that it 'categorically repudiates the personal worth of the individual'. However, he also holds that the health of the race is paramount. 'The will of the eternal creator' and 'the iron logic of nature' both decree that the weak or diseased should be destroyed, that defectives should be prevented from breeding, and that miscegenation should be banned, since it generates cross-breeds and mongrels, who are inevitably inferior. These measures evidently subordinate the individual to the group, but that in no sense diminishes Hitler's advocacy of them. Much as individuality matters, the right to be an individual can, it seems, be granted only very sparingly. The Russians, for example, do not qualify for it at all in Hitler's view. 'Russians,' he observed, 'exist only *en masse*, and that explains their brutality.'[64]

Though Hitler's conclusion here may seem ill-considered, it differs little from H. G. Wells's thoughts about the hordes of black and yellow men in Africa and Asia. To a degree what both Wells and Hitler reflect, and what they appeal to in their readers, are the hostility and loss of focus induced in modern consciousness by a world where populousness defeats the imagination. Given the multitudes by which the individual is surrounded, it is virtually impossible to regard everyone else as having an individuality equivalent to one's own. The mass, as a reductive and dismissive concept, is invented to ease this difficulty.

Population figures were a deeply worrying subject to Hitler, as to other intellectuals. The 'amazing' growth of Germany's population before the war, and the annual increase since then, are key facts upon which the expansionist programme in *Mein Kampf* is based. In his conversation he reverts to the alarming increase in the populations of Russia and India (the latter having gone up by 55 million in ten years, he points out, to 388 million). The phenomenon of Hitlerism was a product of multitudinousness and cannot be imagined without that precondition. In its origins, its methods and its solutions, it was inextricably involved with the concept of the mass. There are, *Mein Kampf* observes, currently 80 million Germans in Europe. After another hundred years there will be 250 million. National policy must ensure that they will not be 'packed together like the coolies in the factories of another continent', but will have space to till the soil. Hitler rejects birth control as a means of limiting Germany's population on the grounds that it weakens the race. Whereas 'natural' birth control (hunger, disease) ensures the survival of hardier types, artificial birth control saves the feeble and the diseased. It is not clear where Hitler got this rather curious idea from, but it seems to be a vague recollection of the common eugenic argument that high culture and education tend to decrease fertility, whereas dirt and poverty are prolific breeders. At all events, Hitler faces the consequences of unchecked population growth uncompromisingly, and with an effort at realism rare among political leaders, who have generally ignored the problem. Since food production cannot go on increasing indefinitely, he points out, 'the day will certainly come when the whole of mankind will be forced to check the augmentation of the human species'. Further, given mankind's usual way of confronting difficulties, there seems little chance of this being effected by peaceful means. 'Nobody can doubt that this world will one day be the scene of dreadful struggles for existence on the part of mankind.' In these conflicts, Hitler predicts, instinct and self-preservation, not humanitarianism, will prevail. Humanitarianism is, in any case, he suggests, only a mixture of timidity and self-conceit, so in the coming fight for food and living space there will be no chance of its surviving. The effect of this argument is to root the politics of brutality firmly in his readers' terror of crowds and numbers. 'Overpopulation compels a people to look out for itself', as he put it in conversation.[65]

Meanwhile, the German masses must be encouraged to develop health and vigour of mind and body. The aspects of national life that Hitler considers in need of reform are identical to those that had attracted the animosity of English intellectuals from Gissing on. The mass media must be rescued from the profiteers, and thoroughly cleaned up. The press, the cinema and advertisements must have 'the stains of pollution removed', and be placed in the service of a 'cultural idea'. There must also be compulsory physical education at school, with plenty of boxing and gymnastics, and a corresponding let-up on purely mental education, so as to stem the weakness and degeneracy of the urban population, who are at present 'unfit for life's struggle'.[66] As we have seen, these plans are congruent with much English intellectual criticism of hollow-chested clerks and office workers – a body of opinion that encompasses, for example, Forster's disparaging remarks about Leonard Bast's physique and D. H. Lawrence's plans for replacing school education with PE and combat training.

In analysing the mass Hitler tended, like other male intellectuals, to identify it as feminine. The psychology of the mass is, he explains, like that of a woman. A woman's inner sensibilities are not under the control of her abstract reasoning, and she feels a vague emotional longing for a strong male to dominate her. So, too, does the mass. The great majority of any nation is 'so feminine in its character and outlook' that its thought and conduct are ruled by sentiment rather than reasoning. In conversation Hitler was generally indulgent and contemptuous in his view of women. They were, he believed, naturally vain and jealous of one another. Motherhood was the only proper occupation for them, and if they did not have children they tended to go off their heads. He did not like to see them trying to grapple with ideas, which were man's domain. 'Man's universe is vast compared with that of woman'; 'Woman's universe is man.' As we have seen, it would be easy to find early twentieth-century intellectuals who fully endorsed these opinions.[67]

Like other intellectuals, Hitler rewrote the mass in a number of different and mutually irreconcilable versions. The mass as woman was one of these, but another was the mass as nation. The second idea flowed readily from the first, for since the female mass desired a strong, dominating male, it was appropriate, Hitler argued, for it to be dominated by a national ruler, who would exploit propaganda, crowd control and other modern means to weld it into an efficient political force. 'The nationalization of the masses' is, he decides, the only solution to the problem of Germany's future. The Nazi movement must keep contact with the masses, adapting its propaganda to the lowest intelligence, and putting across a simple message, on the same principle as soap advertising. Given that the masses are, in effect, 'the crowd of simpletons and the credulous' who believe what they read in newspapers, it is important to stop them being misled. Accordingly the state must control newspapers with 'ruthless determination', never allowing itself to be deterred by 'the will-o'-the-wisp of so-called freedom of the press'.[68]

For Hitler an alternative to imagining the mass as a woman or nation was to imagine it as children – 'a vacillating crowd of human children' – just as H. G. Wells imagined Kipps and his kind. However, this did not make much difference to the recommended means of winning it over. Shapes, colours and simple ideas were of prime importance. Hitler, who had read Le Bon on crowds, took immense trouble over appeals to mass psychology, such as the design of the Nazi flag. He decided on the swastika symbol, and the exact size of the white circle relative to the red background, only after 'innumerable trials'.[69]

Another respect in which Hitler's fantasies about the mass conformed to a common intellectual pattern was in his division of the mass into the bourgeoisie, which, like all intellectuals, he despised, and the workers, for whom (like some leftist intellectuals) he expressed profound veneration. The Nazi movement, he declares, must not hope for anything from 'the unthinking herd of bourgeois voters'. It will draw instead on the 'working masses', eliminating their distress and raising their cultural level. The bourgeoisie are stupid, cowardly and inhibited, but the workers are noble. Hitler has noticed this on several occasions. The shipyard workers gave him an 'extraordinary impression of nobility' at the launching of the *Tirpitz*, and the Krupp steelworkers at Essen seemed to him 'stamped with the hallmark of nobility'. In the early days of the movement he made sure members came to meetings without collars or ties, believing that this 'free and easy style' would win the workers' confidence. As Martin Green has documented in *Children of the Sun*, English leftist intellectuals of the Auden group in the 1930s likewise set about proletarianizing themselves. Auden wore a cloth cap, dropped his aitches and ate peas with a knife; Isherwood drank bad tea and ate chocolates to induce worker-style tooth decay.[70]

The major division Hitler made in the concept of the mass, however, was between the German and non-German masses. Whereas the Germans could be transformed into a national mass movement, no such redemption was possible for foreign masses. The 'stupid masses' in Asia constituted 'a disquieting reservoir of men', poised to come 'foaming down' upon Europe in a 'wave' or 'flood'. Unlike Germans, the Asian masses were 'brutes in a state of nature'. The Jews, of course, occupied a special position among non-German masses in Hitler's mythology. The threat of the mass was distinctively a Jewish threat because the mass was controlled by Jews, or so Hitler persuaded himself. Jews owned the press, 'that dangerous Great Power within the state', and consequently fabricated public opinion. Jews, too, were behind Marxism and socialism, so the doctrine of majority rule, abhorrent to 'the aristocratic principle of nature', could be viewed as a Jewish invention.[71]

But the idea of the Jews and the mass interfused even more closely in Hitler's mind than these relatively rational arguments would justify. He envisaged the Jews as a mass that could infiltrate and corrupt other masses. They were, as he imagined them, numberless – there was 'no limit to the number of such people' – and they infected the masses like a moral pestilence, a 'Black Plague' poisoning human souls. In this respect the Jews could be said to represent, for Hitler, the ultimate mass. They were the perfect heirs of the features of mass being that had been invented by early twentieth-century intellectuals. Amorphous, infinite, subhuman, they became, in Hitler's mythology, the ideal objective for the various dehumanizing drives which the concept of the mass had come into being to justify. It even seems that in Hitler's imaginings Jews were physically constituted out of something resembling a special mass substance. He recalls in *Mein Kampf* how, when arguing with Jewish socialists, 'one's hand grasped only jelly and slime, which slipped through the fingers and combined again into a solid mass a moment afterwards'. Hitler's cult of the body beautiful, and his eagerness that it should be shown, not swaddled in clothes, arose in part from a belief that nakedness or near-nakedness would expose that Jews were indeed physically distinct from normal humans, and would consequently make it impossible for 'thousands of girls to be led astray by Jewish mongrels'.[72]

Contemplating the extermination of Jews was made easier by thinking of them as a mass. Mass transportation, destruction and incineration, and the mass production of fertilizer from their ashes, all acquired a certain appropriateness once the initial proposal that they were a mass – not fully alive people – was accepted. In this sense the Holocaust may be seen as the ultimate indictment of the idea of the mass and its acceptance by twentieth-century intellectuals. The appropriate mode of extermination had, it is worth noting, already occurred to Hitler when he was writing *Mein Kampf*. Many German lives might have been saved during the war, he observes, 'if twelve or fifteen thousand of those Jews who were corrupting the nation had been forced to submit to poison gas'.[73] As for disposal of the bodies, cremation was, as we have seen, firmly linked by intellectuals with the soulless masses some years before Hitler adopted it for his final solution.

In Hitler's rewriting of the mass, the figure who came to represent mass virtue, at the far end of the chain of being from the Jew's mass evil, was the peasant. Ecologically sound and gratifyingly humble, peasants had, as we have noted, been popular with intellectuals since Nietzsche. Gissing, Yeats, Lawrence and E. M. Forster were all, to a degree, peasant-fanciers, and Wyndham Lewis applauded the 'purity and beauty of the peasant vision'.[74] *Mein Kampf* concurs with these intellectuals in opposing industrialization and commercialization, and envisaging that a 'healthy peasant class' will become the basis of the national community. An advantage of this step is that it will put an end to the mental and physical evils of congested urban life.[75]

His attachment to the peasant ideal led Hitler to evolve a green dream of vast German accessions in the Ukraine, colonized by 'sturdy peasants', each of whom would be given a fully equipped farm on condition that he married a countrywoman, not a townswoman. This plan is already formulated in *Mein Kampf*. Eastwards in Russia lies 'the territory on which one day our German peasants will be able to bring forth and nourish their sturdy sons'. The conquest of Russia will allow Germany, 'for centuries to come', to give 'every descendant of our race a piece of ground and soil that he can call his own'. In wartime conversations Hitler frequently returns to this vision, his imaginings recalling the world gardens in the futurist fiction of H. G. Wells. The Ukraine and the Caucasus will become 'one of the loveliest gardens in the world', where 20 million Germans will live, among fields and orchards. They will build windmills all over the Ukraine to grind flour, producing 10 or 12 million tons annually, some of which will be turned into spaghetti in specially constructed spaghetti factories sited near the wheatfields to save on transport. Hitler was, of course, an ardent vegetarian, and was fond of discoursing on the harmfulness of cooked food, which, he believed, caused cancer. However, he seems to have been prepared to allow his peasants to eat cooked spaghetti, though raw fruit and vegetables would provide much of their diet.[76]

The Ukraine, he predicted, would make the Reich self-supporting in everything but coffee. Fish would come from the Black Sea, oil from the Caucasus, and citrus fruits from the Crimea, which would also be planted with 100,000 acres of rubber. The Pripet marshes would supply reeds, and cultivated nettles would (a Hamburg firm had assured Hitler) yield a cellulose much superior to cotton. The environment would be treated with reverence. Care would be taken not to deface the landscape with high-tension wires, electric-railway cables and the like.[77]

Another blemish that would have to be removed was, of course, the 'ridiculous hundred million Slavs' who at present occupied the site of Hitler's Ukrainian garden. His plan was that they would be, as he put it, 'isolated in their own pigsties'. This meant that they would be supplied with no hospitals, health service, hygiene facilities, doctors or dentistry. Vaccination and even soap would be withheld in order to encourage epidemic diseases which, it was hoped, would wipe them out. The only medical supply to which they would have access would be contraceptives, to curb their breeding. They would not be taught to read or write (though sometimes Hitler conceded that it might be convenient if they learned just enough to allow them to recognize road signs). In every settlement there would be a loudspeaker to relay selected news items and play cheerful music. The Slavs would be excluded from the 'handsome villages', connected by autobahns, in which the Germans lived. But they would perform 'humble tasks' for their conquerors, and supply organized slave-labour to till the soil.[78]

The contention, then, that Hitler's ideas on culture were trivial, half-baked and disgusting can be allowed only if the same epithets are applied to numerous cultural ideas prevalent among English intellectuals in the first half of the twentieth century, some of which are still espoused today. The superiority of 'high' art, the eternal glory of Greek sculpture and architecture, the transcendent value of the old masters and of classical music, the supremacy of Shakespeare, Goethe and other authors acknowledged by intellectuals as great, the divine spark that animates all productions of genius and distinguishes them from the low amusements of the mass – these were among Hitler's most dearly held beliefs. His contempt for 'gutter journalism', advertising and 'cinema bilge', his espousal of the aristocratic principle, and his comparison of the 'dunderheaded multitude' with women and children, are other features that readers of this book will have no difficulty matching in intellectual discourse. To such readers, his various rewritings of the mass – as exterminable subhumans, as an inhibited bourgeois herd, as noble workers, as a peasant pastoral – will also be familiar intellectual devices. The tragedy of *Mein Kampf* is that it was not, in many respects, a deviant work but one firmly rooted in European intellectual orthodoxy.

Postscript

Wednesday, 26 February 1941 Yesterday in the ladies' lavatory at the Sussex Grill at Brighton I heard: She's a little simpering thing. I don't like her. But then he never did care for big women. He has wonderful white teeth. He always had. Its fun having the boys . . . If he don't look out he'll be court martialled. They were powdering and painting, these common little tarts, while I sat, behind a thin door, p–ing as quietly as I could. Then at Fuller's. A fat, smart woman, in red hunting cap, pearls, check skirt, consuming rich cakes. Her shabby dependant also stuffing. They ate and ate. Something scented, shoddy, parasitic about them. Where does the money come to feed these fat white slugs?[1]

When Virginia Woolf wrote this entry in her journal, she had only a short time to live. Madness and suicide were soon to claim her. The harmless chatter she listens to with rage and loathing is curiously reminiscent of the women's conversation that we overhear in the second part of Eliot's *The Waste Land*. The topics are the same – men, teeth, the army. Even the phrasing is echoed ('If you don't give it him'; 'If he don't look out'). Perhaps she unconsciously altered what she heard, assimilating it to that great, central document of modernism.

But whether she did or not, the scene is, of course, invented. The women in Fuller's are not 'slugs'. 'Common little tarts' is an intellectual's rewriting of the occupants of the Sussex Grill lavatory. The invention is strangely self-tormenting. Woolf imagines the women, and is infuriated by what she has imagined. Intellectual figurations of the mass are often, as we have seen, a stimulus to fury, loathing and fear. They are not comfortable things to live with, though they do afford the marginal comfort of assuring the intellectual that he or she is different.

Since intellectual phobias about the mass are, like Virginia Woolf's, circular and self-deluding (for the 'mass' is invented by the intellectual whom the invention gives pain to), they seem, in extreme cases, to be a form of insanity. An intriguing illustration of this is Rayner Heppenstall (1911–81), the friend of George Orwell, Dylan Thomas, Eric Gill, Middleton Murry, etc., who worked for twenty years as a drama producer for the highbrow BBC Third Programme. Heppenstall was in many respects an archetypal early twentieth-century intellectual. He regarded himself as a failed artist, unjustly neglected by a philistine public. He had achieved brief celebrity with his first novel, *The Blaze of Noon*, published in 1939 – the story of a blind man who is also a Nietzsche-reader, hates the weak and disabled, scorns clerks and suburbs. But his later novels met with no comparable success, and his writing became defiantly 'difficult'. Hélène Cixous described him as the founder of the *nouveau roman*. Though his BBC job assured him an ample income, he watched the dwindling proceeds of his writing resentfully. In 1973 he recorded his literary earnings as nil, calculating that the cost of stationery had exceeded his royalties.[2]

In his journals and conversation he finds relief in élitist or racist outbursts against the welfare state, trades unions ('enemies of civilization'), coloured immigrants, new universities and the working class. Like Nietzsche, Wells and other intellectuals, he enjoys contemplating the extinction of large sections of humanity: 'There are a whole race, the Arabs, and a mongrel people, the Irish, upon whom, if it were possible merely by pressing a button, I would happily commit total genocide.'[3] Hitler would have readily understood. But coming from one of the masterminds behind the Third Programme, that bastion of high culture and 'civilized' values, the remark is troubling, and is perhaps best regarded as insane. Heppenstall showed other signs of mental disturbance. He kept a suicide potion, consisting of barbiturates dissolved in vodka, which he periodically gloated over and rebottled. He also engaged in a bitter feud with his neighbours in Deal – an extended family of parents, grandparents and children, whom he objected to on the grounds that they were working class and too numerous. They seem to have done little to arouse his fury, beyond hanging their washing on a line where he could see it, and he admitted that what he hated them for was ultimately just their 'philistinism'. To punish them he lit noxious bonfires and watched, amused, as the mother scuttled out to rescue her washing from the line. When the young husband called and politely remonstrated, Heppenstall told him to 'Piss off'. A policeman then arrived, to inform Heppenstall that bonfires were illegal before 6 o'clock – so subsequently he lit one regularly at 6 each day. He records all this in his journals quite without remorse. In his last (and posthumously published) novel, *The Pier*, he retells the story, concluding it with a scene in which he returns secretly from a continental holiday, enters his neighbours' house and shoots all six adults dead.[4]

Since Heppenstall, at the time he wrote this, was so doddery he could not walk down to the shops, and since, even as a young man, his squeamishness was such that he could not bear to put a bird that a cat had mangled out of its misery, his murderous fantasy seems pathetic rather than dangerous. It hurts no one but himself – like Virginia Woolf's rage in the lavatory – and it is born of impotence. The pain of pursuing an intellectual life amid the coarse intrusions of mass culture gives his writing a permanently wounded air. The individual engulfed by the banalities of tabloid newsprint provided the design of his novel *Two Moons*, published in 1977, which recorded the most tragic event of his life – his son Adam's confinement to a wheelchair, at the age of twenty-eight, as the result of a fall. In the book the details of Adam's accident are conveyed objectively, as news items, and almost lost in a torrent of competing news items that Heppenstall invents or transcribes – crimes, strikes, sporting news, astrological predictions. By this method, at once sardonic and icily impersonal, Heppenstall appropriates his son's hurt, and its relative insignificance in the public arena, as part of his grudge against the mass. The avant-garde technique of the novel excludes ordinary readers. Since it is fabricated out of newsprint, this means Heppenstall can enjoy the irony of turning a mass medium against the mass.

Following Heppenstall has brought me far beyond the limits of my chosen period. The second half of the twentieth century is another story – though Heppenstall's presence in it serves to remind us that the old intellectual prejudices did not die out in 1939, and have not died out yet.

Other things have changed, however. The increase in the world's population that alarmed H. G. Wells and others has accelerated to an unexampled degree. When Wells wrote *The Shape of Things to Come* in 1933, he predicted optimistically that there might be a world war, followed by epidemic and famine, in the mid-1950s, in which half the world's inhabitants would be wiped out, so that by 1960 the global population might have dropped to a little under 1 billion (1,000 million). In fact, almost exactly the opposite has happened. By 1960 the global population was heading towards the 4 billion mark, a figure it reached by 1975. This means that in the fifty years from 1925 to 1975 the world's population doubled, not, as Wells hoped, halved. By 1990 it had climbed to 5.3 billion. The current estimate for 2025 is 8.6 billion. Such figures and rates of increase have never been experienced before. No one can tell how the planet will feed and accommodate such hordes, or whether the ecosystem can survive the levels of pollution they will generate.

A sober estimate of the immediate demographic future by two leading academic experts warns:

If population doesn't slow down spontaneously it will have to be stopped by some sort of catastrophe, either man-made, microbial, or nutritive. Nuclear warfare is one obvious method of cutting back population but has the disadvantage that it could easily cause sufficient global contamination to extinguish the human race. Plague could be almost as devastating: it is unlikely that any bacterium could cause a numerically significant epidemic nowadays, but it is not hard to imagine a virus infection that could have a 95 per cent mortality. Myxomatosis, a disease for which there is no treatment, caused this sort of drop in the rabbit population in many areas of the world in the 1950s. Famine is the ultimate sanction, but if it comes to that it will hardly be acting alone: in the apocalypse the four horsemen ride together.[5]

It will be seen that these solutions to the problem bear a close similarity to those suggested by H. G. Wells in his various futurist fictions. For that matter, the academics' conclusion agrees broadly with Hitler's warning in *Mein Kampf*:

The day will certainly come when the whole of mankind will be forced to check the augmentation of the human species . . . Nobody can doubt that this world will one day be the scene of dreadful struggles for existence on the part of mankind.[6]

The population problem that concerned Hitler and dismayed Ortega y Gasset when he wrote *The Revolt of the Masses* was, of course, almost negligible compared to the fearsomely reduplicating megalife that threatens us today. The European population of 460 million that elicited Ortega's protests had swelled, by 1975, to 635 million – a figure itself eclipsed by those for Asia and Africa. Between 1925 and 1975 Asia's population doubled, from 1,150 to 2,300 million. The rate of increase in sub-Saharan Africa rose from 25 per cent in the first quarter of the twentieth century to 45 per cent in the second and 100 per cent in the third. Large parts of Asia and Africa are now doubling their populations every generation. Between 1950 and 1955 the annual increment to the world's population averaged 47 million. Between 1985 and 1990 it averaged 88 million, or about 1.7 million new people each week.

Faced with these frightening figures it is almost impossible for us to admit that we are just as responsible for them as anyone else. Yet it is evident that each of us, as a single human being, adds exactly as much as every other human being to the total. Almost inevitably our instinct will be to protest that the fault lies elsewhere – with those who have large families; with the irresponsibly procreative Indians and Chinese. This automatic impulse to exclude oneself from the statistics corresponds closely to what early twentieth-century intellectuals felt when they contemplated the 'masses'. Feeling it ourselves should make us sympathize more with the intellectuals' predicament, however repellent we may find the cultural attitudes they favoured and the remedies they proposed.

The remedies the twenty-first century will perfect can only be guessed, but it seems clear that they will entail the recognition that, given the state of the planet, humans, or some humans, must now be categorized as vermin. In case this sounds alarmist, we should remind ourselves that it is already the situation in Bogota, Columbia, where for the last ten years the police and hired death squads have been hunting down and killing street children, many of whom now live in the city's sewers to avoid extermination.[7]

Another change that has occurred in the second half of the twentieth century, of much less moment than population growth but still significant for our subject, is the advent of television, and the transference, at least in Europe and North America, from a predominantly written to a predominantly televisual culture. Intellectuals have opposed the spread of television just as vociferously as they condemned newspapers in the early part of the century. 'I don't see how any civilized person can watch TV, far less own a set,' pronounced W. H. Auden in 1972.[8] However, it is evident that for the majority of people television has immensely extended the opportunity for knowledge. It has also given the majority, in Britain at any rate, unprecedented access to traditional culture, not only through such star ventures as Kenneth Clark's *Civilization*, or the BBC Shakespeare series, but through countless everyday drama productions and documentaries. It is almost certainly true to say that thanks to television, the proportion of the British population that has actually seen drama performed is greater than in any previous age. Following this trend, 'culture' has made itself more widely available in other respects, too. In contemporary poetry, for example, obscurity is no longer the rule. Eliot's dictat that modern poetry must be difficult has been set aside. The leading poets writing in English in the second half of the twentieth century, Larkin, Hughes and Heaney, have all written poems that – though not written with a juvenile readership in mind – can be readily appreciated by schoolchildren.

But just as the spread of literacy to the 'masses' impelled intellectuals in the early twentieth century to produce a mode of culture (modernism) that the masses could not enjoy, so the new availability of culture through television and other popular media has driven intellectuals to evolve an anti-popular cultural mode that can reprocess all existing culture and take it out of the reach of the majority. This mode, variously called 'post-structuralism' or 'deconstruction' or just 'theory', began in 1960s with the work of Jacques Derrida, which attracted a large body of imitators among academics and literary students eager to identify themselves as the intellectual avant-garde. To establish its anti-popular status it was necessary for 'theory' to define itself in opposition to the prominent features of the popular media, such as television. Foremost among these is intelligibility. Whereas television must ensure that it can be understood by a wide and not necessarily highly educated audience, 'theory' must ensure that it cannot. Partly by copying the turns of phrase and peculiar verbal usages of Derrida and other practitioners, it has managed to evolve a language that is impenetrable to most native English-speakers.

A second popular feature it has succeeded in combating is human interest. A factor in television's breadth of appeal is its focus on personality. In its cultural coverage this generally takes the form of interviews with writers, actors or directors, and programmes about authors' and artists' biographies. 'Theory', on the other hand, dismisses such biographical approaches as trivial and irrelevant. It denies that there is any ascertainable connection between authors or artists and the meaning of the works they produce. In these respects, 'theory' is in accord with early twentieth-century aesthetic treatises such as Clive Bell's *Art* and Ortega y Gasset's *The Dehumanization of Art*, which taught, as we have seen, that only people incapable of aesthetic emotion look for human interest and other such 'sentimental irrelevancies' in artistic works, and that 'the passion and pain of the man behind the poet' is the province of the degenerate masses, not the specially gifted minority. 'Theory' (which, it is no surprise to find, often makes obeisance to Nietzsche) teaches that art and literature are 'self-referential' or 'self-reflexive' – that is, they have no relevance at all to the real world or to the life ordinary people lead. This viewpoint is, again, perfectly in accord with the Bloomsbury aesthetes' horror of the 'photographic' realism that the 'gross herd' clamours for – a horror which led Clive Bell, for example, to disdain seventeenth-century Dutch art as a collection of 'chromo-photographs'.[9]

Roland Barthes, whose essay 'The Death of the Author' is generally regarded as a landmark in the late twentieth-century dehumanization of literature, shows other affinities with the old-style intellectuals. In *The Pleasure of the Text* he urges his disciples 'to be *aristocratic* readers' (Barthes's emphasis). In *Mythologies* he 'decodes' various items of popular culture (all-in-wrestling, steak and chips) to show how their real meaning, discernible to the intellectual, escapes the gullible masses. He is the foe of the *bourgeois*, and even more vehemently of the *petit bourgeois*. He hates plastic – 'a graceless material, the product of chemistry, not of nature' – and blames the bourgeoisie for inventing it. The 'natural' material, especially for toys, is, he explains, wood.

It is a familiar and poetic substance, which does not sever the child from close contact with the tree . . . Wood makes essential objects, objects for all time. Yet there hardly remain any of these wooden toys from the Vosges, these fretwork farms with their animals, which were only possible, it is true, in the days of the craftsman.[10]

The craftsman, like the peasant, is envisaged by the intellectual as a respectful, contented, wholly meritorious subordinate, in tune with nature. But the mass (in this case the version of the mass called the bourgeoisie), with its unnatural appetite for plastic (or, in an earlier era, for tinned food), reveals itself as unnatural, and not fully or wholesomely human.

Notes

Preface

1 – See Augustine's *Enchiridion* in J. Rivière (ed.), *Oeuvres de Saint Augustin*, Vol. IX, *Exposés Généraux de la Foi*, Desclée de Brouwer, Paris, 1947, pp. 152, 346–7, and *Contra Duas Epistulas Pelagianorum*, Book 2, Para. 13, in F. J. Thonnard, E. Bleuzen and A. C. de Veer (eds.), *Oeuvres*, Vol. XXIII, 1974. See also the use of *massa* in the Vulgate, Romans 9: 21, from which Augustine derives the term.

1 The Revolt of the Masses

1 – José Ortega y Gasset, *The Revolt of the Masses*, authorized translation from the Spanish, Allen and Unwin, London, 1932, pp. 54, 119–20.

2 – H. G. Wells, *Kipps*, Fontana Books, London, 1961, p. 240.

3 – Ortega y Gasset, op. cit., pp. 11–13, 18, 24, 131–2, 135. His analysis was influenced by that of Oswald Spengler, who saw in the 'fluid masses' of 'parasitical city-dwellers' a sign that the West was nearing the end of its culture cycle. See Spengler's *The Decline of the West*, trans. Charles F. Atkinson, Knopf, New York, 1980, Vol. I, pp. 32–3.

4 – Friedrich Nietzsche, *Thus Spoke Zarathustra*, trans. R. J. Hollingdale, Penguin Books, Harmondsworth, 1961, pp. 75–7, 98, 120, and *The Will to Power*, trans. Walter Kaufmann and R. J. Hollingdale, Weidenfeld & Nicolson, London, 1968, pp. 77, 382, 458.

5 – See David S. Thatcher, *Nietzsche in England, 1890–1914*, University of Toronto Press, 1970, pp. 93, 148, 186, 235; and A. R. Orage, *Friedrich Nietzsche: The Dionysian Spirit of the Age*, T. N. Foulis, London, 1906, and *Nietzsche in Outline and Aphorism*, T. N. Foulis, London, 1907, p. 169.

6 – Flaubert–Sand, *Correspondance*, Flammarion, Paris, 1981,

pp. 342 ff., 350 ff., quoted in Herbert Lottman, *Flaubert: A Biography*, Methuen, London, 1989, pp. 237–8. On the subject of antipathy to the masses among leaders of the Decadent movement such as Huysmans and Whistler, see Patrick Brantlinger, *Bread and Circuses: Theories of Mass Culture as Social Decay*, Cornell University Press, Ithaca, 1983, pp. 113 f.

7 – See Robert Ferguson, *Enigma: The Life of Knut Hamsun*, Hutchinson, London, 1987, pp. 1, 164, 386.

8 – The Education Act of 1870 did not make elementary education either free or compulsory, but it enabled school boards to frame by-laws rendering attendance compulsory, and also to pay school fees in cases of parental poverty. Disraeli's Act of 1876 made it punishable for parents to fail to secure elementary education for their children, and for an employer to employ a child without a certificate of elementary education. The 1880 Act obliged school boards to frame by-laws rendering attendance compulsory, so completing the process of universal compulsory education. Education was not free until 1881, when the Elementary Education Act placed free education within the reach of every child.

9 – H. G. Wells, *The War in the Air*, Penguin Books, Harmondsworth, 1979, p. 229, and *The Outline of History*, George Newnes, London, 1920, p. 647.

10 – Michael Holroyd, *Bernard Shaw, Vol. I, 1856–98. The Search for Love*, Chatto and Windus, London, 1988, p. 79.

11 – Ibid., p. 104.

12 – Hamilton Fyfe, *Northcliffe: An Intimate Biography*, Macmillan, New York, 1930, p. 83. For an intellectual view of Northcliffe, see J. Middleton Murry, 'Northcliffe as Symbol', *Adelphi*, I, 1930.

13 – Helen MacGill Hughes, *News and the Human Interest Story*, University of Chicago Press, 1940, pp. 106, 255.

14 – Nietzsche, *Thus Spoke Zarathustra*, ed. cit., p. 77, and *The Will to Power*, ed. cit., p. 80.

15 – *Criterion*, xvii, 1938, p. 688.

16 – F. R. Leavis and Denys Thompson, *Culture and Environment: The Training of Critical Awareness*, Chatto and Windus, London, 1933, p. 3.

17 – F. R. Leavis, 'Scrutiny: A Retrospect', *Scrutiny*, 20, 1963, p. 1.

18 – Friedrich Nietzsche, *Beyond Good and Evil*, trans. R. J. Hollingdale, Penguin Books, Harmondsworth, 1973, pp. 147–9, and *Thus Spoke Zarathustra*, ed. cit., p. 67.

19 – D. L. Le Mahieu, *A Culture for Democracy: Mass Communication and the Cultivated Mind in Britain Between the Wars*, Clarendon Press, Oxford, 1988, pp. 33, 265.

20 Sir Arthur Conan Doyle, *The Hound of the Baskervilles*, John Murray and Jonathan Cape, London, 1974, p. 46.

21 – Peter Ackroyd, *T. S. Eliot*, Hamish Hamilton, London, 1984, p. 248.

22 – F. R. Leavis, *Mass Civilisation and Minority Culture*, The Minority Press, Cambridge, 1930, pp. 3–12, 25.

23 – Michael Millgate (ed.), *The Life and Works of Thomas Hardy*, Macmillan, London, 1984, p. 192.

24 – George Orwell, *Keep the Aspidistra Flying*, Penguin Books, Harmondsworth, 1970, pp. 90–92.

25 – Warren Roberts, James T. Boulton and Elizabeth Mansfield (eds.), *The Letters of D. H. Lawrence, Vol. IV, 1921–4*, Cambridge University Press, 1987, p. 234. For Nietzsche's influence on Lawrence see Colin Milton, *Lawrence and Nietzsche*, Aberdeen University Press, 1987.

26 – D. H. Lawrence, 'Reflections on the Death of a Porcupine', in *Selected Essays*, Penguin Books, Harmondsworth, 1969, p. 65.

27 – D. H. Lawrence, *Kangaroo*, Penguin Books, Harmondsworth, 1971, p. 294.

28 – D. H. Lawrence, *Mornings in Mexico and Etruscan Places*, Penguin Books, Harmondsworth, 1971, pp. 12–13.

29 – D. H. Lawrence, *Selected Letters*, Penguin Books, Harmondsworth, 1950, p. 82.

30 – D. H. Lawrence, *Fantasia of the Unconscious and Psychoanalysis and the Unconscious*, Penguin Books, Harmondsworth, 1971, pp. 144, 180.

31 – James T. Boulton and Andrew Robertson (eds.), *The Letters of D. H. Lawrence, Vol. III, 1916–21*, Cambridge University Press, 1984, p. 160.

32 – Nietzsche, *The Will to Power*, ed. cit., p. 476.

33 – Nietzsche, *Beyond Good and Evil*, ed. cit., p. 70.

34 – Nietzsche, *The Will to Power*, ed. cit., p. 506.

35 – James T. Boulton (ed.), *The Letters of D. H. Lawrence, Vol. I, 1901–13*, Cambridge University Press, 1979, p. 81.

36 – Nietzsche, *The Will to Power*, ed. cit., p. 169.

37 – James T. Boulton and Andrew Robertson (eds.), ed. cit., p. 21.

38 – Donat Gallagher (ed.), *The Essays, Articles and Reviews of Evelyn Waugh*, Methuen, London, 1983, p. 548.

39 – Nietzsche, *The Will to Power*, ed. cit., pp. 389–90, 504.

40 – See W. B. Yeats, *On the Boiler*, The Cuala Press, Dublin, [1939], and David Bradshaw, 'The Eugenics Movement in the Thirties and the Emergence of *On the Boiler*' in Deirdre Toomey (ed.), *Yeats and Women*, 1991, pp. 189–215.

41 – Nietzsche, *Thus Spoke Zarathustra*, ed. cit., p. 67.

42 – Lawrence, *Fantasia of the Unconscious and Psychoanalysis and the Unconscious*, ed. cit., pp. 68, 80–81, 87.

43 – T. S. Eliot, *Christianity and Culture*, Harcourt Brace, New York, 1968, p. 185, and *Selected Essays*, Faber and Faber, London, 3rd edn, 1951, pp. 398, 509, 515–16.

44 – Valerie Eliot (ed.), *The Letters of T. S. Eliot, Vol. I, 1898–1922*, Faber and Faber, London, 1988, pp. 120 (on reading Nietzsche), 161.

45 – George Moore, *Confessions of a Young Man*, Swan, Sonnenschein, Lowrey & Co., London, 1888, p. 225; and Aldous Huxley, *Beyond the Mexique Bay*, Chatto and Windus, London, 1934, p. 101.

46 – Eliot, *Selected Essays*, ed. cit., p. 289.

47 – Valentine Cunningham, *British Writers of the Thirties*, Oxford University Press, 1988, p. 275.

48 – José Ortega y Gasset, *The Dehumanization of Art and Other Essays on Art, Culture and Literature*, trans. Helene Weyl, Princeton University Press, 1968, pp. 5–13.

49 – E. M. Forster, *Howards End*, Penguin Books, Harmondsworth, 1968, pp. 44, 53, 109, 114, 210.

50 – Virginia Woolf, *Mrs Dalloway*, Penguin Books, Harmondsworth, 1973, pp. 14, 136–8, 146–7.

51 – James Joyce, *Ulysses*, Bodley Head, London, 1960, pp. 82–4, 147–89, 257, 302, 304.

52 – Anne Olivier Bell (ed.), *A Moment's Liberty: The Shorter Diary of Virginia Woolf*, The Hogarth Press, London, 1990, pp. 145–6, 148.

53 – See John Betjeman, 'Slough', l.7 in *Collected Poems*, John Murray, London, 4th edn, 1979, p. 22; Norman Sherry, *The Life of Graham Greene: Vol. I, 1904–39*, Jonathan Cape, London, 1989, pp. 241–2; H. G. Wells, *The History of Mr Polly*, Pan Books, London, 1971, p. 145, and *Love and Mr Lewisham*, Harper and Bros., London and New York, 1900, p. 245; George Orwell, *The Road to Wigan Pier*, Penguin Books, Harmondsworth, 1970, pp. 82, 88; Fiona MacCarthy, *Eric Gill*, Faber and Faber, London, 1989, p. 149; and Joseph Connolly, *Jerome K. Jerome: A Critical Biography*, Orbis Publishing, London, 1982, p. 37.

2 Rewriting the Masses

1 – José Ortega y Gasset, *The Revolt of the Masses*, authorized translation from the Spanish, Allen and Unwin, London, 1932, pp. 14, 15, 19, 21, 146.

2 – Michael Millgate (ed.), *The Life and Works of Thomas Hardy*, Macmillan, London, 1984, pp. 141, 247.

3 – Andrew McNeillie (ed.), *The Essays of Virginia Woolf, Vol. III, 1919–24*, The Hogarth Press, London, 1988, p. 3.

4 – Ezra Pound, *The Cantos*, Faber and Faber, London, 1986, pp. 61–7, 613, and Humphrey Carpenter, *A Serious Character: The Life of Ezra Pound*, Faber and Faber, London, 1988, pp. 199, 421.

5 – On Mass Observation, see the bibliography in Angus Calder and Dorothy Sheridan (eds.), *Speak for Yourself: A Mass-Observation Anthology, 1937–49*, Jonathan Cape, London, 1984. In so far as Mass Observation proved anything about the mass, it was that the mass did not exist. Its volunteers on the 'National Panel' seem to be just as individual as anyone else, and include at least one writer of considerable talent, Nella Last; see Richard Broad and Suzie Fleming (eds.), *Nella Last's War: A Mother's Diary, 1939–45*, Falling Wall Press, Bristol, 1981.

6 – See David Bodanis, *Web of Words: The Ideas Behind Politics*, Macmillan Press, London, 1988, pp. 15–38.

7 – Gustave Le Bon, *The Crowd: A Study of the Popular Mind*, Fisher Unwin, London, 1896, pp. xvii–xxi, 3–21, 49, 84–9, etc. On Le Bon, see J. S. McClelland, *The Crowd and the Mob: From Plato to Canetti*, Unwin Hyman, London, 1989, pp. 8, 14, 196–235, 282.

8 – See W. Trotter, *Instincts of the Herd in Peace and War*, Fisher Unwin, 1916, pp. 151, 161–3, 167, 171–80, 196–206. For D. H. Lawrence's comments on Trotter, see James T. Boulton and Andrew Robertson (eds.), *The Letters of D. H. Lawrence, Vol. III, 1916–21*, Cambridge University Press, 1984, p. 59.

9 – Sigmund Freud, *Group Psychology and the Analysis of the Ego*, authorized translation by James Strachey, International Psycho-Analytical Press, London and Vienna, 1922, pp. 5, 10, 82–3, 90–112.

10 – Sigmund Freud, *Complete Psychological Works*, Standard Edition, James Strachey et al. (eds.), Hogarth Press, London, 1953–74, Vol. XXII, p. 221, and Vol. 21, pp. 7–8.

11 – Elias Canetti, *Crowds and Power*, trans. Carol Stewart, Gollancz, London, 1962, pp. 15–22, 48–52, 306–26, 468. For Canetti's recognition of the importance of bacilli ('one of the central myths in the history of human thought') in shaping ideas about the mass, see p. 363.

12 – Virginia Woolf, *Mrs Dalloway*, Penguin Books, Harmondsworth, 1973, p. 93.

13 – See Beaumont Newhall, *The History of Photography*, Secker and Warburg, London, 1982, pp. 128–9.

14 – Charles Baudelaire, *The Mirror of Art*, Phaidon Press, London, 1955, pp. 228–31.

15 – W. B. Yeats, *On the Boiler*, The Cuala Press, Dublin, [1939], p. 25.

16 – Lady Eastlake, 'Photography', *Quarterly Review*, 101, 1857, pp. 442–68.

17 – George Moore, *Confessions of a Young Man*, Swan, Sonnenschein, Lowrey & Co., London, 1888, p. 229; and George Gissing, *The Whirlpool*, Lawrence and Bullen, London, 1897, p. 218.

18 – Walter Benjamin, *Illuminations*, Hannah Arendt (ed.), trans. Harry Zohn, Jonathan Cape, London, 1970, p. 226.

19 – See John House, 'London in the Art of Monet and Pissarro', in Malcolm Warner, *The Image of London: Views by Travellers and Emigres 1550–1920*, Trefoil Publications, London, 1987, pp. 73–98.

20 – See Carpenter, op. cit., pp. 189–90.

21 – E. M. Forster, *A Room with a View*, Penguin Books, Harmondsworth, pp. 65, 46–8.

22 – See P. N. Furbank, *E. M. Forster: A Life, Vol. II, Polycrates' Ring, 1914–70*, Secker and Warburg, London, 1978, pp. 83–4.

23 – E. M. Forster, *A Passage to India*, Penguin Books, Harmondsworth, 1969, p. 212.

24 – E. M. Forster, *Howards End*, Penguin Books, Harmondsworth, 1968, p. 44.

25 – See Warren Roberts, James T. Boulton and Elizabeth Mansfield (eds.), *The Letters of D. H. Lawrence, Vol. IV, 1921–24*, Cambridge University Press, 1987, pp. 8, 10–11, 59, 120, 221, 225, 239, 246, 263, 285, 286, 362, etc.

26 – Friedrich Nietzsche, *Thus Spoke Zarathustra*, trans, R. J. Hollingdale, Penguin Books, Harmondsworth, 1961, p. 258. On Gauguin and peasants, see Caroline Boyle-Turner, *Gauguin and the School of Pont-Aven*, Royal Academy of Arts, London, 1986.

27 – See Malcolm Yorke, *Eric Gill: Man of Flesh and Spirit*, Constable, London, 1981, pp. 27, 270; and Fiona McCarthy, *Eric Gill*, Faber and Faber, London, 1989, pp. 75, 102, 289.

28 – Virginia Woolf, *Mrs Dalloway*, Penguin Books, Harmondsworth, 1973, pp. 90–92.

29 – J. B. Priestley, *Rain Upon Gadshill: A Further Chapter of Autobiography*, Heinemann, London, 1939, p. 40.

30 – See Vincent Brome, *J. B. Priestley*, Hamish Hamilton, London, 1988, pp. 380–81; and Priestley, op. cit., p. 192.

31 – Grahame Greene, *A Sort of Life*, Bodley Head, London, 1971, p. 175; and Norman Sherry, *The Life of Graham Greene, Vol. I, 1904–39*, Jonathan Cape, London, 1989, pp. 264–5, 296–304.

32 – Martin Greene, *Children of the Sun: A Narrative of 'Decadence' in England after 1918*, Constable, London, 1977, pp. 306–62.

33 – Quoted in Valentine Cunningham, *British Writers of the Thirties*, Oxford University Press, 1988, pp. 269–70.

34 – Quoted ibid., p. 275.

35 – George Orwell, *The Road to Wigan Pier*, Penguin Books, Harmondsworth, 1970, pp. 64, 102, 110–14, 125, 185, and *Homage to Catalonia*, Penguin Books, Harmondsworth, 1970, pp. 19, 33.

36 – George Orwell, *Down and Out in Paris and London*, Penguin Books, Harmondsworth, 1970, p. 123, and *The Road to Wigan Pier*, ed. cit., p. 132–3.

37 – Ibid., p. 16.

38 – George Orwell, *Coming Up for Air*, Penguin Books, Harmondsworth, 1970, p. 216.

39 – George Orwell, *Nineteen Eighty-Four*, Penguin Books, Harmondsworth, 1969, pp. 59–60, 107.

40 – See Max Horkheimer, *Critical Theory: Selected Essays*, Herder and Herder, New York, 1972, p. 237; Herbert Marcuse, *The Authentic Dimension*, Beacon, Boston, 1978, pp. 32, 52–3; Theodor Adorno, *Negative Dialectics*, trans. E. B. Ashton, Seabury, New York, 1973, p. 265; and Orwell, *Nineteen Eighty-Four*, ed. cit., p. 215.

41 – Orwell, *Nineteen Eighty-Four*, ed. cit., pp. 174–5.

3 The Suburbs and the Clerks

1 – For the facts in this paragraph see Michael Jahn, 'Suburban Development in Outer West London, 1850–1900', in F. M. L. Thompson (ed.), *The Rise of Suburbia*, Leicester University Press and St Martin's Press, New York, 1982, pp. 23, 94–156; Arthur M. Edwards, *The Design of Suburbia: A Critical Study of Environmental History*, Pembridge Press, London, 1981; *The Times*, 25 June 1904; Noreen Branson, *Britain in the Nineteen-Twenties*, Weidenfeld & Nicolson, 1975, p. 117; and Friedrich Nietzsche, *Thus Spoke Zarathustra*, trans. R. J. Hollingdale, Penguin Books, Harmondsworth, 1969, p. 187.

2 – See S. Martin Gaskell, 'Housing and the Lower Middle Class, 1870–1914', in Geoffrey Crossick (ed.), *The Lower Middle Class in Britain, 1870–1914*, St Martin's Press, New York, 1977, pp. 159–83.

3 – Graham Greene, *A Sort of Life*, Bodley Head, London, 1971, p. 35.

4 – See Humphrey Carpenter, *The Brideshead Generation: Evelyn Waugh and His Friends*, Weidenfeld & Nicolson, London, 1989, pp. 48, 149, and *Vile Bodies*, Penguin Books, Harmondsworth, pp. 199–200.

5 – E. M. Forster, *Howards End*, Penguin Books, Harmondsworth, 1968, p. 316.

6 – Dan H. Laurence (ed.),*George Bernard Shaw: Collected Letters, 1911–25*, Max Reinhardt, London, 1985, p. 367.

7 – See Julia Briggs, *A Woman of Passion: The Life of E. Nesbit, 1858–1924*, Hutchinson, London, 1987, pp. 201, 321–3.

8 – E. M. Forster, *Two Cheers for Democracy*, Penguin Books, Harmondsworth, 1965, p. 68.

9 – C. E. M. Joad, *The Horrors of the Countryside*, Hogarth Press, London, 1931, pp. 8–11, 44.

10 – See Paul Fussell, *Abroad: British Literary Travel Between the Wars*, Oxford University Press, 1980; and Robert Byron, *Letters Home*, Lucy Butler (ed.), John Murray, London, 1991, pp. 174, 219, 233–5, 278.

11 – Q. D. Leavis, *Fiction and the Reading Public*, Chatto and Windus, London, 1932, pp. 181, 210–211; [Cyril Connolly], *The Unquiet Grave: A Word Cycle by Palinurus*, Horizon, London, 1944, p. 26; and Humphrey Carpenter, *The Brideshead Generation*, Weidenfeld & Nicolson, 1989, p. 302.

12 – Norman Sherry, *The Life of Graham Greene, Vol. 1, 1904–39*, Jonathan Cape, London, 1989, pp. 476–7; and Graham Greene, *Brighton Rock*, Penguin Books, Harmondsworth, 1961, p. 37.

13 – Arthur Machen, *The Secret Glory*, Martin Secker, London, [1922], pp. 289–95.

14 – See Martin Green, *Children of the Sun: A Narrative of 'Decadence' in England after 1918*, Constable, London, 1977, p. 371; Peter Ackroyd, *T. S. Eliot*, Hamish Hamilton, London, 1984, p. 143; and Humphrey Carpenter, *A Serious Character: The Life of Ezra Pound*, Faber and Faber, 1983, p. 899.

15 – Alan Heuser (ed.), *Selected Literary Criticism of Louis MacNeice*, Oxford University Press, 1987, p. 87.

16 – G. K. Chesterton, *The Man Who Was Thursday*, Penguin Books, Harmondsworth, 1937, pp. 11–14, and *The Napoleon of Notting Hill*, Penguin Books, Harmondsworth, 1946, p. 153. For Chesterton's politics, see Margaret Canovan, *G. K. Chesterton, Radical Populist*, Harcourt Brace Jovanovich, New York, 1978.

17 – See A. J. Languth, *Saki: A Life of Hector Hugh Munro*, Oxford University Press, 1982, pp. 222, 258, 271; *The Penguin Complete Saki*, Penguin Books, Harmondsworth, 1982, pp. 161, 479; and Friedrich Nietzsche, *The Will to Power*, trans. Walter Kaufmann and R. J. Hollingdale, Weidenfeld & Nicolson, London, 1968, p. 542.

18 – George Moore, *Confessions of a Young Man*, Swan, Sonnenschein, Lowrey & Co, London, 1888, pp. 158–9, 187–90, 222, 229.

19 – See *The Collected Poems of T. W. H. Crosland*, Martin Secker,

1917; and Arnold Bennett, *Books and Persons*, Chatto and Windus, London, 1917, p. 64.

20 – T. W. H. Crosland, *The Suburbans*, John Long, London, 1905, pp. 10–12, 17, 21, 55, 67–9, 202.

21 – See Geoffrey Crossick (ed.), *The Lower Middle Class in Britain, 1870–1914*, St Martin's Press, New York, 1977, p. 20; D. L. Le Mahieu, *A Culture for Democracy: Mass Communication and the Cultivated Mind in Britain Between the Wars*, Clarendon Press, Oxford, 1988, pp. 7–10; Noreen Branson, *Britain in the Nineteen-Twenties*, Weidenfeld & Nicolson, 1975, p. 118; and Kenneth Lindsay, *Social Progress and Educational Waste*, Routledge, London, 1926, pp. 7, 196.

22 – Richard N. Price, 'Society, Status and Jingoism: The Social Roots of Middle-Class Patriotism, 1870–1900', in Crossick, op. cit., p. 95; Geoffrey Crossick, 'The Emergence of the Lower Middle Class in Britain: A Discussion', in Crossick, op. cit., pp. 11–60; Joseph Connolly, *Jerome K. Jerome: A Critical Biography*, Orbis Publishing, London, 1982, p. 75; Norman Sherry, *The Life of Graham Greene, Vol. 1, 1904–39*, Jonathan Cape, London, 1989, pp. 200–205; and Frances Donaldson (ed.), *Yours Plum: The Letters of P. G. Wodehouse*, Hutchinson, London, 1990, pp. 24, 36, 42 etc.

23 – See Crossick, op. cit., p. 33; Hugh McLeod, 'White Collar Values and the Role of Religion', in Crossick, op. cit., pp. 61–88; T. S. Eliot, *The Waste Land: A Facsimile and Transcript of the Original Drafts*, Valerie Eliot (ed.), Faber and Faber, London, 1971, p. 45; and H. G. Wells, *The War in the Air*, Penguin Books, Harmondsworth, 1979, p. 244.

24 – Shan F. Bullock, *Robert Thorne: The Story of a London Clerk*, T. Werner Laurie, London, 1907, pp. 138, 177, 249, 278, etc.

25 – E. M. Forster, *Howards End*, Penguin Books, Harmondsworth, 1968, p. 109.

26 – See George Bernard Shaw, Prefaces to *Man and Superman* and *On the Rocks* in *Complete Prefaces*, Paul Hamlyn, London, 1965, pp. 158–9, 162, 176, 187, 353–4, and *Misalliance* in *Complete Plays*, Paul Hamlyn, London, 1965, pp. 628–33; also David S. Thatcher, *Nietzsche in England, 1890–1914*, University of Toronto Press, 1970, pp. 175–214; and Friedrich Nietzsche, *The Will to Power*, trans. Walter Kaufmann and R. J. Hollingdale, Weidenfeld & Nicolson, London, 1968, p. 467.

27 – Richard N. Price, 'Society, Status and Jingoism: The Social Roots of Middle-Class Patriotism, 1870–1900', in Geoffrey Crossick (ed.), *The Lower Middle Class in Britain, 1870–1914*, St Martin's Press, New York, 1977, pp. 89–112.

28 – H. G. Wells, *The History of Mr Polly*, Pan Books, London, 1963, p. 197.

29 – See Robert Crawford, *The Savage and the City in the Work of T. S. Eliot*, Oxford University Press, 1987, pp. 133–6; and Craig Raine (ed.), *A Choice of Kipling's Prose*, Faber and Faber, London, 1987, pp. 152–76.

30 – See Bevis Hillier, *Young Betjeman*, John Murray, London, 1988, p. 341; Frederick Locker, *London Lyrics*, Chapman and Hall, London, 1857; H. O. Meredith, *Week-Day Poems*, Edward Arnold, London, 1911; Douglas Goldring, *Streets and Other Verses*, Selwyn and Blount, London, 1920, p. 52; and F. O. Mann, *London and Suburban*, G. Bell and Sons, London, 1925, pp. 2–7.

31 – See John Betjeman, *Collected Poems*, John Murray, London, 1979, pp. 154, 205, 212–13, 356–7; Philip Larkin, 'Betjeman en Block', in *Listen: A Review of Poetry and Criticism*, 3(2), Spring 1959, pp. 14–22. Betjeman's suburban hates are documented at length in his 'Diary of Percy Progress' articles for *Night and Day*, see the issues of 15 July, 5 August, 19 August, 18 November and 16 December 1937.

32 – My paragraphs on Stevie Smith are indebted to Frances Spalding, *Stevie Smith: A Critical Biography*, Faber and Faber, London, 1988, pp. 10–15, 66, 95, 101; see also Jack Barbera and William McBrien (eds.), *Me Again: Uncollected Writings of Stevie Smith*, Virago, London, 1981, pp. 101–2.

33 – Anita Brookner, *Lewis Percy*, Jonathan Cape, London, 1989, pp. 135, 147, 214.

34 – Charles Tomlinson, 'The Middlebrow Muse', *Essays in Criticism*, 7, 1957, pp. 208–17.

4 Natural Aristocrats

1 – James T. Boulton and Andrew Robertson (eds.), *The Letters of D. H. Lawrence, Vol. III, 1916–21*, Cambridge University Press, 1984, p. 143.

2 – W. B. Yeats, *Essays and Introductions*, Macmillan, London, 1961, p. 221.

3 – For his views on the 'timeless' in literature and the 'established great literature of all time', see T. S. Eliot, *Selected Essays*, Faber and Faber, London, 1961, pp. 14, 397.

4 – Clive Bell, *Art*, Chatto and Windus, London, 1914, p. 241.

5 – Ezra Pound, 'The New Sculpture', *Egoist*, 16 February 1914, pp. 67–8.

6 – For the opinions in this paragraph see Friedrich Nietzsche, *Beyond*

Good and Evil, trans. R. J. Hollingdale, Penguin Books, Harmondsworth, 1973, pp. 71, 102-3, 121, 149, 185; *The Anti-Christ*, in *Twilight of the Idols and The Anti-Christ*, trans. R. J. Hollingdale, Penguin Books, Harmondsworth, 1968, p. 118; *Daybreak: Thoughts on the Prejudices of Morality*, trans. R. J. Hollingdale, Cambridge University Press, 1982, p. 86; *The Will to Power*, trans. Walter Kaufmann and R. J. Hollingdale, Weidenfeld & Nicolson, London, 1968, p. 386; and *Thus Spoke Zarathustra*, trans. R. J. Hollingdale, Penguin Books, Harmondsworth, 1961, pp. 74, 91.

7 – For the opinions in this paragraph, see Nietzsche *Beyond Good and Evil*, ed. cit., pp. 43, 57, 69, 71; *The Anti-Christ*, ed. cit., pp. 156, 161-2, *The Will to Power*, ed. cit., pp. 208, 363, 390, 401, and *Ecce Homo*, trans. R. J. Hollingdale, Penguin Books, Harmondsworth, 1979, p. 59.

8 – See Nietzsche, *The Will to Power*, ed. cit., p. 149, and *Twilight of the Idols*, ed. cit., pp. 46, 55, 69.

9 – See Nietzsche, *Beyond Good and Evil*, ed. cit., p. 175, and *The Will to Power*, ed. cit., pp. 32, 363.

10 – See Nietzsche, *Thus Spoke Zarathustra*, ed. cit., pp. 122, 173, 196, and David S. Thatcher, *Nietzsche in England, 1890–1914*, University of Toronto Press, 1970, p. 130.

11 – See Richard Ellmann, *Oscar Wilde*, Hamish Hamilton, London, 1987, p. 288; and Clive Bell, op. cit., 1914, pp. 32-3.

12 – See Nietzsche, *Beyond Good and Evil*, ed. cit., p. 95, *The Will to Power*, ed. cit., pp. 235, 277, 283, *Twilight of the Idols*, ed. cit., pp. 31, 36-7, *Ecce Homo*, ed. cit., p. 54, and *Thus Spoke Zarathustra*, ed. cit., p. 61.

13 – James T. Boulton (ed.), *The Letters of D. H. Lawrence, Vol. I, 1901–13*, Cambridge University Press, 1979, p. 503; Nietzsche, *The Will to Power*, ed. cit., p. 495.

14 – Nietzsche, *Beyond Good and Evil*, ed. cit. p. 127; and D. H. Lawrence, *The Lost Girl*, Penguin Books, Harmondsworth, 1970, p. 35, and *Lady Chatterley's Lover*, Penguin Books, Harmondsworth, 1971, p. 287.

15 – D. H. Lawrence, *Fantasia of the Unconscious and Psychoanalysis and the Unconscious*, Penguin Books, Harmondsworth, 1971, p. 247, and *Selected Essays*, Penguin Books, Harmondsworth, 1969, p. 247.

16 – Nietzsche, *The Will to Power*, trans. Walter Kaufmann and R. J. Hollingdale, Weidenfeld and Nicolson, 1968, p. 277.

17 – Warren Roberts, James T. Boulton and Elizabeth Mansfield (eds.), *The Letters of D. H. Lawrence, Vol. IV, 1921–4*, Cambridge University Press, 1987, pp. 227, 277.

18 – D. H. Lawrence, *Selected Essays*, Penguin Books, Harmondsworth,

1969, pp. 64–5, 90, and *Aaron's Rod*, Penguin Books, Harmondsworth, 1968, pp. 326–8.

19 – Nietzsche, *The Will to Power*, ed. cit., p. 277.

20 – D. H. Lawrence, *The Trespasser*, Penguin Books, Harmondsworth, 1969, p. 35, and *St Mawr and The Virgin and the Gipsy*, Penguin Books, Harmondsworth, 1971, pp. 57–8, 216.

21 – See Clive Bell, *Civilization*, Chatto and Windus, London, 1928, p. 74.

22 – Bell, *Art*, ed. cit., pp. 25, 29, 39, 68–9, 80, 94, 192, 242, 261.

23 – Bell, *Civilization*, ed. cit., 204–6, 210, 218–19, 240, 243.

24 – Ibid., pp. 219–28.

25 – Ibid., pp. 233–7.

26 – Bell, *Art*, ed. cit., pp. 54, 65, 69; and John Middleton Murry, *Things to Come*, Jonathan Cape, London, 1928, p. 175, and *To the Unknown God*, Jonathan Cape, London, 1924, pp. 159–92.

27 – Jack Barbera and William McBrien (eds.), *Me Again: Uncollected Writings of Stevie Smith*, Virago, London, 1981, p. 157; Evelyn Waugh, *Brideshead Revisited*, Penguin Books, Harmondsworth, 1976, p. 134; and Humphrey Carpenter, *The Brideshead Generation*, Weidenfeld & Nicolson, London, 1989, p. 378.

28 – See Graham Greene, *Brighton Rock*, Penguin Books, Harmondsworth, 1961, pp. 5, 7–10, 13, 36, 45, 81, 89–90, 114, 128–9, 133, 236.

29 – George Orwell, *Collected Essays, Journalism and Letters*, Vol. IV, Penguin Books, Harmondsworth, 1970, p. 499.

30 – Norman Sherry, *The Life of Graham Greene, Vol. I, 1904–39*, Jonathan Cape, London, 1989, p. 646; and T. S. Eliot, *Selected Essays*, Faber and Faber, London, 1961, pp. 419–30.

31 – See Marie-Françoise Allain, *The Other Man: Conversations with Graham Greene*, Bodley Head, London, 1983, pp. 161, 172.

32 – See Aldous Huxley, *Music at Night*, Chatto and Windus, London, 1931, pp. 82, 204, and *On the Margin*, Chatto and Windus, London, 1923, pp. 48–50.

33 – Aldous Huxley, *The Doors of Perception*, Chatto and Windus, London, 1954, pp. 11–12, 25–9, 53, and *Adonis and Alphabet*, Chatto and Windus, London, 1956, p. 166.

34 – Grover Smith (ed.), *Letters of Aldous Huxley*, Chatto and Windus, London, 1969, p. 345.

35 – Aldous Huxley, *Brave New World*, Penguin Books, Harmondsworth, 1970, pp. 39–40.

36 – Ibid., p. 173

37 – Nietzsche, *Beyond Good and Evil*, ed. cit., pp. 53–4.

38 – Huxley, *Brave New World*, ed. cit., p. 7.

39 – Ibid., pp. 182, 185.

40 – George Steiner, *Real Presences: Is There Anything in What We Say?*, Faber and Faber, London, 1989, p. 223.

5 George Gissing and the Ineducable Masses

When he is the author of a work listed here, George Gissing is referred to as GG.

1 – A. C. Young (ed.), *The Letters of George Gissing to Eduard Bertz*, Constable, London, 1961, pp. 151–2.

2 – GG, *By the Ionian Sea: Notes of a Ramble in Southern Italy*, Chapman and Hall, London, 1901, pp. 118–19.

3 – See, for example, GG, *Workers in the Dawn*, Vol I, Remington and Co., London, 1880, p. 162.

4 – See, for example, ibid., p. 170, *Thyrza: A Tale*, Vol. I, Smith, Elder and Co., London 1887, p. 101, and *Demos: A Story of English Socialism*, Vol. I, Smith, Elder and Co., London,1886, pp. 78–80.

5 – Pierre Coustillas (ed.), *The Letters of George Gissing to Gabrielle Fleury*, New York Public Library, 1964, p. 64.

6 – On the friction between Gissing's belief in determinism and his faith in will power, see David Grylls's perceptive study, *The Paradox of Gissing*, Allen and Unwin, London, 1986, pp. 1–18.

7 – Examples of exceptional working-class characters in Gissing who are born with imagination would include the heroine of *Thyrza*, or Ida in *The Unclassed*.

8 – GG, *Demos*, ed. cit., p. 258, Vol. II, p. 220.

9 – GG, *Our Friend the Charlatan*, Chapman and Hall, London, 1901, pp. 154–8.

10 – See Jacob Korg, *George Gissing: A Critical Biography*, Methuen, London, 1965, p. 105.

11 – *Letters of George Gissing to Members of his Family*, Collected and arranged by Algernon and Ellen Gissing, Constable and Co., London, 1927, p. 44.

12 – GG, *Thyrza*, ed. cit., pp. 28, 148–9.

13 – GG, *Born in Exile*, Vol. I, Adam and Charles Black, London, 1892, p. 128.

14 – GG, *In the Year of Jubilee*, Vol. II, Lawrence and Bullen, London, 1894, p. 139.

15 – GG, *Demos*, Vol. III, ed. cit., p. 281.

16 – GG, *Workers in the Dawn*, Vol. II, ed. cit., p. 191.

17 – GG, *The Private Papers of Henry Ryecroft*, Constable, London, 1905, p. 70.

18 – GG, *The Whirlpool*, Lawrence and Bullen, London, 1897, p. 15.

19 – GG, *In the Year of Jubilee*, Vol. I, ed. cit., pp. 10–15, Vol. II, pp. 181–4, 207.

20 – Ibid., Vol. I, pp. 29–31, Vol. II, p. 160, Vol. III, p. 260.

21 – George J. Romanes, 'Mental Differences Between Men and Women', *The Nineteenth Century*, 123, May 1887, pp. 654–72.

22 – GG, *The Emancipated*, Vol. II, Richard Bentley, London, 1890, p. 233.

23 – Grylls, op. cit., p. 157; and Herbert Spencer, *Principles of Biology*, Vol. II, Williams and Norgate, London, 1898, pp. 512–13.

24 – GG, *Denzil Quarrier*, Lawrence and Bullen, London, 1892, p. 341.

25 – An outstanding example is the Denyer family in *The Emancipated*.

26 – GG, *The Whirlpool*, ed. cit., pp. 39–42.

27 – See Anthony West, *H. G. Wells: Aspects of a Life*, Hutchinson, London, 1984, pp. 238–76; Austin Harrison, 'George Gissing', in *The Nineteenth Century and After*, 355, September 1906, pp. 453–63; and Korg, op. cit.

28 – Korg, op. cit., p. 57.

29 – Coustillas, op. cit., p. 36.

30 – A. C. Young, op. cit., p. 171.

31 – See Jacob Korg (ed.), *George Gissing's Commonplace Book*, New York Public Library, 1962, pp. 52–4.

32 – GG, *The Odd Women*, Anthony Blond, London, 1968, pp. 22, 53.

33 – GG, *The Unclassed*, Chapman and Hall, 1884, Vol. I, p. 247, Vol. II, pp. 37, 287.

34 – Morley Roberts, *The Private Life of Henry Maitland*, Eveleigh Nash, London, 1912, p. 75.

35 – See GG, *The Private Papers of Henry Ryecroft*, ed. cit., p. 181.

36 – Korg, *George Gissing: A Critical Biography*, ed. cit., p. 8.

37 – GG, *New Grub Street*, Bernard Bergonzi (ed.), Penguin Books, Harmondsworth, 1968, p. 187.

38 – See Samuel Vogt Gapp, *George Gissing: Classicist*, University of Pennsylvania Press, Philadelphia, 1936, p. 181.

39 – GG, *New Grub Street*, ed. cit., p. 155.

40 – Gapp, op. cit., pp. 17–18.

41 – GG, *By the Ionian Sea*, ed. cit., p. 6.

42 – Ibid., pp. 7, 13, 33.

43 – GG, *Thyrza*, Vol. I., ed. cit., p. 158.

44 – GG, *Workers in the Dawn*, Vol. III, ed. cit., pp. 94–6.

45 – GG, *In the Year of Jubilee*, Vol. I, ed. cit., p. 130, Vol. II, p. 71, and Vol. III, pp. 174–5, 235.

46 – *A Beautiful World*, I, November 1893, p. 2.

47 – GG, *In the Year of Jubilee*, Vol. I, ed. cit., p. 120.

48 – GG, *The Nether World*, Vol. I, Smith, Elder and Co., London, 1889, pp. 256–73.

49 – GG, *Will Warburton*, Constable, 1905, pp. 113–14.

50 – GG, *New Grub Street*, ed. cit., pp. 43, 65, 82.

51 – Ibid., pp. 494–6.

52 – For the facts in this paragraph, see Norman and Jean Mackenzie, *The Time-Traveller: The Life of H. G. Wells*, Weidenfeld & Nicolson, London, 1973, p. 78; Margaret Drabble, *Arnold Bennett: A Biography*, G. K. Hall and Co., Boston, Mass., 1986, p. 54; Richard Ellmann, *James Joyce*, Oxford University Press, 1969, p. 50; and Peter Keating, *The Haunted Study: A Social History of the English Novel, 1875–1914*, Secker and Warburg, London, 1989, pp. 36–8.

53 – GG, *In the Year of Jubilee*, Vol. I, ed. cit., pp. 101–3, 141, Vol. II, p. 139, Vol. III, pp. 32–5.

54 – See, for example, GG, *Demos*, Vol. II, ed. cit., p. 103; *In the Year of Jubilee*, Vol. II, ed. cit., pp. 147–9, and *The Nether World*, Vol. III, ed. cit., p. 251.

55 – GG, *The Whirlpool*, ed. cit., p. 152.

56 – GG, *Demos*, Vol I, ed. cit., pp. 146, 148, 214.

57 – Ibid., Vol. I, p. 135, Vol. III, pp. 31–4.

58 – Ibid., Vol. III, p. 13.

59 – GG, *Workers in the Dawn*, Vol. I, ed. cit., p. 195, Vol. II, p. 6; *The Unclassed*, Vol. III, ed. cit., pp. 6–7, 290–91.

60 – GG, *Born in Exile*, Vol. I, ed. cit., pp. 63–4, 204, 215–16, Vol. II, p. 150, Vol. III, p. 233; and Korg, *George Gissing: A Critical Biography*, ed. cit., p. 15.

61 – GG, *Our Friend the Charlatan*, ed. cit., pp. 23, 80, 194, 235–6, 408; and A. C. Young, op. cit., pp. 172, 273.

62 – GG, *The Emancipated*, Vol. I, ed. cit., pp. 199–200.

63 – A. C. Young, op. cit., p. 33.

64 – For the instances in this paragraph see GG, *The Odd Women*, ed. cit., p. 34, *The Nether World*, Vol. I, ed. cit., pp. 47, 86, Vol. II, p. 291, Vol. III, pp. 42–3, *New Grub Street*, ed. cit., p. 404, *Demos*, Vol. I, ed. cit., p. 61. David Grylls, op. cit., p. 54, notes Gissing's debt to Arnold White's *The Problems of a Great City*, Remington and Co., London, 1886. But White's emphasis is statistical and objective; he does not provide Gissing with individual observations such as I have listed.

65 – GG, *The Nether World*, Vol. I, ed. cit., pp. 176–7.

66 – GG, *The Unclassed*, Vol. III, ed. cit., pp. 187, 203.

67 – Korg, *George Gissing's Commonplace Book*, ed. cit., p. 54.

68 – GG, *Workers in the Dawn*, Vol. III, ed. cit., pp. 192–3.

6 H. G. Wells Getting Rid of People

When he is the author of a work listed here, H. G. Wells is referred to as HGW.

1 – See J. M. Rawcliffe, 'Bromley: Kentish Market Town to London Suburb, 1841–81', in F. M. L. Thompson (ed.), *The Rise of Suburbia*, Leicester University Press and St Martin's Press, New York, 1982, pp. 28–91.

2 – HGW, *The New Machiavelli*, Penguin Books, Harmondsworth, 1966, pp. 33–9.

3 – HGW, *Kipps*, Fontana Collins, London, 1961, p. 240.

4 – HGW, *A Modern Utopia*, Chapman and Hall, London, 1905, p. 180.

5 – HGW, *The World of William Clissold*, Ernest Benn, London, 1926, p. 237.

6 – HGW, *The Open Conspiracy: Blue Prints for a World Revolution*, Victor Gollancz, London, 1928, pp. 80–88.

7 – HGW, *Apropos of Dolores*, Jonathan Cape, London, 1938, p. 61.

8 – HGW, *The World of William Clissold*, ed. cit., p. 772.

9 – HGW, *Tono-Bungay*, Pan Books, London, 1972, p. 82.

10 – HGW, *Ann Veronica*, Penguin Books, Harmondsworth, 1968, p. 10.

11 – HGW, *The Wife of Sir Isaac Harman*, Macmillan, London, 1914, pp. 341–2.

12 – HGW, *In the Days of the Comet*, The Century Co., New York, 1906, p. 191.

13 – See HGW, 'A Dream of Armageddon', in *The Country of the Blind and Other Stories*, Nelson, London, 1911.

14 – HGW, *The Wife of Sir Isaac Harman*, ed. cit., pp. 31, 96. On the nightmare future of advertising, see also HGW, 'A Story of the Days to Come', in *Tales of Space and Time*, Harper and Bros., London and New York, 1900, pp. 200–246, and *When the Sleeper Wakes*, Harper and Bros., 1899, pp. 161–2.

15 – See HGW, *In the Days of the Comet*, ed. cit., pp. 101, 123–6, and *The Shape of Things to Come: The Ultimate Revolution*, Hutchinson, London, 1933, p. 196.

16 – HGW, *Kipps*, ed. cit., p. 201.

17 – HGW, *The World of William Clissold*, ed. cit., pp. 784, 794–9.

18 – HGW, *Marriage*, Macmillan, London, 1912, pp. 508, 526.

19 – HGW, *Apropos of Dolores*, ed. cit., pp. 51–2.

20 – HGW, *The World Set Free: A Story of Mankind*, Macmillan and Co., London, 1914, p. 280.

21 – HGW, *When the Sleeper Wakes*, ed. cit., pp. 65, 68, 140, 239–59.

22 – HGW, *Anticipations of the Reaction of Mechanical and Scientific Progress upon Human Life and Thought*, Chapman and Hall, London, 1901, pp. 81–2, 211–12.

23 – Ibid., pp. 287–90.

24 – Ibid., pp. 298–9.

25 – Ibid., pp. 300–301.

26 – Ibid., pp. 280, 317.

27 – HGW, *Mankind in the Making*, Chapman and Hall, London, 1903, pp. 37, 64, 72, 99–111.

28 – HGW, *A Modern Utopia*, ed. cit., p. 135.

29 – Ibid., pp. 141–5, 184–91.

30 – See HGW, 'The Empire of the Ants', in *The Country of the Blind and Other Stories*, ed. cit.

31 – HGW, 'The Sea Raiders', in *The Plattner Story and Others*, Methuen, London, 1897.

32 – HGW, in *The Country of the Blind and Other Stories*, ed. cit.

33 – HGW, *The First Men in the Moon*, George Newnes, London, 1901, p. 137.

34 – HGW, *The Time Machine*, Pan Books, London, 1953, p. 92.

35 – HGW, in *Tales of Space and Time*, ed. cit.

36 – HGW, in *The Country of the Blind and Other Stories*, ed. cit.

37 – HGW, *The First Men in the Moon*, ed. cit., p. 36.

38 – HGW, *The War of the Worlds*, Pan Books, London, 1975, p. 112.

39 – Ibid., pp. 158–68.

40 – Ibid., p. 143.

41 – HGW, *The War in the Air*, Penguin Books, Harmondsworth, 1967, pp. 242–3.

42 – Norman and Jean Mackenzie, *The Time Traveller: The Life of H. G. Wells*, Weidenfeld & Nicolson, London, 1973, p. 298.

43 – HGW, *The Shape of Things to Come*, ed. cit., pp. 220, 236–7, 239.

7 H. G. Wells Against H. G. Wells

When he is the author of a work listed here, H. G. Wells is referred to as HGW.

1 – HGW, *The First Men in the Moon*, George Newnes, London, 1901, p. 311.

2 – See HGW, 'Of a Book Unwritten', in *Certain Personal Matters*, Lawrence and Bullen, London, 1898, pp. 170–71.

3 – See HGW, *Marriage*, Macmillan, London, 1912, p. 499, *The Food of the Gods and How It Came to Earth*, Macmillan, London, 1904, pp. 316–17, *The World Set Free: A Story of Mankind*, Macmillan, London, 1914, p. 28, and *The Discovery of the Future*, Fisher Unwin, London, 1902, p. 95.

4 – See, for example, HGW, *The Time Machine*, Pan Books, London, 1953, p. 76, and *The War in the Air*, Penguin Books, Harmondsworth, 1967, p. 248.

5 – HGW, *Anticipations of the Reaction of Mechanical and Scientific Progress upon Human Life and Thought*, Chapman and Hall, London, 1901, p. 53.

6 – HGW, *A Modern Utopia*, Chapman and Hall, London, 1905, p. 116.

7 – HGW, 'A Story of the Days to Come', in *Tales of Space and Time*, Harper and Bros., London and New York, 1900, p. 212.

8 – HGW, *The New Machiavelli*, Penguin Books, Harmondsworth, 1966, p. 44.

9 – Ibid., p. 56.

10 – HGW, *Tono-Bungay*, Pan Books, London, 1964, pp. 130–31.

11 – See HGW, *The World of William Clissold*, Ernest Benn, London, 1926, pp. 285–6, 286–7.

12 – HGW, *The Outline of History*, George Newnes, London, 1920, p. 667.

13 – HGW, *The Food of the Gods and How It Came to Earth*, ed. cit., p. 238.

14 – HGW, *The Island of Dr Moreau*, William Heinemann, London, 1896, p. 217, 219.

15 – HGW, *When the Sleeper Wakes*, Harper and Bros., London and New York, 1899, pp. 236–9.

16 – HGW, *Star Begotten*, Chatto, London, 1937, p. 184.

17 – HGW, *The Research Magnificent*, Macmillan, London, 1915, pp. 45, 202, 212.

18 – See HGW, *The New Machiavelli*, ed. cit., p. 114, and *Marriage*, ed. cit., p. 324.

19 – HGW, *Tono-Bungay*, ed. cit., p. 222, and *Kipps*, Fontana Books, London, 1961, p. 135.

20 – HGW, *The World of William Clissold*, ed. cit., p. 414.

21 – HGW, *The History of Mr Polly*, Pan Books, London, 1965, pp. 22–3, *Kipps*, ed. cit., p. 12, *The Wheels of Chance*, J. M. Dent, London, 1896, pp. 268–73, *The War in the Air*, ed. cit., p. 114.

22 – See HGW, *The History of Mr Polly*, ed. cit., pp. 24, 39, 45, *The Wheels of Chance*, ed. cit., pp. 139, 273, and *Kipps*, ed. cit., pp. 44–5.

23 – HGW, *Mankind in the Making*, Chapman and Hall, London, 1903, p. 69.

24 – HGW, *Love and Mr Lewisham*, Harper and Bros., London and New York, Chapter 24.

25 – HGW, *The History of Mr Polly*, ed. cit., pp. 88–93.

26 – HGW, *Tono-Bungay*, ed. cit., p. 27.

27 – HGW, *Kipps*, ed. cit., pp. 208–14.

28 – HGW, *The Wheels of Chance*, ed. cit., p. 85.

29 – HGW, *The History of Mr Polly*, ed. cit., p. 141.

30 – HGW, *Kipps*, ed. cit., pp. 182, 238.

31 – Ibid. p. 265.

32 – HGW, *The Island of Dr Moreau*, ed. cit., p. 219.

33 – HGW, *Tono-Bungay*, ed. cit., p. xvi.

34 – See HGW, 'In the Abyss', in *The Plattner Story and Others*, Methuen, London, 1897.

35 – HGW, *The First Men in the Moon*, ed. cit., p. 87.

36 – HGW, *The Wheels of Chance*, ed. cit., p. 45.

37 – Richard Jefferies, *After London: or, Wild England*, Cassell and Co., London, 1885.

38 – Helen Corke, *In Our Infancy: An Autobiography, Part I, 1882–1912*, Cambridge University Press, 1975, pp. 127, 160, 179.

39 – E. M. Forster, *Howards End*, Penguin Books, Harmondsworth, 1968, pp. 111–12.

40 – HGW, *Tono-Bungay*, ed. cit., p. 199.

41 – HGW, *Anticipations*, ed. cit., pp. 211–12.

42 – HGW, *Kipps*, ed. cit., p. 286.

43 – See Norman and Jean Mackenzie, *The Time Traveller: The Life of H. G. Wells*, Weidenfeld & Nicolson, London, 1973, p. 437.

44 – HGW, *A Modern Utopia*, ed. cit., p. 384.

45 – Ibid., p. 265.

46 – HGW, *The World of William Clissold*, ed. cit., pp. 87–92, 120.

47 – HGW, *The Shape of Things to Come: The Ultimate Revolution*, Hutchinson, London, 1933, p. 430.

48 – HGW, *Tono-Bungay*, ed. cit., p. 151.

49 – HGW, *The New Machiavelli*, p. 112.

50 – Ibid., p. 165.

51 – Ibid., pp. 260–61.

52 – HGW, *The Wife of Sir Isaac Harman*, Macmillan, London, 1914, p. 356.

53 – HGW, *Marriage*, ed. cit., pp. 412–13.

54 – Ibid., p. 373.

55 – Mackenzie, op. cit., p. 221.

56 – HGW, *The World Set Free: A Story of Mankind*, Macmillan and Co., London, 1914, pp. 215–21.

57 – HGW, *The Shape of Things to Come*, ed. cit., pp. 386–99.

8 Narrowing the Abyss: Arnold Bennett

When he is the author of a work listed here, Arnold Bennett is referred to as AB.

1 – For details of Bennett's early life see Margaret Drabble, *Arnold Bennett: A Biography*, G. K. Hall and Co., Boston, Mass., 1986, pp. 1–60; and AB, *The Truth About An Author*, Constable, London, 1903.

2 – See Drabble, op. cit., pp. 108–9, 289–93; and Valerie Eliot (ed.), *The Letters of T. S. Eliot, Vol. 1, 1898–1922*, Faber and Faber, London, 1988, p. 169.

3 – Drabble, op. cit., pp. 79–84, 191, 251; and AB, op. cit., p. 150.

4 – AB, op. cit., pp. 135–50, 178.

5 – AB, *Fame and Fiction: An Enquiry into Certain Popularities*, Grant Richards, London, 1901, p. 3.

6 – AB, *Books and Persons, Being Comments on a Past Epoch, 1908–11*, Chatto and Windus, London, 1917, p. 78.

7 – AB, *Fame and Fiction*, ed. cit., p. 123.

8 – AB, *Books and Persons*, ed. cit., pp. 89–101.

9 – AB, 'The Elections and the Democratic Idea', *English Review*, February 1910, pp. 552–60.

10 – See Drabble, op. cit., pp. 160–66, 245–6, 253–4, 287, 313; and AB, *Books and Persons*, ed. cit., pp. 9, 27, 38–9, 65, 209, 321.

11 – AB, *Books and Persons*, ed. cit., p. 280; and Drabble, op. cit., p. 247.

12 – AB, 'The Limits of Dominion', in *Elsie and the Child and Other Stories*, Alan Sutton, 1985, p. 242, and *Helen with the High Hand*, Alan Sutton, Gloucester, 1983, pp. 19–20.

13 – *Hilda Lessways*, Methuen & Co., London, 1911, p. 282.

14 – AB, *The Card*, Penguin Books, Harmondsworth, pp. 78–96.

15 – AB, *Elsie and the Child and Other Stories*, ed. cit., p. 78.

16 – AB, *Hilda Lessways*, ed. cit., pp. 139–40.

17 – AB, *These Twain*, Methuen & Co., 1916, p. 315.

18 – AB, *The Old Wives' Tale*, Penguin Books, Harmondsworth, 1988, p. 119 ('1/11' indicates 1s. 11d.).

19 – AB, *Journalism for Women: A Practical Guide*, John Lane, London and New York, 1898, pp. 3–7, 68.

20 – AB, *Literary Taste: How to Form It. With Detailed Instructions for Collecting a Complete Library of English Literature*, New Age Press, London, 1909, pp. 9–12.
21 – AB, *Clayhanger*, Penguin Books, Harmondsworth, 1989, p. 302.
22 – AB, *Hilda Lessways*, ed. cit., in pp. 113, 137.
23 – See AB, *What the Public Wants*, in *English Review*, Special Supplement, July 1909.
24 – AB, *A Great Man*, Chatto and Windus, London, 1904, pp. 116, 224.
25 – AB, 'The Perfect Creature', in *Elsie and the Child and Other Stories*, ed. cit., pp. 206, 214.
26 – AB, *The Truth About an Author*, ed. cit., pp. 88–9.
27 – AB, *The Man from the North*, Bodley Head, London, 1898, pp. 102–3.
28 – Ibid., p. 108.
29 – Ibid., pp. 262–4.
30 – AB, *Lilian*, Cassell and Co., London, New York, Toronto and Melbourne, 1922, p. 10, and *Buried Alive: A Tale of These Days*, Chapman and Hall, London, 1908, pp. 114–17, 134–9, 209.
31 – In a letter to Frank Harris, 30 November 1908, quoted in Drabble, op. cit., p. 157.
32 – AB, *Clayhanger*, ed. cit., pp. 40, 42, and *The Old Wives' Tale*, ed. cit., p. 139.
33 – AB, *Clayhanger*, ed. cit., p. 263.
34 – AB, *The Old Wives' Tale*, ed. cit., p. 42.
35 – AB, *Clayhanger*, ed cit., p. 103.
36 – AB, *The Old Wives' Tale*, ed. cit., pp. 135, 144.
37 – AB, 'Elsie and the Child', in *Elsie and the Child and Other Stories*, ed. cit., p. 23, and *Riceyman Steps*, Cassell and Co., London, 1923, p. 161.
38 – AB, 'Elsie and the Child', ed. cit., pp. 3, 6–7, 23.
39 – Ibid., p. 8.
40 – Ibid., p. 20.
41 – AB, *The Old Wives' Tale*, ed. cit., p. 138.
42 – D. H. Lawrence, *St Mawr and The Virgin and the Gypsy*, Penguin Books, Harmondsworth, 1950, p. 216.
43 – AB, *These Twain*, Methuen & Co., London, 1916, pp. 410–11.
44 – AB, *The Old Wives' Tale*, ed. cit., p. 31.
45 – Ibid., p. 247.
46 – AB, *Hilda Lessways*, ed. cit., p. 32.
47 – AB, *The Pretty Lady*, Alan Sutton, Gloucester, 1987, p. 52.
48 – AB, *The Old Wives' Tale*, ed. cit., pp. 31, 43, 88, 558–9.

49 – AB, *Clayhanger*, ed. cit., 291, 368.

50 – AB, 'The Mysterious Destruction of Mr Ipple', in *Elsie and the Child and Other Stories*, ed. cit., p. 182.

51 – AB, *Hilda Lessways*, ed. cit., p. 90.

52 – Ibid., p. 322.

53 – AB, *Clayhanger*, ed. cit., p. 50.

54 – Ibid., p. 235.

55 – AB, *Riceyman Steps*, ed. cit., p. 278.

56 – Cyril Connolly, *Enemies of Promise*, André Deutsch, London, 1948, p. 116.

57 – Jeffrey Meyers, *The Enemy: A Biography of Wyndham Lewis*, Routledge, London, 1980, pp. 89–91.

58 – Carole Angier, *Jean Rhys*, André Deutsch, London, 1990, pp. 112, 166.

59 – Humphrey Carpenter, *A Serious Character: The Life of Ezra Pound*, Faber and Faber, London, 1988, pp. 455–6.

60 – AB, *The Old Wives' Tale*, ed. cit., pp. 204, 209–10, 215.

61 – Ibid., p. 217.

62 – Ibid., p. 235.

63 – AB, 'Baby's Bath', in *The Grim Smile of the Five Towns*, Penguin Books, Harmondsworth, 1986, p. 22.

64 – Ibid., p. 73.

65 – AB, *The Old Wives' Tale*, ed. cit., p. 305.

66 – Ibid., p. 67.

67 – Ibid., p. 141.

68 – Ibid., p. 107.

69 – Ibid., p. 82.

70 – AB, *The Pretty Lady*, ed. cit., p. 135.

71 – AB, *Clayhanger*, ed. cit., pp. 391, 393.

72 – AB, *The Man from the North*, ed. cit., p. 148.

73 – AB, *Anna of the Five Towns*, Chatto and Windus, London, 1902, pp. 17–18.

74 – AB, *Whom God Hath Joined*, Methuen & Co., London, 1906, p. 5.

75 – AB, *Anna of the Five Towns*, ed. cit., p. 164.

76 – AB, *Clayhanger*, ed. cit., p. 421.

77 – AB, *The Old Wives' Tale*, ed. cit., p. 275.

78 – Ibid., p. 615.

79 – Andrew McNeillie (ed.), *The Essays of Virginia Woolf, Vol. III*, 1919–24, Hogarth Press, London, 1988, pp. 420–27.

80 – Ibid., p. 428.

81 – AB, *Hilda Lessways*, ed. cit., p. 293.

82 – Ibid., p. 336.

83 – AB, *The Old Wives' Tale*, p. 349.
84 – Ibid., p. 389.
85 – Ibid., p. 481.
86 – Ibid., p. 64.
87 – Ibid., p. 528.
88 – Ibid., p. 421.
89 – Ibid., p. 453.
90 – Ibid., p. 34.
91 – McNeillie, op. cit., p. 432.
92 – AB, *The Card*, ed. cit., pp. 143–50.
93 – AB, *Clayhanger*, ed. cit., p. 178.
94 – AB, *The Card*, ed. cit., p. 146.
95 – See Witold Rybczynski, *Home: A Short History of an Idea*, Heinemann, London, 1988, pp. 160–69.
96 – AB, *These Twain*, Methuen & Co., London, 1916, p. 9.
97 – AB, *Literary Taste*, ed. cit., pp. 9, 22, 27.

9 Wyndham Lewis and Hitler

When he is the author of the work listed here, Wyndham Lewis is referred to as WL.

1 – Jeffrey Meyers, *The Enemy: A Biography of Wyndham Lewis*, Routledge, London, 1980, pp. 76, 119, 120, 133, 146, 224–5.
2 – Ibid., pp. 71, 78, 88.
3 – Ibid., p. 92.
4 – Ibid., pp. 99–100.
5 – Reprinted in Julian Symons (ed.), *The Essential Wyndham Lewis*, André Deutsch, London, 1989, pp. 25–30.
6 – WL, *Tarr*, The Egoist Ltd., London, 1918, pp. ix–x.
7 – WL, *The Art of Being Ruled*, Chatto and Windus, London, 1926, p. 120.
8 – WL, *Tarr*, ed. cit., pp. 215–16, and *The Art of Being Ruled*, ed. cit., p. 123.
9 – See Meyers, op. cit., p. 88.
10 – WL, *Men without Art*, Cassell and Co., London, 1934, pp. 26, 32, 36, 118–23.
11 – Ibid., pp. 259–63.
12 – WL, *Time and Western Man*, Harcourt, Brace and Co., New York, 1928, pp. 30, 442, and *The Art of Being Ruled*, ed. cit., p. 264.
13 – WL, *The Art of Being Ruled*, ed. cit., pp. 95, 271, 275.
14 – Ibid., p. 275.
15 – WL, *Time and Western Man*, ed. cit., p. 315.

16 – WL, *Men without Art*, ed. cit., pp. 170–78.
17 – WL, *Time and Western Man*, ed. cit., pp. 214, 428.
18 – Ibid., p. 32.
19 – WL, *Men without Art*, ed. cit., p. 89.
20 – WL, *Time and Western Man*, ed. cit., pp. 37, 229.
21 – Ibid., p. 380.
22 – Ibid., p. 386.
23 – Ibid., p. 258.
24 – WL, *Men without Art*, ed. cit., p. 127, and *Time and Western Man*, ed. cit., p. 258.
25 – WL, *The Art of Being Ruled*, ed. cit., pp. 164–5, *Men without Art*, ed. cit., p. 183, *The Apes of God*, Nash and Grayson, London, [1932], p. 403, and *Time and Western Man*, ed. cit., pp. 8–26.
26 – WL, *The Art of Being Ruled*, ed. cit., p. 384.
27 – Ibid., p. 118.
28 – Ibid., pp. 111, 177.
29 – Ibid., pp. 101–4.
30 – WL, *Men without Art*, ed. cit., pp. 295–6.
31 – WL, *The Art of Being Ruled*, ed. cit., p. 53.
32 – WL, *Time and Western Man*, ed. cit., pp. 306, 309, 353.
33 – See Sigmund Freud, *Complete Psychological Works*, Standard Edition, James Strachey *et al.* (ed.), Hogarth Press, London, 1953–74, Vol. XXII, p. 221.
34 – WL, *Time and Western Man*, ed. cit., pp. 304, 309, and *Paleface: The Philosophy of the Melting-Pot*, Chatto and Windus, London, 1929, p. 106.
35 – WL, *The Art of Being Ruled*, ed. cit., pp. 35–7, 167–8, 259.
36 – Ibid., p. 89.
37 – WL, *Paleface*, ed. cit., pp. 221–2.
38 – WL, *The Art of Being Ruled*, ed. cit., pp. 418–21.
39 – Ibid., pp. 96, 155, 374.
40 – WL, *Paleface*, pp. 74–9.
41 – Ibid., p. 82.
42 – Ibid., p. vi.
43 – Ibid., p. 65.
44 – WL, *The Apes of God*, ed. cit., p. 443.
45 – WL, *Paleface*, ed. cit., pp. 233–5.
46 – Ibid., p. 258.
47 – Friedrich Nietzsche, *Daybreak: Thoughts on the Prejudices of Morality*, trans. R. J. Hollingdale, Cambridge University Press, 1982, pp. 141, 274.
48 – Meyers, op. cit., p. 230.

49 – WL, *Left Wings Over Europe, or How to Make a War About Nothing*, Jonathan Cape, London, 1936, p. 248.

50 – WL, *Count your Dead: They Are Alive, or a New War in the Making*, Lovat Dickson, London, 1937, pp. 41–5, 77.

51 – WL, *Hitler*, Chatto and Windus, London, 1931, pp. 32, 48.

52 – Ibid., p. 42.

53 – WL, *The Art of Being Ruled*, ed. cit., pp. 147, 155.

54 – Ibid., p. 370.

55 – WL, *Hitler*, ed. cit., p.65.

56 – H. R. Trevor-Roper (ed.), *Hitler's Table Talk, 1941–44*, Weidenfeld & Nicolson, London, 1953, p. xxiii.

57 – Adolf Hitler, *Mein Kampf*, trans. James Murphy, Hurst and Blackett, London, 1939, pp. 32–41, 60.

58 – Hitler, *Mein Kampf*, ed. cit., p. 321, and *Table Talk*, ed. cit., pp. xxix, 242, 372, 507, 709.

59 – Hitler, *Table Talk*, ed. cit., pp. 320–21, 605.

60 – Hitler, *Mein Kampf*, ed. cit., pp. 219, 221, 243, 295–6, and *Table Talk*, ed. cit., p. 251.

61 – Hitler, *Mein Kampf*, ed. cit., p. 331.

62 – Ibid., pp. 296, 321.

63 – Ibid., pp. 65, 79, 321.

64 – Ibid., pp. 238–40, 268, and Hitler, *Table Talk*, ed. cit., p. 327.

65 – Hitler, *Mein Kampf*, ed. cit., pp. 121–8, 200–201, 541, and *Table Talk*, op. cit., pp. 207, 618.

66 – Hitler, *Mein Kampf*, ed. cit., pp. 210–11, 216.

67 – Hitler, *Mein Kampf*, ed. cit., pp. 48–54, 161, and *Table Talk*, ed. cit., pp. 352–3, 359.

68 – Hitler, *Mein Kampf*, ed. cit., pp. 151–61, 206, 282.

69 – Ibid., pp. 161, 410; and J. S. McClelland, *The Crowd and the Mob: From Plato to Canetti*, Unwin Hyman, London, 1989, p. 282.

70 – Hitler, *Mein Kampf*, ed. cit., p. 286, and *Table Talk*, ed. cit., pp. 256, 413, 435, 491; and Martin Green, *The Children of the Sun: A Narrative of 'Decadence' in England after 1918*, Constable, London, 1977, p. 336.

71 – Hitler, *Mein Kampf*, ed. cit., pp. 55, 62, 83, and *Table Talk*, ed. cit., pp. 40, 42, 128.

72 – Hitler, *Mein Kampf*, ed. cit., pp. 60, 345.

73 – Ibid., p. 553.

74 – WL, *Men without Art*, ed. cit., p. 290.

75 – Hitler, *Mein Kampf*, ed. cit., pp. 127–8.

76 – Hitler, *Table Talk*, pp. 16, 68–70, 115, 125, 410, 623, and *Mein Kampf*, ed. cit., p. 541.

77 – Hitler, *Table Talk*, ed. cit., pp. 34, 42, 306, 400.

78 – Ibid., pp. 15, 33–4, 69, 128, 319, 425, 588, 617.

Postscript

1 – Virginia Woolf, *A Moment's Liberty: The Shorter Diary*, Anne Olivier Bell (ed.), Hogarth Press, London, 1990, pp. 502–3.

2 – Jonathan Goodman (ed.), *The Master Eccentric: The Journals of Rayner Heppenstall, 1969–81*, Allison and Busby, London, 1986, pp. 111, 188.

3 – Ibid., p. 117.

4 – Ibid., pp. 192–3; and Rayner Heppenstall, *The Pier*, Allison and Busby, London, 1986.

5 – Colin McEvedy and Richard Jones, *Atlas of World Population History*, Penguin Books, Harmondsworth, 1978, p. 350. My population figures are drawn from this work and from *1988 Demographic Yearbook*, United Nations, New York, 1990, and *World Population Prospects, 1990*, United Nations, New York, 1991.

6 – Adolf Hitler, *Mein Kampf*, trans. James Murphy, Hurst and Blackett, London, 1939, pp. 121–8.

7 – See the testimony of Jaime Jaramillo, *Independent*, 10 June 1991, p. 12.

8 – See George Plimpton (ed.), *Writers at Work: The Paris Review Interviews*, fourth series, Secker and Warburg, London, 1976, p. 264.

9 – See José Ortega y Gasset, *The Dehumanization of Art and Other Essays on Art, Culture and Literature*, trans. Helene Weyl, Princeton University Press, 1968, p. 9; and Clive Bell, *Art*, Chatto and Windus, London, 1914, pp. 25, 39.

10 – See Roland Barthes, *Mythologies*, trans. Annette Lavers, Paladin Books, London, 1973, pp. 54–5, 98, 140, 152, and *The Pleasure of the Text*, trans. Richard Miller, Basil Blackwell, Oxford, 1990, p. 13.

Index

Adorno, Theodor 43, 89
advertising, attitudes towards 38, 105–6, 157, 158, 190, 203, 208; Wells's views on 120–1, 132, 133, 134, 137–8
arts, the, attitudes towards 17–18, 32–3, 80, 82, 86, 157, 188–9, 198–200

Barthes, Roland 216
Baudelaire, Charles 31, 84–5
Bell, Clive 71, 74–5, 153; Art 215–16; Civilization 80–2
Bennett, Arnold 57, 109, 182; background 152–4; Anna of the Five Towns 169, 173; 'Baby's Bath' 171–2; Buried Alive 162; The Card 157, 160, 179–80; Clayhanger 163–4, 168–70, 173, 174, 179; 'Elsie and the Child' 164–5; Fame and Fiction 154–5; Grand Babylon Hotel 154; A Great Man 159–60; Helen with the High Hand 157; Hilda Lessways 158, 159, 167, 169, 175, 176; Journalism for Women: A Practical Guide 158; Literary Taste: How to Form It 158; Lilian 162; The Man from the North 153, 154, 160–2, 173; 'Morning at the Window' 164; The Old Wives' Tale 158, 163, 164, 166–8, 171–2, 174–5, 176–8; 'The Paper Cap' 157; 'The Perfect Creature' 160; The Pretty Lady 167, 172; Riceyman Steps 164, 170; These Twain 158, 166, 180; The Truth About an Author 154; What

the Public Wants 159; Whom God Hath Joined 173
Betjeman, John 21, 66–7
Brookner, Anita 69; Lewis Percy 69
Bullock, Shan F., Robert Thorne: The Story of a London Clerk 60–2
Byron, Robert 50

Canetti, Elias 29–30; Masse und Macht 30
Cattell, Raymond B., The Fight for Our National Intelligence 13
Chesterton, G. K. 137, 146; The Man Who Was Thursday 53–4; The Napoleon of Notting Hill 54
Conan Doyle, Arthur 64, 109; Sherlock Holmes 8–9, 16, 64
Connolly, Cyril 170; The Unquiet Grave 51
cremation 51, 206
Criterion, The 7, 9, 25, 52, 109, 182
Crosland, T. W. H. 59, 60, 61; The Suburbans 57–8, 60

Daily Express 7
Daily Mail 6, 7, 8, 12, 58
Daily Mirror 8

education (and literacy) 5–6, 15–16, 27, 58, 61–2, 65, 86, 203, 214–15; Bennett's views on 155–6, 157, 158–9; Gissing's views on 93–101, 102–3, 110; Lewis's opposition to 190, 192; Wells's views on 138, 141–2, 151